Lucian Randall's previous books include the biography of Vivian Stanshall, *Ginger Geezer*. He lives in London.

Further praise for *Disgusting Bliss*

'Painstakingly detailed . . . Randall offers a feast of anecdotes. It feels as if he has interviewed everyone Morris has ever worked with . . . Rich with behind-the-scenes knowledge . . . Randall is not afraid of examining the controversy that surrounded Morris once the shows were aired . . . and we end up with a fascinating account of a working life' *New Statesman*

'A meticulous biography' *Evening Standard*

'The most sustained impression to date of Morris's character, as well as his working practices' *Guardian*

'A timely contribution to the sum of our knowledge about this extraordinarily private man' *Sight and Sound*

★★★★☆ *Telegraph*

★★★★☆ *Sunday Express*

'Does a fine job of telling us just what he got up to and what he got away with' *Word*, 'Book of the Month'

'Book of the Week' *Time Out*

By the same author

Ginger Geezer: The Life of Vivian Stanshall (with Chris Welch)

'You need never have heard Bonzo Dog Doo-Dah Band song to enjoy this terrific biography' *The Times*

'Compelling portrait of troubled funnyman' *Uncut* magazine

'Lays bare an often horrible life . . . His comic gifts were never just funny, but savage and elegiac by turns, and the book evokes Stanshall's celebration of mad Englishness, with its Dada-surreal vision of Edwardiana and the late 1920s' *Sunday Times*

'Hooked me' Christopher Hirst, Books of the Year, *Independent*

DISGUSTING BLISS

The Brass Eye of
Chris Morris

LUCIAN RANDALL

**SIMON &
SCHUSTER**

London · New York · Sydney · Toronto

A CBS COMPANY

First published in Great Britain in 2010 by Simon & Schuster UK Ltd
This paperback edition published by Simon & Schuster UK Ltd, 2011
A CBS COMPANY

1 3 5 7 9 10 8 6 4 2

Simon & Schuster UK Ltd
1st Floor
222 Gray's Inn Road
London
WC1X 8HB

www.simonandschuster.co.uk

Simon & Schuster Australia
Sydney

PICTURE CREDITS
Courtesy Simon Armour: 1
© ITV/ Anglia: 2
© *Radio Times*: 3, 4
Courtesy Neil Hillard: 5, 6
© Radio Bristol: 7
© Emily Andersen: 8, 9
© Stephen Sweet: 10
© BBC Archive: 11, 12
© Fremantle/ Talkback: 13, 14, 15, 16, 17
© Camera Press: 18
Courtesy of David Quantick: 19, 20
© Rex Features: 21

A CIP catalogue copy for this book is available
from the British Library.

ISBN: 978-1-84739-180-3

Typeset by M Rules
Printed in the UK by CPI Cox & Wyman, Reading, Berkshire RG1 8EX

For Ewelina Chrzanowska, whose passionate art
is an inspiration and for her unshakable belief in me

CONTENTS

ACKNOWLEDGEMENTS

Huge amounts of thanks to Chris Morris for putting up with the idea of this in the first place and for giving permission to everyone to talk, without which it would have been impossible. Thanks to Chiggy for supplying so much information and insight and patiently channelling endless requests to Chris. Additional research by Ian Greaves and Justin Lewis. They provided a wealth of detail and their advice has been invaluable. Thanks, too, to Chas Newkey-Burden for his generous help in answering so many questions. Neil Kennedy at Cook'd and Bomb'd (www.cookdand bombd.co.uk) and many on its buzzing forum have been so helpful and have shared an unmatchable archive of rare and wonderful material.

David Miller and Hannah Westland at Rogers, Coleridge and White got the book off the ground in record time and have been enthusiastic backers ever since. Andrew Gordon saw the potential in it at Simon & Schuster where Mike Jones later took it on and Rory Scarfe edited it. But it wouldn't have got anywhere without the original spark from both Tim Brown and Jonathan Maitland – who gets another thank you for providing so much information on the Bristol years. The incredibly generous support of Peter

Mangold over the last couple of years has kept me going, as has the encouragement and friendship of Alex Robertson, Amanda Grace and the boys, Gus and Dan. I spent many months working at the Village Underground in Old Street, where everyone, particularly Tom and Jack Foxcroft and Obi Mgbado, were unfailingly inspiring and cool.

Thanks for advice and information to Jonathan Amos; Simon Armour; Roger Avery; Louis Barfe; Johnny Beerling; Moazzam Begg; James Burton; Dorothy Byrne; Nick Canner; Steve Gandolfi; Russell Grant; Duncan Gray; Mark Harrison; Richard Hearsey; David Hendy; Jonathan Hewat; Nick Higham; Shirley Hunt; Adrian Jay; Oliver Jones; Peter Kessler; David Knight; Roger Lewis; Richard Lindley; Laurence Llewelyn-Bowen; Craig Oliver; Mark Pilcher; Simon Price; Jane Reck; Bob Satchwell; Matt Sica; Carol Smith and Valerie Ward.

Much gratitude to those who gave many generous helpings of their insight and knowledge, particularly Armando Iannucci; Tom Morris; Matthew Bannister; Peter Baynham; Trevor Dann; Patrick Marber; Charlie Brooker; Prash Naik; Andrew Newman; Dave Schneider; John Armstrong and Steve Yabsley. Many thanks for key interviews and assistance: Roger Alton; Ben Baird; Nick Barraclough; Steve Breeze; Dawn Burford; Greg Burton; Jane Bussmann; Seamus Cassidy; Greg Day; Sally Debonnaire; Greg Eden; Jane Edwards; Kevin Eldon; Matt Elliott; Rebecca Front; Paul Garner; Andrew Glover; Phil Godfrey; Mark Graham; Andy Gray; Russell Hilliard; Margaret Hyde; Dave Jones; Robert Katz; Hugh Levinson; Graham Linehan; Dick Lunn; Doon Mackichan; Ali MacPhail; Ian Masters; Arthur Mathews; John Mulholland; Rebecca Neale; Richard Norley; Sean O'Shea; Clive Priddle; David Quantick; Roy Roberts; Holly Sait; Sarah Smith; James Serafinowicz; Tristram Shapeero; Rachel Sherman; Jane Solomons;

ACKNOWLEDGEMENTS

Adrian Sutton; Adam Tandy; Amon Tobin; Steven Wells and Jonathan Whitehead.

Extracts from TV Go Home © Charlie Brooker/Zeppotron, 2000, reprinted by permission. Other extracts and quotations by kind permission of Armando Iannucci and Robert Katz.

DISGUSTING
BLISS

INTRODUCTION

360-Degree Swivel

WHEN *BRASS EYE* WAS BROADCAST ON CHANNEL 4 IN 1997, Chris Morris came under attack on a daily basis, accused of pulling apart the very fabric of British culture, claims that would be made even more loudly in 2001, when the show's *Special* was broadcast. One tabloid even printed his contact details and urged the public to phone him to tell him what they thought of his 'brass eye'. Though he had become used to hearing that his work was unacceptable over the years, there was something personal and sustained about the reaction to *Brass Eye*. But rather than change his number, Morris simply recorded a new answering machine message.

'Hello, you've reached the newsdesk,' he said. 'Please leave your message after the tone.' It seemed as if the newspaper had printed its own number in error. The sputtering fury of callers was abruptly transmuted into the less immediately gratifying emotion of rather petulant complaint.

'He was entirely nerveless,' Morris's friend, broadcaster Nick Barraclough, told one newspaper. Jo Unwin, Morris's partner, read the piece and later told him, 'You've got that so wrong. He's afraid of the dark.'

Charlie Brooker has been a writing partner of Morris and says, 'He seemed to find it like an annoying change in the weather. He didn't seem like somebody who was stressed or under house arrest.'

The answering machine message was a classic piece of misdirection that echoed what Morris did best in his broadcast work. Programmes such as *Brass Eye* avoided easy targets and popular shots. If you noticed its creator at all, he would be standing to one side, subtly directing the unwary into traps that they had every opportunity to avoid. Celebrities, politicians, authority figures. Nobody was off-limits. No topic was untouchable.

It divided the reception to shows like *Brass Eye* across unusual lines. As important as the humour was the question of whether or not you thought what Chris Morris did was allowable. Was it OK to use subjects such as drugs, sex and the decline of morals in society to make jokes about the way they were portrayed in the media? The answer didn't come in generational terms. You didn't have to be older to feel uncomfortable about the way he got stars to endorse entirely fictitious charities and, if you went through the whole series and the 2001 *Special* on paedophilia without thinking at least once that something, somewhere was indefinably, slightly, watch-through-your-fingers wrong, you were either doing very well or, more likely, hadn't taken it all in on the first go and would later pay closer attention and pick up something ghastly and troubling. If still funny.

For something so clear and loud, *Brass Eye* gave away almost nothing about its origins. Chris Morris never told you what to think, and he gave away little of his motivation. You could believe almost anything about the show and its creator – the two seemed interchangeable – and there were no shortage of theories. He was the tiresome prankster out to shock. He was a contemporary satirist who was presenting a critique of modern media. He was misanthropic, a loner who was too clever for his own good. It was as if *Brass Eye* arrived fully formed and perfected its mixture of shiver and laughter with the 2001 *Special*.

The most obvious starting point for the style which he made his own is *On the Hour*, the show on which Morris made his first major national appearance some ten years earlier. And yet even this is not clear cut. This part of the story belongs as much to Armando Iannucci. It was he who pulled together a group of ambitious and talented young performers to pioneer the eerily accurate style of news comedy with Morris.

Each member of the group was fiercely talented and ambitious and all went on to phenomenal success in comedy and elsewhere in the 1990s. But there was something compelling about Morris's own story and the way that he would push at what was acceptable wherever he was which has made him such an enduringly fascinating figure. He developed his own style as much as his fellow *On the Hour* performers, but unlike them he had never worked on the comedy circuit. And so no account of his trajectory in the 1990s would be complete without a diversion to cover his early career in local radio, where he learned to love the medium and to tear it apart with a surety that came from intimacy.

His is a chronology which is a career in reverse, launched with a conventional success in *On the Hour* and becoming ever less predictable and more inventive, working only to his own agenda. It's not something that someone who wanted to be a star could have done. Morris didn't join his colleagues as they went to even greater success with the various incarnations of Alan Partridge. Instead he stayed just under the surface of general popular awareness, still broadcasting, but returning to radio and rehearsing the techniques he would bring to *Brass Eye*.

Morris himself has a reputation for being both hard to pin down and extremely approachable, rumours which are true in equal measure. It was hard to see how a book like this could work without his involvement. His circle of friends is very protective, and it seemed impossible to imagine that they would talk without his approval. Exactly one year after first being contacted, he arranges a meeting at his management company.

In person, with his black trousers, a long scarf and coat to keep out a February chill and the hair that away from the smoothed-down anchorman style is a mass of curls, he retains the youthful air of a tall, enthusiastic student. The impression is of someone fascinated by people in general, by what motivates them, what they do and how they do it. We discuss comedy, books and how he feels about this one in particular. He's not sure that he wants to revisit what were often draining episodes in his past. And, having greatly overrun our allotted time, we move outside, but continue talking halfway down the street, about what he's doing, where he's finding his inspiration at the moment. He thinks he's unlikely to be interviewed. But the channels of communication are open, he promises, making a channel-of-communication kind of gesture as he disappears. He hasn't responded to any further requests.

His agent Chiggy was surprised by the silence, if only, she said, because he more usually declined such requests immediately. And that made it suddenly clear – this was as good as it would get. Morris was not saying 'no'. I began to contact friends and colleagues, who all went back to him and were all given permission to contribute. Writer David Quantick received an email from Morris in which 'in typical fashion he claims not to mind so long as I don't tell any wildly inaccurate stories'.

As a picture of him gradually came into focus, so, too, did it seem that as much as those around him knew him as he built his distinctive body of work over the 1990s, he didn't share everything with everybody, even his closest allies. There was never a time when he had been completely open and in a way it would have been more misleading if he had been now. There was always some detail that nobody was aware of at the time, something he would be smuggling on to a programme or a legend about himself that he wouldn't correct and that would lead to fresh misapprehensions. This reluctance to come into the open was a key part of what drove him to create programmes which were in a constant state of shift, challenging not only those who took part, but also the audience and frequently the broadcasters. It was an effect he called '360-degree swivel'. As much as an account of Chris Morris, this is also the story of the many plausible worlds he created – and how so many willingly followed him as he beckoned them in.

1

No News = Good News: Balls

ON THE HOUR MADE A STRIKINGLY ASSURED DEBUT IN AUGUST 1991. You might even have listened to the first few minutes and not been entirely sure that it wasn't one of the news programmes that it set out to parody rather than a comedy in its own right. The production was authentic in every detail, from music to the delivery of the presenters. It was only the absurdity of what they were reporting that gave it away. In its wake, topical comedies – taking a wry or, worse yet, a sideways look at the week's news – suddenly seemed hopelessly outdated and unsophisticated when the medium itself was the subject. And not before time. Pretentious, self-important and riddled with parochial obsession, news programmes had never been questioned in such detail before. Let alone by a show that impudently assumed the slick confidence of its targets just to undermine them.

The programme was presided over by Chris Morris's demon presenter character, sharing his name and so believable that it was hard to tell where it ended and he began. There was an unassailable confidence to his performance which was apparent to those he worked with as much as it was to the audience when the show was broadcast. But occasionally the mask slipped. When he had to create an outside broadcast for the second series, Morris took his audio gear and a clipboard on to the roads around Broadcasting House. From here, the item called for him to be recalled to the studio as the result of a technical problem. He tapes himself barging back into the BBC and records a genuine exchange with a security guard who wants to see his pass – 'I'm bursting with news – if you stop me, I'll explode' – and takes the lift without ever pausing for breath. But he later admitted to producer Armando Iannucci that while his fellow BBC employees stood in audible silence as he crisply reported on origami attacks in an art gallery, he'd felt rather silly.

You wouldn't have noticed any signs of discomfort in the broadcast programme. Iannucci says that Morris 'acts confidence very well'. Throughout the two series, he bullied fellow presenters and punctured the conventions of radio news. He was by far the most prominent figure on the programme, only Steve Coogan's Alan Partridge as memorable. To the casual listener it would have sounded very much the *Chris Morris Show* in all but name, but the idea to take the format of news itself had come from Armando Iannucci and it was he who assembled and drove the team that worked alongside them. The cast worked from the framework that the two would create and which Morris would use and develop in much of his work throughout the decade.

Then twenty-eight, his invitation to join the show had come the previous year in the form of a speculative letter from Iannucci, a 26-year-old producer of such stalwart Radio 4 comic institutions as *The News Quiz* and *Week Ending*. Iannucci was extremely inventive and technically very adept and, like Morris, worked very much on his own terms. Yet he was more amenable to playing the bureaucratic constrictions of the BBC system and to accepting the conventions of publicity, obligingly trotting out the same anecdotes for different interviewers with polished charm. His self-deprecating tones were often employed to communicate the same kind of exasperation at the more ridiculous aspects of the media, but his character was more that of the eyebrows-raised insider who would subvert rather than sabotage. When he talks about working in BBC comedy but having to attend a general production training course at the insistence of the corporation, he expresses his attitude to the notion by emphasizing 'training course' in a Scottish lilt that suggests amazement at the existence in this world of anything so dull. And yet it was this course that sparked their revolutionary comedy.

Participants learned about news, features, drama and documentary. They had had to make a ten-minute factual programme and Iannucci began to consider the comic potential of his 1990 coursework. 'I thought why not make a short news programme which sounded absolutely authentic but which was gibberish,' he said.[1] Iannucci drew on the verbal tics of other programmes on Radio 4 – *Today*, drama, newsreaders – and the shows he had first listened to when he came to London from Radio Scotland, including *The Way It Is* on Capital Radio, a fast and furious news programme with a noisy soundtrack.

Iannucci sent the resulting ten-minute piece to Jonathan James-Moore, the head of light entertainment at BBC Radio, who suggested making it into a pilot for a full series. The first task was to recruit cast and writers. Iannucci had come across Morris's weekend DJ show on GLR – Greater London Radio – on which he regularly included nonsense stories delivered with authority. 'There's someone who, as well as being funny, is very technically competent,' says

Iannucci, 'so understands how to make something sound like that rather than have to ask a number of people to try and do it.'

Morris drove the ancient, battered Merc he'd had for years to meet Iannucci at BBC Radio in Portland Place. As Morris was illegally parked, they quickly went back to his car. A fruitless cruise for spaces around the block gradually turned into a mobile meeting and the start of a partnership which would last for years. 'We spent about two hours driving around and around Broadcasting House,' said Iannucci. 'And I thought, Well, this is interesting. The fact that I can talk to him for two hours and it just feels normal is a good start, really. And we found we liked the same sort of comedy, so we just clicked instantly.'[2] It wasn't just humour, radio and an interest in news and politics that they had in common. As kids they had both been Jesuit-educated and discovered they shared a couple of the same teachers between their respective schools.

The two worked on a pilot completed in April 1991. As a trusted producer, Iannucci was largely left alone to get on with a show for which there was little direct precedent. Comedy featuring the news tended to be either topical jokes about people in the news or the two Ronnies sat at a desk doing gags in their own voices. Even shows like *Radio Active*, which Iannucci cited as a favourite, alongside *Rutland Weekend Television*, had been recorded with an audience as a sketch show without going into the minutiae of the business of broadcasting news. The *On the Hour* team struggle now to recall much in the way of direct influences on the very specific take-off of the genre. There was nobody doing that improvisational, serious approach to spoofing – at least not in the UK. If there was anything at all, for the likes of Dave Schneider and Armando Iannucci, it was to be found from the US in the 1984 movie *This is Spinal Tap*, the closest cousin in terms of the approach. Its target might have been rock music – specifically heavy metal on the road being quite a ridiculous sight in all its self-regarding pomposity – but like *On the Hour* it seemed very much as if it could be true and clearly had an affection for the adolescent obsessions of metallers and a feel for the inherent tragedy of the ageing rocker.

On the Hour was to be a magazine show featuring news, sport, weather, finance, environment news and special features. Morris was the anchor, the main presenter, and also played other reporters and interviewees. As in real news shows, his items would be edited and dropped in as complete 'packages'. Then there was a team of writers and actors who worked almost exclusively with Iannucci. With the overall shape of the programme dictated by Morris and Iannucci, they created the rest of the regular reporters and characters. Ideas either supplied by the writers or less frequently worked up in rehearsals would be developed through improvisation in the studio, and the humour was to come through the contrast between the straight performances and the nonsense content. The choice of cast and writers was vital to the success of a show that was not going to rely on filling a half-hour slot with topical gags for its humour.

'Most producers try to follow trends,' explains comic and *On the Hour* writer Richard Herring. 'Armando is really excellent at understanding what good comedy is and who is a good comedian.' Iannucci didn't just call in the latest sensations from the Edinburgh Festival or select from actors' directories like *Spotlight*. He had amassed a bunch of friends through performing comedy since his days at university in Oxford and knew people through his production work, and he was equally prepared to search outside the industry to find exactly the right people for the job. Iannucci's cast didn't have to have a background in performing – one of the first to be involved wasn't even interested in making comedy a full-time career. Andrew Glover had been a long-time friend and partner with

Iannucci deep in the mines of student comedy but had given it up to follow his dream as a management consultant.

Glover met Iannucci just days after starting at University College in Oxford. They wrote at college together and were in separate undergraduate revue shows at the 1985 Edinburgh Fringe. As Iannucci began work on a PhD the following year, they performed regularly as A Pair of Shorts. Even then Iannucci had a quality that marked him out from fellow student performers. 'He was always a bit more demanding of himself,' says Glover of the young comic. 'If something feels at all obvious, he'll want to put three twists in it.' Having contributed some material for Iannucci who started his career at Radio Scotland, he supplied material for *Week Ending* when Iannucci helmed it. They continued the informal relationship into *On the Hour*, Glover enjoying the process of writing for the show without the pressure of it being a primary source of income. Amiable and smart, he would be relaxed about moving further away from the core of the *On the Hour* group as his very sensible career at washing-powder giants Procter & Gamble grew more demanding.

Rather more serious about the idea of making a go of it was Dave Schneider, another Oxford graduate who had occasionally joined Iannucci in A Pair of Shorts after Glover's departure. Schneider had studied modern languages after attending the City of London School. 'Armando was bloody good. Voices, impressions, stupidness,' says Schneider. 'There is a slapstick quality to Armando as well, which people don't associate with him.' The two would bunk off the Bodleian Library to spend time in coffee bars chatting about comedy and friends who had gone professional. Among Schneider's own comedy heroes was Danny Kaye, like him a Jewish comic with a physical aspect to his act which inspired Schneider as he included clowning around in his live show, wrestling with tables or playing a talentless magician. Both he and Iannucci favoured surreal material and Schneider started to research around Yiddish theatre for a PhD, but neither he nor Iannucci completed their higher studies. While Iannucci went to Radio Scotland, Schneider acted at the National Theatre and ended up on TV's *Up To Something!*, a forgotten sketch show with Shane Richie for which Iannucci was also a writer. Schneider was around for the flickering initial ember of *On the Hour* that Iannucci made for his BBC production course and has a vague recollection of contributing an interview with a brain-damaged boxer.

The permutations of friends from Iannucci's Oxford days became more tangled with the addition of Stewart Lee and Richard Herring, two comics who had met at the university. Iannucci used masses of their material on *Week Ending*, a show the pair regarded with mixed feelings. It was good to have a professional outlet, but, although Iannucci had freshened up the format, they still found it embarrassingly formulaic. Worse, as new, young writers they were featured in documentaries about it. They got their own back with an *On the Hour* sketch ripping up what they saw as the old show's worst excesses of predictable caricatures and groaning puns, 'Thank God It's Satire-Day'. The bile was real. After a year on *Week Ending*, Richard Herring had got to the point where he hid in one of the crates used to store newspapers in the writers' room to avoid a meeting. 'I just couldn't face writing shit topical satire,' he explains.

Patrick Marber was another performer for whom *On the Hour* came at just the right time. He'd worked with Iannucci before, including a brief coinciding stint on the inevitable *Week Ending*. Marber's own style of humour was much influenced by Ben Elton and Rik Mayall who he saw perform at his Oxford college in 1983. 'Formatively, hilariously funny,' says Marber, who also started out on the stand-up circuit. But he was always aware that he was just filling time.

'I decided that I enjoyed doing this thing,' he says. '"I want to be a serious writer, but I haven't written anything, so I will bide my time doing comedy until I write my great work." I think that was my general overview.' He kept on what was becoming a performing treadmill, including a yearly stint in Edinburgh, but it was becoming painfully obvious to him that he wasn't in the league of such contemporaries as Eddie Izzard. Marber took a year off around 1990 to live what he thought would be the life of a novelist in Paris, during which time Iannucci called up to ask him to be in *On the Hour*. Which turned out to be good timing, because Marber had failed to write his book and felt he was doing little more than standing by watching his friends preparing one-hour shows to propel them into stardom. 'I didn't have the talent to go all the way as a stand-up. I didn't have the ambition . . . I just didn't want it,' he says.

Iannucci and Morris's show represented a particularly welcome change for Doon Mackichan. She had been appearing in Radio 1's sketch show *The Mary Whitehouse Experience*, in its later series produced by Iannucci, starring David Baddiel, Rob Newman, Steve Punt and Hugh Dennis, and had found it a rather depressing experience. There were few enough good comedic roles around for women and *Mary Whitehouse* was no exception, the female performers feeling they were left with whatever the men didn't want to say. If *On the Hour* had a male perspective, it was dictated more by the newsroom setting than by the rest of the cast. The production of the show would be a collaborative process in which everyone could get something in – as long as they spoke up loud enough. Rebecca Front was another occasional *Mary Whitehouse* performer who was recruited. Iannucci had also produced a radio series for a double act in which she appeared.

In addition, Front knew Marber from a 1984 Oxford revue show called *Stop the Weak*, in which they'd done knockabout, physical comedy. And, independently of Iannucci, Marber and Mackichan knew of each other from the stand-up circuit, where both of them had come across the most well known of all the cast and writers, Steve Coogan. He was the one member of the team who hadn't come across or worked with Iannucci in one of his many roles, but he came recommended. Coogan had been a great mimic from his childhood days, had started doing impressions as part of his stand-up while studying drama at the polytechnic in his home town of Manchester and walked straight into a contract to do voices for *Spitting Image*. By the time *On the Hour* came along, he had also appeared in the Royal Variety Performance and, like Patrick Marber, whom he had met at the Edinburgh Festival in 1990, was frustrated by the limitations of what he was doing.

'I was known as a sort of cut-price Rory Bremner. Reliable, but limited,' he said. 'I knew that impressions made people laugh and were a short cut to approval from an audience, but I respected other comedians because they got laughs without doing impressions, which meant they had to work a lot harder, and that what they were doing was more substantial. It wound me up. I wanted that respect.'[3]

Into this potent brew of youthful ambition, burgeoning success and sweaty impatience Armando dropped a couple of veteran *New Musical Express* writers. David Quantick and Steven Wells were a few years older than most of the others, had been working in the music press since the early 1980s and regarded their mostly lesser-known colleagues with a mixture of condescension and disdain. 'I just remember thinking, What a bunch of losers,' says Quantick. 'These people will never make it.' His partner felt the same.

'I wanted to produce the show!' Wells recalls. 'I was an arrogant and incredibly frustrated rock writer.' Although Quantick had also written for *Spitting Image*, he and Wells had been recruited on the strength of their *NME* column, called Culture Vulture, Ride the Lizard, or whatever they felt like each week once they'd got completely stoned and filled it with topical music parodies. An item in their column about classical music which included the assertion that it largely involved tiny guitars played under the chin particularly appealed to Iannucci, who felt it was good for the journalistic side of the show to have writers who were funny but as music writers weren't primarily gag men: 'More of a way of doing funny non-fiction,' he explains.

As an actor rather than a comedian, Rebecca Front also contributed to the straight feel of the show, though she was initially uncomfortable with the improvisation. 'I thought I wouldn't be funny enough,' she explains, 'but Armando talked me out of it . . . Well, sort of shoved a microphone in front of me and made me get on with it, to be specific.'

In that first meeting, Iannucci handed out copies of his sketches and played an excerpt of the original programme he'd done for his training course. Richard Herring's notes survive to reveal how advanced the thinking from Morris and Iannucci already was. Amid his doodles were 'vox pops', 'news-clips – false – spurious', 'real clips', 'professional liars' and 'is it specially written or true. News events.'

Armando Iannucci and Steve Coogan encountered each other for the first time when the cast first assembled in the studio. 'I was slightly nervous because he was very quiet,' said Iannucci. 'Then we switched the microphones on and he was very funny . . . I now see that his strangeness was actually a matter of being a bit reserved with people he doesn't know.'[4]

For his part, Coogan felt what could have been a sideways move in going to radio had been vindicated. 'Working with Iannucci was a revelation. He really did reshape things for me . . . I remember thinking, 'I've been looking for this all my life. We knew we were on to something,' he later said.[5]

From briefing to broadcast, the feel of the show remained remarkably unchanged, but Iannucci couldn't be entirely sure of how the people he knew separately or in different permutations would work together. But his instinct had been spot on. They gelled almost instantly. It helped that, apart from Quantick and Wells, they were all in their late twenties. Less tangibly, the core members of the team were all Catholic – Morris, Iannucci, Coogan and Mackichan – or Jewish – Schneider, Front and Marber. As Armando recalls with a laugh, it was 'the Judaeo-Catholic conspiracy against the English Establishment . . .' Or the *On the Hour* conspiracy against the media mainstream – the cast had a track record in ignoring fashion even back when they were students. 'Alternative' was the buzzword and stand-up the most obvious route to fame when they were coming up in the mid-1980s and their Oxford revues and physical comedy had seemed almost wilfully out of step. It was a stubborn attitude to following their own instincts that informed *On the Hour*. They rejected the idea that you could have filler material as long as there was a better joke along in a minute. Easy laughs were dropped no matter how topical or populist they might be if it seemed they compromised the tone of the show – whatever that might turn out to be.

The writers were in the dark, having to feel their way to what worked rather than rely on tested standbys. They might tell Iannucci they had ruled out a particular avenue because it didn't seem to work, only for him to realize that was exactly what he wanted. Even the best initial ideas could be reworked through improvisation. It would be hard to work out exactly who was responsible for any one item.

'It's an approach I've always been keen on,' said Iannucci, 'being non-proprietary about your work. Not saying, "No, you can't change that, because that's mine and I've spent four months getting that line right."[6]

Morris provided up to a third of the writing of most shows himself and hijacked unused GLR studios at night for his own performances, refining them, multitracking voices and creating his own effects, while Iannucci worked with the rest of the cast to structure the show and create the rest of the material. It was cheap enough to keep the tapes running, so he did, just in case there was a piece of genius that couldn't be recaptured.

'It was like being in a little lab, really,' says Patrick Marber. Just like in a real news programme, sessions were edited down by Iannucci until the best bits remained. The technique formed the basis for the way that he and Morris would both work over the years.

Working alone, Morris rarely needed to be in the main meetings. For much of the first series of *On the Hour* and into the second one he remained something of an unknown quantity to most of the cast and writers and an intimidating figure from a distance: 'A bit daunting,' confirms Rebecca Front, 'because he is effectively a rather tall brain, but he's charming with it, so that helped.'

It wasn't until the show transferred as *The Day Today* to BBC2 that Morris and the others integrated as they all had to appear in front of the cameras at the same time. The freedom of radio was that Morris could be spliced into the final programme without its being audibly apparent that he didn't work his material in with the group.

Carol Smith was Iannucci's production assistant for *On the Hour*. '[Morris] would go off and he'd come back with a five-inch spool of tape and that five-minute piece would be on there, and then he'd play it to us in the studio and that was it,' she says. 'It was in, and we couldn't touch it, because it was so densely produced and so layered and . . . you couldn't get a blade in.' It meant that Morris could get away with smuggling in material which nobody could then remove. 'You literally could not get a blade in anywhere to edit and so, y'know, there were some extraordinary things in there, but they went out.'

Iannucci was the one who cut across all the various groups – communicating the shape of the show to the writers and the cast. Patrick Marber recalls, 'He said, "Look, there's a way of performing comedy where the jokes are very much told and I want you to bury the humour. I want you to do funny voices but I don't want them to be too funny. I want you to improvise funny things but don't be looking for the humour, just trust that it will come."' Their very serious approach won *On the Hour*'s creators a reputation for being unapproachable. Inspired by the concept of the show, they did all seem as if they had a lot to prove.

'We were all full of the flush of youth and we thought we were the young turks,' said Coogan.[7]

'I don't think there was a single person there who wasn't an alpha male,' recalls Steven Wells. As self-confessed 'ageing Trot', he had marched with the Anti-Nazi League and seen The Clash perform for Rock Against Racism in Hackney's Victoria Park in the late 1970s. While *On the Hour* wasn't politically motivated, all of the team took inspiration from a clarity of purpose in the show's concept which was as bold as any campaigning.

'I think there is a lot of anger, I think it's very accessible to comedians,' says Dave Schneider, 'and certainly to that group of comedians.' They took their lead from the top. 'There's a sort of "from the pulpits" quality to them [Morris and Iannucci] . . . vengeful angels.'

The approaches of the members of the cast didn't always agree. Steven Wells identified the generation that Stewart Lee and Richard Herring belonged to as being more cynical than his as a punk – but individually each knew they had earned the right to be there and that the team worked well together. Armando Iannucci treated everyone decently and inspired loyalty – both he and Chris Morris were motivated by doing something interesting rather than only becoming well known, so the rest of the cast felt comfortable in trying out ideas even when they fell horribly flat.

Morris wove the real world into *On the Hour* in the shape of phone calls he made in presenter character to such outsiders as the vet asked to comment on the news that dangerous dogs were to be fitted with rubber skulls – 'It wouldn't be able to bite a child's face off, then?' he asks, to the vet's bafflement. The sound quality of the real interviews was virtually indistinguishable from scripted phone calls performed by the cast, Iannucci recording those through an actual phone rather than simply adding a filter effect to a microphone. Genuine archive recordings jostled with performed sports reports taped with real commentator lip mikes to give the voice an authentic nasal quality. Items from American reporters like Rebecca Front's Barbara Wintergreen were compressed and distorted to sound like a cheap import.

The organic production method meant that nobody could be quite sure what they had until the moment of broadcast. Some of the team hadn't even heard Chris Morris's contributions. Even he and Iannucci didn't know how well it would work until the last piece had been completed. There was no laugh track, no audience, no punchlines and no traditional gags. That would be as true of the eventual series, which was commissioned to go out between August and September that year, as it was of the pilot. That sense of flux, that it was something that was going out live, helped to mark it out from other comedy shows.

'It then felt like it was a whole world,' says Iannucci, 'and I think you can only do that if you genuinely get lots of different voices

contributing.' Up to a point – the overall parameters were not nego-
tiable. 'I think I once in my youthful brashness made some
suggestions about how things should be directed to Armando,'
laughs Steven Wells, 'but he probably just blinked and thought,
Who the fuck are you? and took no notice whatsoever.' *On the Hour*
had come at a time when everyone connected with the show was
ready to take the opportunity it represented. The rather unusual
and protracted production process allowed the core team to create
in a way they hadn't quite worked out for themselves.

'There was so much gratitude that we were in this thing,' says
Marber, 'and Armando and Chris were the primary creative entities.
Helping it be the thing it was, you know. They were gods to us. We
just did what we were told, really. I was just coming up with gags that
I thought were funny to support their vision. I never really thought
about how the news was presented, to be honest. I didn't really care.
That wasn't my agenda; mine was just to do the job.'

When it came to doing the actual series, there was hardly any
stylistic difference from the pilot. Ahead of the driving theme music,
Morris set the tone with a gravelly welcome that got progressively
more ridiculous over the two series, playing the main presenter as an
amalgam of Jeremy Paxman and *Today* presenters, with the tragic
tones of Michael Buerk at his most human-interested.

'Everyone had done Paxman,' said David Quantick, 'but nobody
had listened to the weird way Michael Buerk talks, his strange dying
fall, and they picked up on all that.'[8] Comedy clubs for years after
echoed with stand-ups bolstering a weak gag by emphasizing the
final words with that mock pathos.

Each show started with the headlines with a realistic form and
rhythm: 'Life peer in wind tunnel disaster', 'International string
lengths agreed' or 'Sri Lankan diplomat expelled for copying rice'. The
news itself would often be read by Morris as an adenoidal Radio 4

continuity announcer, surreal stories with sound effects underneath distracting from the solemn tones. All the horrors of radio news in one show. Reports were faded up too quickly or not at all. Strange noises bled through from outside the studio, papers were rustled as attempts to read the news were continually interrupted and undermined.

There was one noticeable absence. In the pilot, Morris says, 'Now it's time for Bill with some sports news', and producer Iannucci makes a rare appearance, cutting in as editor from the control room to say there was no sports news. It wasn't until they prepared for the main series that Iannucci asked Steve Coogan if he could do a sports reporter. Tempting though it was to do an impersonation, they wanted to focus, as with other aspects of the show, on the generics of the species. 'And Steve opened his mouth and Alan Partridge flew out,'[9] said Iannucci. The voice was defensive, someone who felt rather inferior to the other thrusting reporters on the show and as if he were anxious to prove he was a proper journalist. 'It was very strange because . . . everyone in the room knew who it was. We knew the life story of this person, his frustrations at being seen as just a news reporter, when in fact he wanted to be taken seriously. But not so seriously he'd be seen as a serious news guy; he had more of a light entertainment ambition. Very quickly someone said he was a Partridge. And someone else said, "Yeah, and he's an Alan." Alan Partridge came out in minutes.'[10] From the very beginning he was recognizably the character who would find fame with his own chat show and, more immediately, he proved to be a great foil for Morris. Their stilted newsroom banter became an increasingly strained and awkward highlight as the series progressed. Alan was quickly as strong a character as Morris's presenter, for ever awkwardly interviewing female athletes, strangely obsessed both with the propensity for sportsmen and women to have groin strain – 'I've been told it's a bit like a guitar string snapping' – and male athletes in their changing rooms.

Alan soon had a back story. Items with him were often improvised, although Patrick Marber, whose writing partnership with Coogan was developing, would flesh him out with specific points to Coogan such as asking where he thought Alan would shop. Stewart Lee and Richard Herring wrote for his scenes, all the contributors engaging in absurdly detailed discussions about his life, down to the most plausible place he might come from (Milton Keynes was suggested as a comedy staple before settling on Norwich – a solid town, they decided, but also amusing).

Other regular reports included environmental news from the green desk of Rebecca Front's Rosie May, her segment complete with soothing new-age muzak and the plaintive songs of whales. There was a trite religious thought for the day from Patrick Marber as Monsignor Treeb-Lopez, and Morris brought Wayne Carr, a vacuous pop correspondent he'd been doing for years on his own radio shows.

On the Hour was an immediate success, with overwhelmingly good reviews in all the nationals, and it would remain a favourite with its creators.

'We had a real hoot doing *On the Hour*,' Iannucci says now. 'Because it was the first and it was fresh territory. Nobody had been there before. I have very fond memories of that time.'

It sounded enough like a respectable Radio 4 show not to frighten the regular audiences but had an undercurrent of subversion you could pick up on if you were listening closely. You could be amused at the more affectionate aspects of its mockery of BBC radio or you could pick up on the harder stuff. There were a few listeners who thought the show was real and wrote into Radio 4's *Feedback* to express their disgust at the mocking of religion, politics or sport. But this was balanced when an item about an evangelical American radio station offering an alarm to scare away liberals and homosexuals prompted a listener to congratulate the team on their stand against degenerates.

The show proved popular in newsrooms with its degree of accuracy that BBC media correspondent Nick Higham calls 'spooky', though Morris thought its favourable reception was more to do with the way that its existence confirmed to reporters that they were as important as they had always believed themselves to be. *On the Hour* arrived at a time when news broadcasting was expanding massively. Rolling news was the big thing and its champions had marked Radio 4's frequency as potential Lebensraum under the BBC's radio news boss Jenny Abramsky and deputy director general John Birt. Sky had just started its rolling service in the UK, and CNN had been doing it for years in America. During the first Gulf War, in 1991, Abramsky diverted Radio 4's FM frequency to what some parts of the BBC uncharitably referred to as 'rolling bollocks'.

Eventually, Radio 5 would be sacrificed to news, but the success of *On the Hour* gave the management of Radio 4 entertainment another handy 'stick to beat news with', according to radio historian David Hendy. 'Though there were a few keen on the idea of more news,' he says, 'I think the majority among those running Radio 4 – and plenty among those making programmes – would have been very pleased by the show.'

'There was just a general sense of newsiness being a bit loud,' agrees Iannucci. The Gulf's embedded journalists, endless expert analysis, time-filling speculation and the feeling that war had come to be presented as if it were a computer game provided material for *On the Hour*'s own war special, a highlight of a triumphant series.

Jonathan James-Moore, an inspiration for many upcoming

comics at the BBC, came down to congratulate the team during the first run. It could have signalled the first step on the road to a conventional comedy career for all of the team in the BBC, perhaps even to *On the Hour* becoming one of the station's perennial favourites. But there would be only one more series of *On the Hour* before its creators turned their attention to other opportunities, not least taking on the tics of television news. Even then it would have to be on their terms.

Morris would be instrumental in providing the confidence to keep true to the spirit of the show. There was a sense of apartness to what he did that even the casual listener could detect. His sections were the results of a practised radio professional working in his own medium to his own agenda rather than a comic performer working in collaboration. He wasn't playing a role in the way that his fellow cast members were.

Morris had never been a comedian or an actor, but had spent his working life in radio, observing everything that it entailed – the backstabbing of the newsroom, the banter of local reporters desperate for a story that would catapult them into national networks and the station staff who had to cover for the sort of mistakes from which *On the Hour* got so much of its comedy. Legends about what he had got away with during that time – and what he hadn't – were already growing by the time of *On the Hour*. It was that grounded understanding of how radio worked which made him so well placed to subvert it.

2

MAN STEPS OFF PAVEMENT

CHRIS MORRIS WAS BORN ON 15 JUNE 1962 IN THE VILLAGE OF Buckden, Cambridgeshire, to parents who were both doctors. His father, Michael Morris, was the local GP, and his mother, Rosemary Parrington, had taken on what were then expected duties of a doctor's spouse as a full-time, unpaid administrative assistant in the surgery. She was also largely responsible for looking after Chris and his brothers in their early years. Tom was two years Chris's junior and Ben was four years younger. It was a secure and stable upbringing, which would be reported by the *Daily Mail* in the wake of *Brass Eye* with something approaching disappointment. 'For a self-appointed scourge of the Establishment,' they said, 'Chris Morris has the most conventional of backgrounds.'[1]

His colleague and friend, broadcaster Trevor Dann, suggests such early exposure to the realities of medical conditions around him would have been just the sort of thing to give the boy a down-to-earth attitude to life, which later influenced the boldness of his approach to his work and his choice of subject matter. It's a theory that provokes a boom of laughter and a swift dismissal from Chris's brother Tom.

'That conjures up an image of some kind of Rabelaisian house-hold with a sort of oak operating table and people hacking off legs,' he says, like Chris authoritative and direct in his speech, 'which wasn't the case.' But the thought prompts him to consider the other mainstay of Chris's upbringing, the family's long-standing connection with farming and rural life.

Both of the boys' parents grew up on farms in East Anglia. Michael Morris's family came from the Saxmundham area of Suffolk, and Rosemary's came from Colchester in Essex. When they were married, the Morrises initially lived in a combined house and surgery in the village, but after a separate clinic was built they bought a large and ramshackle Victorian farmhouse which, although it was not any longer a working agricultural concern, nevertheless retained chickens, geese, pigs, sheep and dogs. Chris became used to such sights as rabbits being hunted for dinner by cats. It was a lesson in the realities of life to rival anything he might learn from his parents' trade. Those rabbits which had only been half-killed would later have to be put out of their misery. Life on the old farm fostered an interest in animal life which culminated in Morris reading zoology at university.

The three boys got on 'averagely' well, remembers Tom, the age gap more noticeable when they were younger – Chris and Tom 'were better matched as fighters, so we probably fought more than either of us fought with Ben'. They became much closer as they grew up.

They had an extended family they visited regularly – not only both sets of grandparents but also Rosemary's sister and all but one of Michael's four sisters, who all had their own families. Michael and Rosemary also took the boys on regular holidays.

Secure though their home environment was, Michael inevitably had less involvement with the boys' upbringing than Rosemary as a result of his demanding position as the old-fashioned village doctor. He worked long hours and frequently at weekends. Chris's mother went back to work in 1974 as he approached his teens, when she was employed by the local authority in community medicine.

Though the boys had a sciences background with seemingly not a hint of the arts in which all three would later make their careers, their father in his own way played a role, centre stage, in the village community. Buckden was only a few miles from Huntingdon and reasonably close to Peterborough and Cambridge itself, but Michael Morris was the first call for most locals. The GP's role was to be compassionate but clear-eyed in his dealings with the public. He would know the most intimate details of most of the residents, their most private physical and mental concerns, often giving out general advice as much as prescriptions and being someone whom the whole village could confide in. It gave him responsibility and power in equal measure as he was implicitly trusted by so many. Chris's work would later play on notions of authority and frequently featured the medical trade, particularly the doctor in *Blue Jam* whose apparent omnipotence covered disastrous flaws. At one moment he would be patronizingly ordering a female patient in and the next recoiling in horror at the sight of her daughter because he's apparently never seen a child before and thinks she's some kind of unnatural dwarf woman.

Michael's own cultural interests lay more in the classics, which he had absorbed into an encyclopaedic mind alongside his medical studies, while Rosemary had studied English before she went into medicine, and enjoyed theatre. Storytelling was a prominent feature of the boys' upbringing. 'You can never tell how important things are, can you?' says Tom Morris now. 'But certainly I can very vividly remember my dad reading us stories from when we were under ten.

I can remember on one holiday being read *Watership Down* aloud, all of it, in nightly episodes. And I can remember being read a version of *The Odyssey*. And we used to love it.'

The regular routine of family life was abruptly disrupted when the boys got to the age of ten and were sent to boarding school. Chris and Tom went to Stonyhurst College near Clitheroe in Lancashire and Ben went to Ampleforth College, a Benedictine school way up on the edge of the moors north of York. Their parents wanted them to receive a Catholic education and Stonyhurst, where Michael had been a pupil between 1944 and 1949, had an intriguingly radical past. It was founded in Europe in the late sixteenth century as a training centre for priests who were going to go undercover to support disenfranchised Catholics and foment revolution. In the late 1960s the headmaster fostered a creative ethos at the school through attracting music, English and drama teachers who were distinguished in their fields.

'By the time we got there, it wasn't at all like that,' says Tom. 'There was just a skeleton of this great liberal imagination that had moved on. It wasn't a very good school – looking back on it, it was a shambles.' It was saved by the few teachers who had stayed on from the heights of the previous years. One of the surviving elements of the old regime was a requirement that everyone had to learn an instrument for their first year. It rooted the pupils in musicality from an early age. Chris started on the double bass and later moved to the bass guitar. Tom learned the trombone.

Chris started his Stonyhurst College school career at St Mary's Hall, a feeder prep school in the grounds of Stonyhurst itself. His was a small class who were encouraged to think of themselves as the elite among children who were all pretty bright and driven. There were about fifteen to twenty of them in that group who formed tight friendships that lasted throughout their school careers. They received a more intensive schooling than most and were generally marked out for glory in the top sets at the main school. All prep pupils took the general entrance exam at thirteen, though St Mary's was a special scholarship class with a £100 prize for the smartest.

'There was probably a high degree of arrogance in our year. Most of us thought it would all fall into our laps,' says Phil Godfrey, a friend of Morris and fellow St Mary's pupil. 'We would be merciless whenever there was a teacher who couldn't handle us.' Morris's class was characterized by a lot of eccentric talent; all the pupils were trying to assert themselves, and he didn't seem to be marked out for success more than anyone else. There were other pupils who went on to have prominent careers in law and in the music business and seemed at the time to be more likely to make a name for themselves, though Morris did well in the sciences and was popular and gregarious. They were useful traits to have at the school.

Stonyhurst was an isolated and small community. Some of the parents, in the forces or working overseas, had effectively parked their offspring there. Morris was one of those whose parents had sent him through choice, because they felt he would receive the best education, but it wasn't easy for anyone.

'You had to be fairly emotionally tough,' says Phil Godfrey. 'I certainly wouldn't send my kids there. There was an air of religious oppression. You were praying every two hours, it seemed. By the time we left we were telling each other we wouldn't need to go to church for another thirty years.'

There were some imaginative approaches to spirituality at the school, and the Jesuit way of education had an impact on all the pupils. Morris and his friends were naturally inquisitive, and their restless thinking was encouraged.

'We were difficult to pin down,' says Godfrey. 'We were rejecting all the Jesuit values.' It was a common reaction, but the head teacher later told Godfrey that they had been particularly 'awkward'. Their set was more rebellious, made more fun of the teachers and later on there were more big drinkers among them than among the rest of the school population.

The education could be quite overwhelming for some, particularly the many Stonyhurst students whose roots were an unsettled part-Irish, Spanish and Maltese or Gibraltarian. Morris was part of the Establishment, with his Middle England village background. He had a natural sort of confidence on which the Jesuit teachers built, reinforcing how privileged the students were to be receiving such a high standard of education.

Morris's inner core seemed to give him a physical assurance as well. He had a birthmark on his face and later very apparent acne, but friends and colleagues throughout his life barely noticed their presence. Years later, a journalist friend doing a programme on removal techniques for birthmarks asked if Morris would be interested in trying it. He was told not to worry; it wasn't a problem. At school Morris also got along with a false tooth he had from prep school until he got a proper replacement in his late teens. He used the fake to make faces and would drop it out for comic effect. The original tooth came out in a fierce under-twelves inter-school rugby tackle that resulted in a hospital trip.

Morris also played cricket and the game became an early obsession for him, leading him to practise with friends with a rolled-up newspaper. Jeff Thompson, the fast bowler, was such an idol that Morris was nicknamed after him, but his enthusiasm outmatched his ability and he never made the first team. In the holidays the Morris brothers played cricket in the garden and watched test matches, and Chris would spend hours impersonating cricket commentary. He was also able to do a good impression of Mick Jagger, distinguishing himself by being able to do the mouth. The Rolling Stones were then hitting their peak of creativity with *Exile on Main Street* and *It's Only Rock 'n' Roll* and Morris preferred them to the groups his friends were into – the likes of Led Zep, Floyd, Genesis and Yes, whose progressive sounds were an inescapable feature of the early 1970s all over the UK.

Up on the edge of the moorlands of Lancashire, it was harder to keep up with pop culture that wasn't on the national radar. Even developments in London often passed them by, though Phil Godfrey recorded radio shows with a tape machine and a mike when he returned there during holidays. Through him, Morris got to hear Capital Radio, albeit in lo-fi. The station had been set up in the early 1970s as one of the first legal commercial alternatives to BBC radio. It was home to Kenny Everett, whose pioneering use of multitracking, bizarre characters and mastery of the technical aspects of radio were allied to a fierce irreverence. The Capital shows were a revelation for Morris. Everett was not only a renegade but a technical perfectionist, using his own studio so he could record chorused jingles. His shows featured improvised comedy and a barrage of ridiculous voices. He sang along with records and was an instinctively brilliant DJ.

Equally inventive was the literary comic favourite of both Tom and Chris, a collection of hoax letters sent by Humphry Berkeley as a Cambridge undergraduate in 1948. His creation was a headmaster of fictional Selhurst School he called Rochester Sneath, whose requests to real heads affectionately poked fun at the pompous instincts of the private teaching profession and spurred many of them to respond to the most unlikely requests.

The Master of Marlborough College was asked how he managed to 'engineer' a royal visit. 'I did nothing whatever to engineer the recent royal visit,' he wrote back crossly. 'No doubt the fact that the King's Private Secretary, the Lord Chancellor and the Archbishop of

Canterbury are all Old Marlburians had something to do with the matter.'[2]

The surreal nature of Sneath's demands provided clues for those not quite so caught up in the dignity of their position. The head of Wimbledon College agreed to perform an exorcism, saying he would need a 'Bell, Book and Candle, a gallon of holy water and a packet of salt. The latter is required for sprinkling on a certain part of the ghostly anatomy, so it should be loose and capable of being taken up in pinches.'[3] The Cambridge college authorities were less amused when the hoax was revealed and a deluge of headmasterly complaints followed. Berkeley was sent down for two years, though it was made clear on his return that unofficially the senior fellows thought his endeavour was quite funny. An otherwise upstanding member of the Establishment, Berkeley went on to be a MP and writer and waited a respectable twenty-five years before publishing the letters as *The Life and Death of Rochester Sneath* in 1974.

Morris's early comic favourites also included the Goons and the comic musical stylings of the Bonzo Dog Doo Dah Band, whose lead singer, Vivian Stanshall, was a major influence, though in interview Morris was later reluctant to name heroes as such. 'The temptation is to create an ideal football team of all-comers, but I don't find it works like that,' he said.[4] But he liked Peter Cook and at school appreciated the sweary humour of Cook and Dudley Moore's Derek and Clive. Morris was drawn to verbal humour, though the noise and rhythm of comedy came before the words.

Like many of his friends, Morris was into drama. He appeared in school plays, and Tom was also involved with theatricals but found it a frustrating experience. 'I certainly had direct conflict with the authorities at the school about creating work, making theatre, which defined the experience for me,' says Tom. He wanted to put on various shows and events but there wasn't a system to support it.

Permission had been given in the 1960s for a show that wasn't kind to the teachers, but Tom's headmaster turned a similar request from him down without discussion. The school promoted the academic abilities of its students but just seemed no longer geared to bringing the best out of the pupils in the way it had.

Having kept up with his music, in the sixth form Chris joined a band with his friend Simon Armour. 'We called the band Nosmo King,' says Armour, 'because I had a No Smoking sign and cut it in half. It was also a bit ironic, because in those days we all used to slip out to the woods to smoke.' Their set included classics like Santana's 'Samba Pa Ti', 'Message in a Bottle' by The Police and – a particular favourite for Morris – the Rolling Stones's 'Sympathy for the Devil'.

'I'm sure to hear it nowadays would be painful,' says Simon, 'but the constant playing gave us a better idea of rhythm and harmony – and how to keep playing your guitar when someone pours a pint over it.' Twice a year the Jesuits shipped in a busload of girls from a Preston school for a disco. 'I can imagine they went back to their rooms and prayed nothing serious happened. Of course, for us this was like heaven, with unlimited booze and girls everywhere.'

Chris also played bass in the school's official sixth-form dance band, Upper Syntax and Poetry. Head of history Tom Muir used to train and organize the front line, comprising trumpets, clarinets and trombones, including Tom Morris, while teacher and school archivist David Knight organized the rhythm section of guitar, bass and drums. Both Morrises were, recalls Knight, 'wayward': 'Chris neither sought nor, indeed, needed any advice. He was less malleable to my own suggestions than was usually the case with boy musicians. But then he was more competent than most, so I would like to think of this as merely a comment rather than a criticism. I believe that Tom Muir had a similar experience with Chris's brother Tom.'

Chris read sciences at A-level, and David Knight says Stonyhurst teachers remembered 'a bright boy from the top class who did well but less than spectacularly academically', though this was in the context of a school where most of the pupils were, on average, pretty good. Yet Morris didn't seem to be set on a particular direction in life at that point. Tom would win an exhibition for Pembroke College, Cambridge, but Chris took up zoology at Bristol University in 1980. Having been a fan of children's TV staple Johnny Morris and his *Animal Magic* anthropomorphism, it was amusing and a bit of a thrill to be going to study in the town from which his namesake had broadcast his most famous programme.

Among his fellow Bristol zoology students was Mark Pilcher: 'Chris had long bushy hair – almost touching his shoulders at one stage, I think. I have a photograph of all the students in 1980 and, now I look at it, Chris has one of, if not *the* biggest, most stripy tie of all the undergraduates.'

Morris shared a house in the Clifton area of Bristol with legal student Caroline Leddy, who would be a long-time friend and much later work on producing *Brass Eye*. A cousin of Morris from America also lived there. She was training to be a medic and went out with a music student named Jonathan Whitehead. Though he and Morris didn't get to know one another at that time, Whitehead was later to become a friend and key musical collaborator. Both were bassists in bands, Morris playing in Expresso Bongo, a rhythm and blues outfit in the mode of the Stones.

Morris was still into the Bonzo Dog Band and began using one of their techniques for fun. The Bonzos had once gone out near their studio to record vox pop interviews on such nonsense notions as the importance of the 'shirt'. The resulting confused responses from the public were used to lead into an album track of the same name. Morris took a big reel-to-reel tape recorder to the streets of Bristol for his own interviews on similar subjects which he played back to friends in his room. 'He asked daft questions and was surprised that he got all these really serious answers,' says Phil Godfrey.

A student revue put on by Morris's department targeted the staff in one of the items. 'There was a tall, thin lecturer in botany who had a funny haircut and an odd way of pronouncing certain words,' says Mark Pilcher. 'Great ammunition for Chris.'

In the summer of his third year Morris produced a project on lizards under the general supervision of tutor Roger Avery, who can now recall little detail of either the work or the student who produced it. As at Stonyhurst, Morris hadn't particularly stood out in his year for good or bad. He graduated with a 2:1 in 1983 and headed back Cambridge way to home in Buckden.

The most striking thing about the direction of all three Morris brothers as they started out on their careers was the way they'd had a family background in medicine, had been strong in sciences as students, but then moved decisively into the arts where both Tom and Chris made their own distinctive impact. Tom studied renaissance drama and poetry at Cambridge and then wrote plays and began working out of the theatrical mainstream, becoming artistic director at Battersea Arts Centre in London. By 2009 he was artistic director at the Bristol Old Vic and as respected as Chris for determinedly forging his own path. He has no idea at all why they ended up in similar areas and sees as many differences as shared characteristics.

'My route through alternative theatre is a matter of taste which may connect with his choice of work,' says Tom, 'but is far more open to the influence and inspiration of what other people are doing in the field than his extraordinarily self-contained approach and process. I regard us as very different kinds of people within our slightly similar creative fields.' At Battersea Arts Centre, Tom Morris was 'a bit further away from the creative anvil, so the work that I did and enabled to happen at Battersea was very much inspired by a sense of boredom with what I perceived to be the Establishment in theatre. There were artists who could be challenged to work in different ways. And if I hadn't been Chris's brother, then he would have been one of the artists whom I was trying to challenge in those ways to reinvent the rules of theatre in whatever way was appropriate to what he wanted to say.'

Back home with a degree in zoology, Morris took a job in Cambridge's thriving main market. Andy's Records had started on a single stall, but while they kept the original pitch where Morris worked, they had become a major company that was on the verge of establishing itself as a dominant chain of shops in the east of England. If you wanted to work on the stall, you had to be a graduate and have a broad knowledge of music. It was a rite of passage for musicians on the busy Cambridge scene, Morris himself among them.

Andy's working day required an odd mix of the cerebral and brute force. It was a long journey in from Buckden, and the market started at 7 a.m. each day, which felt earlier to the staff on a weekend when they'd been out the night before. They would all pull on steel-toe boots and set about unloading the records as fast as possible. Box after box, thousands of records, from a truck that could hold seven and a half tons. It was non-stop all day. The punters knew their stuff and the staff needed to be able to chat on their level, field their questions, find out their interests and get them into new artists. All the while they knew that even at the end of a good day the extensive supply of vinyl would be largely undiminished and would if anything be looking rather heavier as it waited to be reloaded.

Staff bonded through a studenty take on the relentless black humour and mockery that characterized market trader life. On bustling shopping days, the area was a favoured hunting ground for TV and radio crews soliciting public opinion. Whenever they were in earshot, the staff would all shout something rude for the microphones. 'Knob!' was Morris's favourite.

It wasn't long before he found himself the focus of that special trader humour. He had sold the last copy of an album by The Clash and, making a note to reorder it, misread 'Litho in Canada' as some kind of live album, when it referred to the place of manufacture. This passed as a hilarious comedy opportunity for his workmates, and Morris became known as 'Litho'. But he always joined in with the general banter and, if he was quieter and more considered than the other staff, he was as willing to do the physical work as anyone.

Market life inspired a sketch in the first episode of *On the Hour*. 'There's been mixed reaction to the news that pedestrians are to be banned from Cambridge city centre,' reported Morris. 'The council ruling follows concern over congestion in the city's increasingly crowded streets. Market traders are up in arms, claiming that already recession-hit trade will dry up completely if no one is allowed to walk within half a mile of their stalls. But the council are unrepentant. "There's no pleasing these tossers," said a spokesman this morning. "You clear the streets so they can unload their vans and they turn around and crap in your face."'[5] When Morris left Andy's, he was presented with a history of lithography from an academic bookshop in town.

Morris was himself active in local bands. He played funky bass in the Exploding Hamsters, made up of students from the university, a slick, brass- and percussion-led dance outfit. In a similar vein were Somewhere in the Foreign Office, with trumpet, trombone, guitar and two lead singers, a bunch of young, talented musicians out for a good time and loosely kept in check by Mark Graham, who at almost thirty was able to pull seniority on most of them. The band's finest hour came through their agent, who specialized in military gigs and booked their uptempo rhythms into RAF, USAF and Royal Navy bases in the very north of England and in Scotland – including Marham, Lossiemouth, Faslane and Swinderby. They set up in the canteen while the chairs and tables were cleared away and, *Spinal Tap*-style, frequently played to an audience as small as thirty, one of whom could be relied on to loudly request 'Freebird' while the rest sat with their feet up. None of the musicians took the project too seriously. Singer Steve Breeze kept his fellow musicians amused by telling the audience they were off on an arena tour but just doing a few warm-up gigs first. Morris and the other band members would try not to crack up as the base personnel appeared to take everything at face value.

All ten of the group crammed into a Fiat Ducato van with their equipment and tents, the budget not stretching to hotels. Being constrained to canvas led to some unforgettable moments, like the big beach fire under the aurora borealis on the coast of Scotland and a night at a hippie commune called Findhorn. The band were allowed to stay, even though they confessed the next gig was at a nuclear base, on the understanding that they promised to beam 'psychic rays of love' to the military staff on the base.

There were no egos on the road – everyone got on well, acted as their own roadie and made up rude songs for the long journeys, when they weren't playing Thomas Dolby's 'I Scare Myself', a favourite from 1984's *The Flat Earth*. They shared a sense of humour influenced by the Pythons and the ubiquitous filth of Derek and Clive. Chris would bring out his impersonations of Jagger and Richards in which he was joined by Steve Breeze.

Morris generally stuck to bass duties in the band, though he was able to turn his hand to a number of different instruments. He was beginning to find himself as a young man. The acne he'd suffered was clearing up, though Morris seemed to Mark Graham to be capable of being quite sensitive – 'I just remember him being a happy soul,' says Graham.

Morris was popular and always surrounded by girls at the gigs. 'He had a sort of animal charm about him,' says Steve Breeze. 'The whole thing about him was his magnetism. It was quite strange for a guy who was a really nice bloke.' It was a carefree time, with no real responsibilities. But the band knew there were too many of them to have a realistic chance of making a living; they were too talented to wait around and they drifted apart, finally concluding with one last festival gig.

Over the summer of 1984 Morris got a gig playing bass for the Cambridge Footlights Revue. The four-piece band featured a number of different drummers and Cambridge students Hugh Levinson and Roy Margolis. With his red-spotted necktie, which he said was a family heirloom, Morris fitted in well with the university crowd and could easily have passed for one of its posher members. The show they accompanied, directed by Nick Hancock and featuring Steve Punt, was called *The Story So Far,* a series of sketches with the common theme of a setting in a futuristic Britain led by a president. The band swiftly got to grips with the repertoire, and doing a proper sixty-date tour of the country was another blast of fun for Morris. If churning out the same numbers got a little dull on some nights, the musicians would amuse themselves by swapping instruments or trying to make the cast corpse by wearing wigs and delivering comic asides during scene changes, and Morris was invariably at the centre of the mischief. He would make up nonsense words and phrases, which he dropped randomly into conversations, and was particularly fond of impersonating a cast member who sang with a noticeably warbly vibrato.

The climax of the tour was at the Edinburgh Festival for a three-week run, which was sold out despite a very bad review in *The Scotsman*. The glory of the Footlights had faded somewhat since a high point in 1981 when Stephen Fry and Hugh Laurie had been principal members and taken a career-launching show to Edinburgh which included Emma Thompson and Tony Slattery. But it was still a prestigious name, and some of the 1984 cast members were very aware of being in the boiler room of comedy and were determined to make it. They swapped notes with Footlights alumni Slattery and Neil Mullarkey and would sit around plotting strategies and having intense discussions about what constituted a joke.

Not Chris Morris. He showed no interest in using the festival or the band as a way of getting into comedy. He was enjoying just being the hired musical help for the summer. Morris's former university housemate Caroline Leddy was also at the festival. She performed in The Millies with Richard Vranch, Donna McPhail and Jo Unwin – who almost a decade later would become Morris's partner. But as early as that trip to Edinburgh, Chris confessed to his Footlights friends that he had 'a thing' about Unwin, and all agreed she looked particularly spectacular on stage in The Millies when she and Leddy came out in slinky catsuits. The seats in the venue were just loose chairs arranged in ranks, and Morris, startled by the vision, shifted his chair sharply and fell over backwards.

But the Footlights tour would be Morris's last major musical adventure. His interest was beginning to be diverted elsewhere. Back in Cambridge, he contributed bass and ideas to Steve Breeze's main project, a band signed to RCA. Morris just didn't have the time for the sessions in Breeze's mum's garage. His replacement was Neill MacColl, half-brother of Kirsty.

Morris's attention had been diverted to Radio Cambridgeshire, where Somewhere in the Foreign Office's other singer, Jane Edwards, had been working since the station started back in May 1982.

Underfunded and staffed by just twenty, Radio Cambridgeshire was already struggling. Edwards worked there casually, more for fun than anything else, just another outlet for a creative musician. She worked on *Stop It I Like It*, hosted by a presenter named Nick Barraclough and broadcast from the station's radio car, as well as making up silly things in the studio. As Somewhere . . . started their Scottish adventure, she heard she'd got the chance to play with the founders of Squeeze and knew that she couldn't continue with the radio work.

Morris was impressed by the way she juggled a music career with radio and liked the idea of doing something similar himself. Jane offered to introduce him to the station. She'd already got jobs there for sixth-form college friends Rachel Sherman and Dawn Burford. None of them was paid, and it was all rather basic work, but for young people exploring their options it felt like a great creative freedom. It was arranged that Morris would spend an early morning watching Nick Barraclough and his breakfast team.

Barraclough was a smart, talented broadcaster who was passionate about his folk and country-based music. Articulate and warm, he had been brought up locally and played professionally in bands for ten years before making his radio debut with Radio Cambridgeshire. He regularly had people in on work experience but the arrival of Chris Morris was memorable. For the whole morning Morris sat in, Barraclough felt he was being watched with unnerving intensity. Most young hopefuls concentrated for a maximum of fifteen minutes before the glamour of BBC local radio wore off and they began to fidget, glaze over or read the morning papers. But as they chatted after the show, Morris quizzed Barraclough on certain techniques he'd observed. He was soon invited back. Nick was an encouraging figure who liked to see what people could do, and Morris demonstrated attractive qualities – he was bright, eager to learn and young. In other words, cheap.

Well-spoken Morris was soon recording 'packages' – two- or three-minute local stories. It was something like an apprenticeship. He read the news, made documentaries and learned how to edit. Everything was on quarter-inch tape, which would be marked with a wax chinagraph pencil before a razor blade was used to cut the tape and it was spliced back together – the basis of all the techniques he would use, from building up basic packages to later more complicated editing for comic effect. And until digital technology took it all on to computer, it was the only way of doing things. 'You could sit in that station all night and just fiddle about in the production area, turn tapes around, speeding stuff up and down,' says Nick Barraclough. 'Frankly, the technical side of radio is easy, if you've got common sense. But to do it the way that Chris did it, to *think* of it . . .' The process of editing was physically demanding. Robert Katz, who later wrote with Morris, creates a vivid image of how advanced his skills would become when they worked together in London, talking of an obsessive approach to the art of editing: 'the sheer complexity of his audio montage style used only analogue technology. Sometimes his fingers would be covered in dried blood the next day.'

Dawn Burford had taken over from Jane Edwards in the radio car and Morris joined as her driving partner, working out how everything functioned and checking for overhead power lines so that the cumbersome telescopic aerial was extended up to something like twenty or thirty feet without causing unnecessary electrocution to either of them. His progress at the station was monitored by its managing editor, Ian Masters, and Morris was taken on as a freelance with rolling short-term contracts of around three months.

The greatest chunk of output at the station was chokingly parochial, and there wasn't enough of it. The BBC provided funding for only six hours of broadcast time and, in order for the fledgling station to have any chance to establish itself, it needed to stay on air from 6 a.m. to 10 p.m. It was not unusual for staff to work an eighteen-hour shift, which was if nothing else an opportunity for someone starting out to find inventive ways of creating programmes of a higher quality than the budget allowed. Morris, absorbed in the work, regularly stayed into the small hours.

He graduated to presenting a drive-time show, having begun to fill in for absentees after six months at Radio Cambridgeshire: 'I can remember tuning in one Christmas time,' says Ian Masters, 'listening to him and thinking, Yeah, that was good. That was a good show. This boy will go somewhere providing he perseveres and is willing to step along the hard way.'

Morris got to know his way around the studio so well that presenters would come to him for tech support before they went to the BBC engineers. Colleague Jonathan Amos remembers Morris using rather unorthodox methods to solve a problem during an outside broadcast one freezing February. 'The mast on the radio froze solid – it couldn't be raised to send a signal back to base,' he says. 'Legend has it that Morris climbed up on the top of the vehicle and pissed on the mast to release it.' He was also beginning to pick up on the gulf between news and every other type of programme. 'News regard themselves as the anointed ones, the real reason for the existence of the radio station,' says Nick Barraclough, 'and they see local radio as news bulletins with some waffle in between. So they were incredibly puffed up, self-important . . . and Chris was watching.'

In 1994 Morris told *Melody Maker* about a journalist he called Pat who 'knew all the tricks, how to chat up the police, etc. One day, he came rushing into the studio, shouting, "Chris, Chris, you've gotta listen to this: 'Police are out in force today as the county's roads serve up their traditional pre-Christmas cocktail of carnage.'" I said, "Pat, you *can't* say that." When he did the news, he read, "The roads have served up their traditional pre-Christmas *menu of mayhem,*" smiled at me through the glass, and carried on.'[6]

Nick Barraclough promoted Morris's promising show to Trevor Dann, who presented a Sunday-night show on Radio Cambridgeshire for new and alternative music. At thirty-five, he was an established name with a career including stints as a Radio 1 producer and on BBC2's *The Old Grey Whistle Test.* Within five years, as one of the managers tasked with founding the BBC's London station GLR in 1988, he would be on the lookout for DJs with distinctive styles – by which time Chris Morris would have stepped a considerable distance along the hard way.

Even at Radio Cambridgeshire, Morris was evolving a clear idea of how he wanted to work, as fellow presenter Valerie Ward discovered when they briefly collaborated on an arts programme. 'I think they thought that, as I wanted to produce and Chris was keener on presenting, we would make a good team,' she says. 'We didn't. I wanted to write everything, script it, time it, craft it, include interviews and location packages. Chris just wanted to go with the flow.' They tried to work separately and bring their pieces together. But by the time they met, Morris had often still not decided what he wanted to do. 'I was reduced to tears,' says Ward. Ian Masters recalls, 'Even then Chris's approach to broadcasting was out of the ordinary. Some people asked me if he was a little too "zany". My response was always that I would rather have broadcasters who tried new approaches – even if those approaches failed sometimes. I liked his bright tongue-in-cheek style and his wry humour.'

Morris would use listeners who called in as props for his own sense of humour, rather than draw out their own stories. He wasn't unkind, but he wasn't patient. 'I think he did find it hard to put himself in other people's shoes perhaps,' says Rachel Sherman. 'He was always one step ahead of them, but that wasn't always funny.

Sometimes that was a problem. He can make you feel stupid even though he's not meaning to. If you aren't very secure in yourself, if you don't feel up to matching what he's doing, you could end up feeling a bit pathetic.'

His style was more readily understood by his colleagues. Morris would enthusiastically bound around the studio and had a flippant, public-school sense of fun which made him a popular figure. The absurd constraints of time and budget on the station encouraged a black humour in the creative teams which, as he had on the market stall, Morris fitted into comfortably. He employed his observational skills to capture almost everyone in the station perfectly and without mercy. Ian Masters' headmasterly style and tendency to be pompous made him a particularly rich source of humour for Morris in evening pub sessions. It was only a year or so after Morris joined that he gave a devastatingly cruel and accurate impersonation during a speech on the occasion of Masters leaving, which marked him out among such colleagues as Trevor Dann as someone brimming with comic talent and potential. His confidence was reflected in his appearance, which was usually relaxed and individual, and even when he seemed more interested in what he was wearing he never tried to make a statement and was certainly not a follower of trends. He favoured Harris Tweed jackets and pinstripe or sometimes outlandish paisley shirts, occasionally with bow ties and a blazer, Viv Stanshall-style. He was engaging with friends and always wanted to know what they were doing, why they were doing it and who they were doing it with. 'Which is a rare thing in his business,' says Nick Barraclough, who had quickly established what would become an enduring friendship with Morris. 'Normally people just talk about themselves.' Chris was genuinely curious. But when he opened his mike to address, largely, the housebound and afflicted of Cambridgeshire, all of that remained hidden.

'He could never let down the front,' says Barraclough. 'He was always playing a part when he was broadcasting. I don't think he could ever just be him, really. The thing about local radio is that you've *got* to put your personality across and you've got to disrobe everything. If you don't open up, then you'll be no good at all, and Chris is by definition any number of people except himself.' It would always be hard for close friends to work out how much of that broadcasting persona was worked out in advance and what was simply down to how he felt on any particular day. Perhaps he didn't even have it all figured out himself. 'They just thought I was being ironic,' he later said of those early days, 'and I don't quite understand why.'[7]

Dawn Burford was not won over by his style. She thought her driving partner was full of himself. It wasn't right that he was so off-hand with the public, she insists – that despite the fact that many of the audience had, even in her own words, the intelligence 'of a broom handle', the staff should make allowances. She remembers being dispatched in the radio car to cover a craft fair where stall-holders would be eager to discuss their crocheting and knitware with the smart young types from the BBC. Morris was horrified. 'What are we doing here?' he said to Burford despairingly. 'It's full of smelly old women. I can't do this.' He dumped the recording gear on her and, she says, 'sodded off for a bit'. It was almost as if he couldn't bring himself to do it. Whatever his destiny held, he seemed to know even then, it wasn't smelly old ladies, although they would provide material for *On the Hour*. The 'Look Around Your Region' sections would be the heartfelt pokes he delivered at the parochial stories he was doing for real as a young journalist in Cambridgeshire, featuring 'Bang on Target' with 'Michael Bang' and headlines such as 'Hopping lessons for Timmy the amputee badger' and 'How far are we from Kent today?'

A phone call to Radio Cambridgeshire from anyone who appeared to be more on the wavelength of the young staff was always a cause for celebration in the studio. Morris had been at the station for something like eighteen months when a sixteen-year-old named Paul Garner called in to a competition. He sounded naturally funny and was soon helping out in the studio. It was the start of a friendship and occasional working association between the two that would last years. Garner's primary interest lay in music rather than comedy, and as he planned to make it in the music business he was far from overawed by what Morris was doing and brought an unaffected freshness to his weekend job. But he quickly learned to respect Morris's professionalism. He once came in with a tape of something stupid he'd done and mistakenly played it on a tape machine that interrupted a serious programme. Always imposing, Morris was suddenly a furious figure. Though the storm passed quickly, Garner says, 'I remember being quite frightened of him.'

In later years it would be reported that Morris's own tendencies to cause mischief started at Radio Cambridgeshire. But he was still learning. There simply wasn't the scope to mess around at the under-resourced station and though friends and colleagues have heard all about the stories – often repeated in press profiles – of him filling studios with helium and being fired, in interview they all say that while they are sure it happened, it wasn't there. But it was only a matter of time before he broke out from the budgetary and creative limitations of his first proper show.

In the spring of 1987 Morris sent a reel of his best work off for a position at the BBC station located, coincidentally, in his university town. Radio Bristol advertised for a 'bright and lively broadcaster who can produce and present weekend sequence programmes with flair, pace and imagination . . . Salary around £10,000–£11,000'.[8]

In another coincidence, Morris already knew the man who would hire him, David Solomons, programme organizer at the station. The former sports reporter's daughter Jane was a station assistant at Radio Cambridgeshire, where she was going out with Morris. Yet though it was an appointment which might appear to be a clear case of industry nepotism, quite the reverse was true. Morris's engine was fuelled by a powerful dislike of unfairness and hypocrisy in all their forms. Colleagues at Radio Cambridgeshire remember that he took against his fellow young recruit Emma Freud simply because it was said she'd got work experience at the station only after her father, local MP Clement Freud, had asked Ian Masters. It seems a minor offence – the media is after all rife with far more breathtaking crimes of family, and Emma Freud became a talented broadcaster in her own right – but it was enough to ensure that Morris never quite got on with her. Some years later he contributed an occasional column for the London *Evening Standard*, then edited by a relative of his later partner Jo Unwin, a fact picked up on by *Private Eye* and reported by them in typically arch style. He immediately wrote to the magazine to confirm the piece and volunteer the story of his earlier connection with his employers at Bristol. 'Mr Yentob!' he added in a plea to the controller of BBC1. 'Have you a child for me?'[9]

Quite apart from anything else, Morris's ability and potential on the demo tape were proof enough of his capability. David Solomons had told *Broadcast* magazine that he was looking for someone 'able to take a sideways look at life'.[10] Morris's style – edgier and more irreverent than most – was exactly what they were looking for. Jane remembers that her father was impressed by Morris as a broadcaster: 'I think he greatly admired his imagination, daring and creativity,' she says.

Jane Solomons was born in Yeovil, Somerset, and studied at Reading University. She was also new to the industry and at Radio

Cambridgeshire had become aware of Morris gradually as he took on more shifts before they started to go out together. In interview she is guarded in her description of their relationship, almost as if it were one in which there was more companionship than passion, though they were committed enough to remain a couple even after he got the job at Bristol. For a while it would be a distance relationship, as Solomons had to get work in the area and to sell her Cambridge home before she could move to be with him in the West Country.

Morris stayed in contact with old friends and colleagues when he left. Nick Barraclough would be kept up to date with Morris's new enthusiasms, his discoveries in music, the shape of his first starring show at Bristol and, at length, the increasingly uncomfortable relationship that developed with Bristol's management as Morris began to push at the limits of what could be done with a local radio show.

3

NO KNOWN CURE

A MAVERICK RADIO TALENT, HE WAS SACKED BY THE BBC AFTER inappropriate remarks concerning a government minister and, after almost a year's exile from the airwaves, was hired by Radio Bristol – on the condition that he supplied his tapes from his home studio in advance. Kenny Everett, who had been such an influence on Morris's childhood, made his return to the airwaves in the summer of 1971. Following in his footsteps – albeit sixteen years later – Chris Morris was a long way from making the not dissimilar comments on a contemporary minister that would lead to his own suspension from what Kenny Everett used to call the Beeb. Morris was still learning and Radio Bristol allowed him greater scope to develop as a broadcaster. More solid than surprising, some presenters unchanged in themselves or their format for twenty years, Bristol was longer established than Radio Cambridgeshire and was actively looking for somebody to innovate.

Morris and no-nonsense programme organizer David Solomons developed the concept of what became *No Known Cure*, which started broadcasting in July 1987. The tight budget meant that Morris had to stretch his material to fill live shows on Saturdays and Sundays between 10 a.m. and midday. In October 1988 he took on a Friday 10 p.m. to 12 a.m. slot for the *Late No Known Cure*, the same month he started to do a show for the new London BBC station GLR. He managed to produce both programmes for eighteen months before at last moving up to GLR and the capital on a permanent basis.

Morris was again under short-term contract. Roy Roberts, Radio Bristol station manager, remembers that his new employee arrived with a chequered reputation. 'We knew that he was a slightly risky, or adventurous, proposition,' he says. If Morris's card was already marked, it wasn't clear who at Radio Cambridgeshire tipped them off. Ian Masters' successor, Margaret Hyde, insists that she'd had no problems with him, but he had already begun to get a reputation.

Morris worked alone to create the bulk of the material for his show, starting the working week on Wednesday through to the final show on Sunday. He laboured over every detail, down to composing his own jingles – he could spend an entire day making a brief trail of a quality that went far beyond what was required for local radio. It wasn't unusual for a newsreader hurrying to deliver a late-night broadcast to see Morris hunched over a synthesizer in a room at the front of a former private house where programme-makers congregated between shows.

Steve Yabsley helped out with such tasks as fielding listener calls. He had joined the station in 1986 after having been a packing clerk who hung around the station until they gave him work. Slim, with a narrow face, brown eyes and neat dark hair, he was a local boy and naturally funny. On Thursdays Yabsley and Morris repaired to a café to write items together. 'Chris was incredibly focused and he knew his own mind totally,' says Yabsley. 'Everything else was going on around him and he was concentrating on what he was doing. I just think of him as a whirlwind.'

Matt Sica worked at Radio Bristol as an assistant in his teens. 'He took on the show – really grabbed it by the horns. It was a real wrestling match between him and the show. And if the timing was out on anything, it didn't sit well with him.' Morris had ranks of cartridges on which he stored effects and the jingles he'd written. 'Observed from the outside, he was rather comical, because he hid behind a wall of carts and seemed to be doing the job of four or five men.'

The audience didn't quite know what to make of this clear new presence at Bristol. Presenters always had to prove themselves, and Morris's voice in particular wasn't the comfort blanket the listeners were used to. At first his mates called in for the competitions until the show established a fan base.

Morris might not have been playing in bands any more, but he diverted his undimmed passion for music into the records he played on the show. He delighted in discovering new music, was a regular gig-goer and gave mix tapes to friends. 'His musical knowledge is phenomenal,' says Nick Barraclough, who received a number of those tapes, 'and [he] has a completely catholic taste. Absolutely open to anything.' Morris shared his passions with the audience. Favourites included Nirvana and the Pixies and They Might Be Giants. While chart hits constituted much of the playlist, he had an instinct for the popular over the populist, though Matt Sica remembers being introduced to Michael Nyman's *Belly of an Architect* and Philip Glass's music for *Koyaanisqatsi*. 'He used to play that in the office as well. He really liked the repetitiveness and the polyrhythms . . . Things like that would get played. For me, it was bizarre stuff for the radio.'

No Known Cure could also be a vehicle to develop parodies of broadcasting clichés, but the heart of the programme was essentially a really good DJ show. Morris gave formulaic features, from competitions to interviews, an imaginative and subversive tweak. Rather than being asked to call in, listeners were expected to be 'bothering' the phones. All the features of a traditional DJ show were there, but each given an emphasis that conveyed the futility of the existence of the local broadcaster and the show itself. It was conspiratorial, drawing the listener in as if they had to make the best of the dross with him. He read out letters and dedications reluctantly, with palpable disdain and affected horror should a caller be gauche enough to sound happy to be talking to him. It looked just as extraordinary as it sounded if you happened to be in the studio with him. 'It was completely new to me to see someone doing radio like that,' says Matt. 'You're seeing somebody perform, doing something that is, in effect, verbal mime. Morris's energy was quite outstanding.' His jingles lurched tipsily, he dropped snatches of amusing vocal samples on to records or faded himself in playing along on a synth like a demented five-year-old. 'You weren't sure if he'd lost it! Or whether he was being funny 'cos it looked so odd. You're only listening to one thing, but watching it – it was a mixture. You couldn't quite believe what you were seeing, so you didn't bother listening to it, 'cos it was more fun to watch it.'

When the show went out on Fridays, Matt Sica recalls, 'I had a particular job of going to the office where Morris worked in the daytimes, to record on cassette *Week Ending*, and that had to be religiously done. To go up, and sit and wait. All the other jobs downstairs were put aside, because I had to wait for the cassette to finish, turn it round and put it back in the player as quickly as possible . . . I think it fitted in to the genre of show that we were doing for a while. Whether or not it gave Morris ideas, or inspired him for ideas, I don't know. It was more than a passion of just listening to *Week Ending* 'cos of being on while he was on air.'

There were guests on the show, and some interviewees came from a comedy club that had opened in Bristol, Julian Clary and Jerry Sadowitz among the disparate bunch. 'I don't know if I went to see Les Bubb first, or Les Bubb came to see us,' says Matt Sica, 'but somehow I came across Les Bubb – and then he became associated with the show. Arthur Smith also became sort of "Listen to this – this guy's funny" and strange poet Ivor Cutler.'

In later years, Peter Fincham, the executive producer of many of Morris's TV shows, would say that Morris's humour came from working alone in the studio rather than honing a stand-up act himself in front of an audience, but Morris worked the crowd, albeit remotely. Callers were props in his humour. They might be encouraged to win a prize by guessing what an object was from clearly unconnected and unhelpful clues, and Morris would be mock-outraged at any attempt at obviously humorous answers. Unlike a stand-up comedian, Morris had the refuge of being able to cut his audience off, yet there was the sense of the show as a club. As at Radio Cambridgeshire, he simply seemed to expect that everyone could keep up.

Unsuspecting members of the public on the street were regularly used for Morris's Feedback Reports slot. People would give their thoughts on anything from 'wind obedience' (commenting on the conclusions of 'Professor Gus T. Day') to official moves to limit the time people take to say things. Most interviewees fumbled their way to agreeing with whatever he said, but one managed to produce a stream of consciousness that seemed to come from Morris's own universe. He was a trolley collector at the local Sainsbury's called Steve who was soon christened Sergeant

Murphy. His rapid-fire responses featured on Morris's radio programmes for years.

Then there was 'Ten ideas to change the world', co-written with Steve Yabsley and delivered by the golden voice of local broadcaster Michael Alexander St John-Gifford over Pachelbel's stately 'Canon in D Major'. It was a thought for the day for the deranged – the point was that there was no point. Each idea and meandering digression made less sense than the subjects up for discussion in the Feedback Reports, but the writing was packed with delightfully surreal imagery and given apparent authority through St John's irresistible solemnity: 'Coalescing a mild stir in the public gallery by actually frowning your face off' was one idea, 'Calling for absolute silence after the sorbet, then dissolving rather beautifully into a rude finger' another. Michael St John, as he was known by everyone, would be another regular voice on Morris's shows for years to come.

Morris used his repertoire of impersonations and created Wayne Carr, a smug DJ of the sort that Paul Whitehouse and Harry Enfield later popularized with their Smashie and Nicey characters. Wayne Carr ('WC on the radio') would be Morris's alter ego throughout his DJ career, popping up to misinterpret news headlines, make banal or offensive observations and interview unknowing celebrities.

On making his return to the city of Bristol, Morris at first rented and then bought a place with a doctor friend he'd known from university. Jane Solomons would share the house with him before buying her own place. Morris often took to the streets of Bristol in a rather beautiful Mercedes, cream-coloured and impractically large for the narrow streets between his place and the BBC in Whiteladies Road. It was a distinctive car, if rather old and unreliable, but somehow Morris kept it on the road into the 1990s. He was an enthusiastic cyclist and played tennis and remained a keen if, friends remember, rather wayward bowler in cricket. Morris had his own take on the 1980s look which hadn't developed greatly in his move from Cambridgeshire. 'Always with a bow tie! Literally, bow tie, a stripy shirt quite often and a V-neck,' says Matt Sica. 'Absolutely loved it – and trainers. Just wonderfully took the piss. It was like power-dressing at local radio. Cravats as well; he also wore cravats.'

Morris attracted a like-minded bunch of friends, sharp, funny and well attuned to the absurdities of life in local radio. Many were around his age, twenty-five, such as Jonathan Maitland, a warm and charmingly ambitious reporter, nicknamed Nath by Morris. Hugh Levinson, who had played guitar in the 1984 Footlights revue show, joined Bristol as a local radio trainee partly at Morris's suggestion. Having graduated in 1985 with no idea of what he wanted to do, Levinson spent a year in Japan teaching English before deciding to follow his friend. Clive Myrie went on to be a foreign correspondent. The gang also included Steve Yabsley and bringing up the average age was John Armstrong. Tall and slightly untidy, Armstrong had come up through newspapers and a variety of local, national and London-based radio and was one of the newsreaders at the station who shared Morris's irreverence for their working environment.

Maitland remembers that Morris's attention was slightly distracted by another of their friends, Julie Sedgewick: 'She was well fit and everyone fancied her,' he says. 'You'd have to have been gay or asexual not to have felt a bit of a twinge. She looked like I imagined Cathy from *Wuthering Heights* to have looked. In the end, Clive went out with her.'

Other friends came from his university days, and Jane Solomons remembers a time characterized by a busy social circle, as much drawn from outside the media as from the BBC, and lots of good conversation. Morris was a great host with a skill in cooking beyond the range of the average twenty-five-year-old. 'My impression of Chris at the time was as a sort of bon viveur,' says Steve Yabsley, inspired to develop his own fare by Morris's versatility with herbs, garlic and flavourings. It was nurturing stuff, which he deployed to bring everyone together and not just during good times. When Jonathan Maitland had relationship problems, he ended up on Morris's doorstep one night. 'He opened the door and I burst out crying,' says Maitland, 'pretty embarrassing for a bloke.' But Morris was sweet and caring. Having grown up to be self-reliant through Stonyhurst, he nevertheless had an instinctive understanding of people and their problems. 'I just spilled it all out to him, and he was just very kind and knew how to deal with it,' says Maitland. 'He was in touch with his feminine side.'

There were also more raucous get-togethers. 'We had a really good party at my place, really good,' says Maitland. 'Tasty women and loads of drink. And Chris jumped out of the window and a hedge broke his fall. So he got lots of people to do this hedge-jumping thing. Undergraduate high jinks . . . but very funny.'

Jonathan Maitland was also a natural show-off and, although a news journalist, as aware as Morris of the inherent ridiculousness of his trade. 'He and Chris would often taunt each other on air,' remembers Sica. 'One would whisper abusive things down the other's cans [headphones], or buzz them just as they were about to go on, or stand outside the door and wave frantically as if it was some sort of emergency . . . play around like that. I remember once, Maitland was reading the news and Morris had his mike on, rustling his papers, taking big deep breaths before Maitland's sentences, to make it sound like he was nervous, or breathe deeply, or saying things under his breath.'

The domain in which Maitland worked was largely populated by a race more savagely ambitious and self-important than anyone in TV. They were fanatical about making news local. Morris later said that in December 1988, 'When Lockerbie happened in the Radio Bristol newsroom and somebody discovered that a local woman had been involved there was a, "Yes!" So it is quite hard to take it all seriously, but I was trying very hard to be well behaved.'[1]

Newsroom editor Mark Byford was an ongoing comedic obsession for Morris and Maitland as a BBC management textbook made flesh. He paced the newsroom when anything exciting happened and indicated his approval for a story by announcing in his Yorkshire accent, 'That's good telly! That's good telly!' Byford always seemed destined for great corporation things – and indeed went on to be deputy director general.

For all its absurdities and puffed-out peacocks, Radio Bristol would remain home for some of Morris's friends. Aside from a stint on Radio 4, John Armstrong remains at the station and Steve Yabsley is still a presenter much in Morris's inventive mould. Not so for Morris and Jonathan Maitland: 'I was trying to get out of Radio Bristol like nobody's business,' says Maitland. When he eventually achieved escape velocity it was to make it first as a reporter on Radio 4's *Today* programme and then later on ITV.

Meanwhile, back in his York penthouse flat, as he styled it in his radio shows, was Victor Lewis-Smith, another radio natural who was further down the road to recognition than Morris. Lewis-Smith started out on Radio York in 1983 and went on to contribute to Radio 4 shows as both a broadcaster and a producer. Evolving a breakneck, powerhouse style of his own as a performer of radio comedy, Lewis-Smith created lightning-fast, densely-packed sketches, often linked by manic tape winds. He multitracked multiple characters and did his own jingles in mocking BBC harmonies. He was, said Morris, a 'fully loaded weapon',[2] someone who had also come up through radio rather than stand-up and 'unquestion-ably one of the few who've taken radio by the horns.'[3] But Morris didn't say it until much later in his career.

From their broadcasting citadels in the 1980s, the princes of Bristol and York regarded one another with mutual suspicion. There might have been plenty of room for two talents like theirs to develop in tandem, but as young men with everything to prove it seemed they were trying to occupy exactly the same space, and a mutual loathing developed which, over the years, would be not so much barely disguised as played out in public at every oppor-tunity. 'There was a lot of snideness on both sides,' says John Armstrong.

In 1987 Lewis-Smith was a feature on Radio 4's *Loose Ends*. He poked fun at anyone and everything, from Ned Sherrin downwards. With collaborator Paul Sparks, he would send contributions to the show as late as possible so that they could sneak more contentious material through, a technique Morris would later use to his own great advantage.

Morris and Lewis-Smith followed each other's work very closely. A senior colleague at Bristol observes that for Morris 'it seemed to be quite an obsession'. He was getting national exposure with *No Known Cure* items appearing on Radio 4's *Pick of the Week*, and it was only a matter of time before Ned Sherrin played a clip of one of Morris's tapes on *Loose Ends* in January 1989, introducing it by drily commenting that Lewis-Smith was reportedly 'thrilled' about the 'young broadcaster from the West Country' as a precursor to what indeed was a very direct homage by Morris. He had perfectly caught the manic technical and presentation side of Lewis-Smith, he just hadn't quite found his own voice at that time. But even at what was a fairly embryonic stage, there was a detectable sense of energy, of a ferocious talent ripping through a whole palette of broadcasting techniques, discarding what didn't work and beginning to create something new out of what did.

The process of development brought Morris into ever more frequent clashes with management. He had quickly established something of a familiar relationship with them on joining the station which many other staff never attained, but there was always something of an edge to it. 'Chris is a guy who wants to challenge policies, practices and procedures all the time. And obviously he did so,' says Roy Roberts. 'He tended not to ask if he could do things; he'd try and do things to see what he could get away with.' Up to a point, the battles were something that Roberts himself accepted as a part of working with Morris, whose show was gaining the cult audience the station had hoped for. Morris's prank phone calls, a popular feature on the programme, regularly resulted in complaints. A football pools company went into panic when Morris asked if he could send in his entry after the game had been played. He was passed around the company, who seemed to think they were victims of a serious plot to defraud them, and they threatened Roberts with the police. The problem for the station was that BBC editorial guidelines insisted that people should be told they were to be on air. 'I hope he told them eventually that he'd made the recording for broadcast,' says Roberts, adding less optimistically, 'I'm not sure that he always did.'

It was Morris's irreverent attitude to the news which provided the most frequent battles with senior station staff, with a subversion that took many different forms. He couldn't help it, he later said, it just 'leaked through'.[4] Newsreaders doing a late slot would often get a buzz from Morris over the intercom. 'Your task tonight is to use "colander" in the bulletin,' he'd challenge. When he had to read the news himself in the course of his own programmes, particularly the late-night edition, he would sometimes add his own undermining remarks on the stories of the day. He even did the same to the national news; because that came down a feed one-way from the BBC in London, the newsreader wouldn't have heard such additions as apple munching or newspaper rustling.

'When I was reading the news,' remembers John Armstrong, 'he mainly indulged in comments or noises. Or sometimes just a word – "duffer", "tosspot". Roberts and [programme organizer Malcolm] Brammer used to hate it – undermining authority et cetera, et cetera.' It was almost midnight one Friday, remembers Matt Sica, when they decided to see if they could provoke some reaction from the audience. 'Chris was fed up because nobody was listening, we hadn't had a phone call for half an hour and so he decided to really push the boat out. His voice got quieter and quieter, there was a long pause, and there was this quiet, muttered whisper of "Bollocks". And we just waited. And nothing happened!'

But while his despairing bosses might have disagreed, he wasn't reckless in his mischief. He punctiliously checked the news bulletins to ensure that he wouldn't be playing for laughs over some genuine major tragedy – a small but telling point that was frequently missed out in the retelling of exploits which were already beginning to form part of a growing Chris Morris legend.

It was clear that his wayward inventiveness could not be constrained for long by Radio Bristol. By early 1990 Morris had been doing a weekly commute to London for nearly eighteen months, working on his Sunday show on GLR. It was only ninety minutes up the M4, but the two stations were planets apart in terms of their output. In the capital, Morris found himself working alongside creative presenters with an ambitious view of what radio could be that Bristol never even set out to match. He was still being featured on *Pick of the Week* and was branching out into print, including the successful transferral of some of his best features, such as DJ Wayne

Carr, into amusing interviews with the *NME* in 1990. But though it never seemed likely that Morris would always be content in working only with what Bristol had to offer, when the end came in the early part of that year, it was sudden and unpleasant.

In later press profiles of Morris it would routinely be said that he was sacked after commentating on the news. Like the story about him filling a studio with helium, the version of events went largely unchecked and would become a cornerstone of his reputation for being a dangerous and unstable character, a vile and repeated slur on his professionalism for which the source seemed to be largely Chris Morris. It was what he told friends such as Nick Barraclough who, on hearing what he had been up to, thought it 'a fabulous thing to do, absolutely wonderful', but at the same time told him, 'I'm not surprised you've been sacked!' It was a beguiling image – Morris yanked mid-broadcast from the studio by the burly bodyguards of news and slung out of the BBC.

But Morris was still a freelancer whose contract had to be renewed and, as managing editor Roy Roberts discreetly comments, because of the amount of work he was getting in London he didn't want to stay on. When pushed on the detail, Roberts concedes, 'I guess the accurate thing was that over a period his relationships with those who supervised his work at Radio Bristol got increasingly strained.' It had essentially become impossible for Morris to work at the station any longer. In particular, he'd completely fallen out with programme organizer Malcolm Brammer, who had succeeded David Solomons. It might not have been the summary dismissal of legend, but it was genuinely sour. His final shows were broadcast in early 1990 and by March he had gone. Colleagues remember that there was very little ceremony as Morris gathered the piles of his tapes which he always kept by his desk and swiftly disappeared. The BBC retained nothing of his work.

By the time Morris left for London, he had also split from Jane Solomons, though their break-up was far more amicable. She doesn't cite a particular moment when it ended, just the sensation that they were going different ways. 'We just drifted apart a bit, I suppose,' she says. They had been together four or five years, she remembers, Morris at first commuting from Bristol back to Cambridge at weekends to see her. She remained in Bristol, where she had a successful career at HTV, becoming a presenter for the TV station.

Long after his departure, the presence of Chris Morris hung around the studios of Whiteladies Road as a palpable influence – or like a bad smell, depending on your view of him. Alison MacPhail, who would later be a key member of Morris's production crew on *The Day Today* and *Brass Eye*, started at Radio Bristol some months after he left. She remembers how his greatest moments were still very present in the collective memory. The prank phone calls, the news tweaking, the management baiting. Mostly the tone was admiring – nothing quite like him had ever passed through the station doors – but a fair disapproving few conceded the management point of view and thought he had got above himself.

Newspapers later still came sniffing around for gossip about him in the wake of *Brass Eye*, and his friends took the opportunity to play along by loyally making up things which were frequently printed wholesale in the newspapers. Steve Yabsley claimed that Morris drank in the studio and managed to get the *Independent* to believe that he had an addiction to garlic and once came to work having cooked a chicken with twenty cloves. Even manager Roy Roberts could never quite bring himself to refute the story of Morris filling a studio with helium at Bristol. In reality, just as staff at Radio Cambridgeshire still believe the incident took place, only somewhere else, Roberts knows that Morris didn't do it on his watch. But it was almost as if by perpetuating the myths, those around Morris were sharing in his impish spirit. And even those whose job it was to keep him in check could never resist finding out how that felt.

4

RAW MEAT RADIO

IN OCTOBER 1988 A NEW AND DISTINCTIVE VOICE WAS HEARD in London. When GLR started broadcasting, it made the assumption that its listeners were intelligent but also liked rock and good pop music – and that all three things weren't mutually exclusive. Chris Morris was part of the launch, and GLR would go on to play a prominent part in his career for the next five years. The capital's BBC predecessor, Radio London, had failed even after a series of relaunches, and the new station was given the freedom to do what it wanted. It took a risk on unknown presenters and those who had been in the wilderness for various reasons to assemble a line-up who were positively encouraged to be daring.

Morris did a Sunday show alongside his Radio Bristol programmes until 1990 and after that would leave GLR for extended periods to work on the first and then second series of *On the Hour*. But he kept returning to the station until the middle of 1993, by which time filming had begun on *The Day Today*.

The station boss was Matthew Bannister, who had worked in the

BBC and on Capital Radio in both news and entertainment. His programme organizer was Trevor Dann, a former colleague. They didn't hesitate in getting rid of existing staff where they felt they wouldn't fit in with the new ethos. There was arrogance in their idiosyncratic vision of the new station and by the time they had the place looking the way they wanted it they had lost some of their audience – but those who remained loved it. It became a sort of club for those who appreciated its mix of current affairs and music.

'It wasn't aimed at a literate minority,' says Trevor Dann, 'but the truth is that Matthew and I both felt, possibly instinctively, that we needed to raise the intellectual level of traditional local radio to win an audience at all in London.'

DJs such as Emma Freud, Dave Pearce, Annie Nightingale, Johnnie Walker and Tommy Vance were soon joined by Danny Baker, an established telly name taking his first steps in radio. He was produced by a young Chris Evans, hot off the train from radio in Manchester. In defiance of radio etiquette, Danny Baker broadcast standing up. On his first day he excitedly banged the table in the studio, shouting, 'This is raw meat radio!' and 'There's a new sheriff in town!' Evans told him to stop and Baker retorted that he would walk out rather than be told what to do. Evans had to explain that it was simply that the mikes were rattling on the table and nobody could hear a word he was saying.

Quickly a fan of Baker, Morris commented on air, 'It's the sort of programme about which one day people will be saying, "Did you ever hear that?" They will be exchanging treasured tapes for return on pain of death if they're broken.' They would also be saying very similar things about his own show.

Morris had come to GLR through Trevor Dann, with whom he kept in contact after their days together at Radio Cambridgeshire. He'd sent the station a tape he made for the twentieth anniversary of

BBC local radio in November 1987. 'Neighbour shall be unspeakable unto neighbour,' he wrote on the case. The tape included a spoof of local news which anticipated *On the Hour* by some four years and was very recognizable for Matthew Bannister. He had created and co-presented Capital Radio's news programme *The Way It Is*, itself providing inspiration for Armando Iannucci in devising his news parody. 'We wanted people who shared our view that quite a lot of the things that happen on local radio are a bit crap,' says Matthew Bannister. '[Morris] seemed like a natural fit.'

Morris was hired on a freelance basis, given total freedom on the show, though as Trevor Dann observes, 'even if I'd asked him to, he wouldn't have followed the rules'. After Dann himself took over the station, Morris called him at home just as he should have been starting his live Easter Monday show in 1991. He'd got a colleague to cover for his first few minutes on air by announcing that he had been held up in traffic and pretended he was calling from Scotland to tell Dan to find an immediate replacement. Something in Dann, a form of inbuilt Morris-warning system, let him know that all wasn't right and he guessed at the last minute – correctly – that he was supposed to oblige with an hysterical outburst.

Morris slid into his show late, breezily explaining to the audience, 'I'm not here,' before introducing a tape of the freshly recorded conversation which concluded with him taunting the bemused Dann: 'You didn't seriously think I'd come in, did you?' There was a short, anguished silence before Dann wordlessly hung up and, back on the show, Morris cued in Bowie's 'Queen Bitch', contentedly repeating to his listeners, 'I'm not here . . .'[1]

'He was always doing this kind of stuff, always upsetting people,' says Dann. 'Even if you fly with him, he's still going to kick you. He will always push it to the point where it is dangerous.' In April 1993, just a month before Morris's final show on GLR, an IRA bomb went off in Bishopsgate, and on that day's show Morris made a direct reference to it when a caller joked that she was so disappointed to get a competition question wrong she was going to kill herself. 'All right,' says Morris, 'well, go to Bishopsgate.'[2]

'The weekend scheduling is inevitably very different on local radio stations, because there's nobody there,' says Trevor Dann. 'So the reality is that presenters turn up and press the button and pretty much do what the fuck they like.' Morris broadcast his show without assistance. 'When I brought him in to do Friday afternoons, I think we did give him a producer, but I don't know who he was. It wouldn't have been anyone he ever spoke to. He'd have been very dismissive.'

Morris's GLR programmes shared much with *No Known Cure* – right from the multilayered, breakneck jingles, cut up and manipulated so even his name was obscured. But it was so much more suited to being broadcast in London. The capital inevitably attracted the knowing, the chaotic and the surprising, and in its sprawl there was always room for something to come shrieking out of some side alleyway to give you a shock. That was the nature of the city and what GLR reflected so well. Morris's show was constantly shifting, impossible to pin down. Bristol listeners would have recognized features such as 'Ten ideas to change the world' with Michael Alexander St John, the interjections of Sergeant Murphy and Feedback Reports.

An occasional contributor to GLR was Paul Garner, who had kept in contact with Morris since meeting him at Radio Cambridgeshire while a teenager doing voluntary work. He played himself on air, willing to be as silly as he could be while helping Morris out generally, ad-libbing and doing competitions. Morris was amused to learn that when Garner had to fly anywhere he would invariably pass time at the airport by seeing if he could get the information desk to page names which made stupid phonetic phrases. Garner would go out to stores and record himself paging names like 'Dawn Doyn' for Morris's show.

Callers to the show were engaged in a similarly brisk, deadpan banter. Morris always sounded most delighted when someone made him laugh despite himself or entered into his world, playing along as if the weirdness were just normal. This was just as true of very young listeners, who were used as part of the comic arsenal in a natural, inclusive way, rather than being handled with the patronizing overdelicacy that was the media's default mode. Morris's default mode was anyway a childlike, mischievous enthusiasm.

In a feature that he later took to his Radio 1 shows, 'kiddy's outing', an outright slander would be delivered at a random celebrity with charming innocence by a very small child. Even the most base-less character assassination sounded endearing when the reader clearly had no idea of the meaning of what they were saying and their main preoccupation was to endeavour to pronounce long words properly – in which respect, kiddy's outing was much like Morris's adult vox pops. In a typical example, one BBC journalist was named as a 'Mekon-headed, sour-faced, constipated news-barker'. For the most part, Morris needed only himself for the humour. He created vivid little characterizations for little mini-sketches. Keith Richards developed from an affectionate impression complete with wheezing laugh and drunken guitar strumming to the point where he would have his own little spot occasionally with surreal musings on current issues.

In July 1990 the GLR show won a Gold Award at the International Radio Festival of New York. That same year Morris and Iannucci started to discuss what would become *On the Hour*. And by the time studio work on that show began in 1991, Morris had found an agent, Caroline 'Chiggy' Chignell at PBJ – the management founded by Peter Bennett-Jones – though not without having to do some persuading.

'We resisted,' she says. 'Partly because I was quite new and I didn't know who he was.' She tried to get rid of him politely.

'I haven't done anything in radio,' she explained.

'Exactly!' Morris replied, delighted. He explained that it would be the gap they had that he could take up. Chiggy relented. 'He's easy to relent to,' she says. 'He's just very persuasive. It's like having the best salesman you can imagine.' Morris energetically set about sealing the deal, treating it as a great game for everyone, but combined his irresistible energy with total clarity about what he wanted. It was an agent's dream. An initial six-month try-out became a permanent arrangement.

On Christmas Day 1990 Morris made his debut appearance on Radio 1 for a one-off show, and early in the new year he left GLR as *On the Hour* took priority. But he continued to do specials and returned in November after the series finished for a further three-month stint.

'He always was part of the team and he ebbed and flowed,' says Trevor Dann. 'His argument, quite legitimately, was: "I can't do this for very long. You know, this is not an act I can do fifty-two weeks of the year" . . . Yeah, and I kind of get that . . . this isn't like being Terry Wogan. You can't just turn up and do it.'

Morris's return was in the form of a three-hour Friday-afternoon show interspersed with news, sport, weather and traffic and an hour-long programme on Sundays. The run concluded at the end of January 1992 when he went to work on the second series of *On the Hour*. The first outing had been such a success that there was a buzz about what would be the final series.

Morris continued to introduce the real world to *On the Hour* with ever more elaborate stunts, including a series of phone calls in which he convinced the *Sun* to buy a story about Neil Kinnock (Steve Coogan) being recorded on a Dictaphone abusing restaurant staff in the middle of the general election campaign. It was not long after the Liberal leader Paddy Ashdown had been exposed for having an affair and it went all the way to a deal, to include substantial cash and a picture of editor Kelvin MacKenzie in a heart-shaped frame. The journalist realized he had been hoaxed only at the point Morris insisted he be quoted as having also seen Kinnock running nude down his hotel corridor in the middle of the night shouting, 'Forget Paddy Pantsdown, I'm Neil Kingcock.'

But he was less successful in an attempt to get the *Today* programme to feature an item about cows coming back to life – it was close, though. Morris called the Radio 4 news programme early one morning shift posing as a freelance reporter from the West Country. His Ted Maul-style character was very much like one of the many real-life local reporters who would try the *Today* show in the hope that selling a story would be a way out of regional broadcasting. It was quite a good way of sneaking an item on the programme, as the approaches tended to be looked on favourably by the show's editors as a way of deflecting criticism of the BBC as being London-centric. Morris and other cast members reported on a herd of cattle which had mysteriously revived at an abattoir after slaughter. No cause was given and the dread acronym 'BSE' was never mentioned, but it didn't need to be. An inevitable, if unconscious, link would be made over the panic about British beef which was still in the headlines when *On the Hour* was recording in May 1992. From mad cow disease to undead cow sickness – not so far-fetched in twitchy times. It was a bank holiday, a thinner day for news, and the night editorial team were convinced.

Then assistant editor Rod Liddle arrived. He was later an editor himself of the show and someone who would become involved in his own brand of BBC controversy during the second Gulf War. But he took one look at 'undead cows' on the running order and spiked the story – he had no way of knowing who was responsible, that he'd outsmarted the man he would himself later cite in a *Time Out* interview as the 'only genius' working in broadcasting.

The fake eventually entered *Today* legend and was still being talked about when the 1992 team gathered for the retirement of their former editor, Phil Harding, in 2007, when the reminiscing turned not to the end of Communism, the first Gulf War or any of the other global stories of the time, but to the ghostly cows from the West Country. Editor Harding could look back on a thirty-eight-year BBC career during which he'd run the World Service, but he himself admitted while laughing that he would have had to resign from *Today* had the story made it through.

The series finished in the only way it could, with Morris's announcement that the show was taking over Radio 4 entirely and for ever for 24-hour 'permanews'. *On the Hour* had immediately established itself as a classic. 'The most brilliant radio comedy to emerge in the last ten years,' said the *Independent* in May, which highlighted the way it combined 'flashes of hallucinatory wit with dazzlingly plausible imitations of the tropes of radio news'.[3]

'I should really remember the date: it was a Saturday morning last summer. I was in bed, dismal at the prospect of *Loose Ends*,' wrote James Hepburn in *The Times*. 'As I reached for the "off" button, a voice like Trevor McDonald's on the plains of Armageddon announced that this was *On the Hour*. Thirty minutes later, I was gazing at the radio with much the same feeling that Keats must have had on first reading Chapman's Homer.'[4] To the delight of doomed, consumptive poets everywhere, *On the Hour* won in the Best Radio comedy category of the 1992 British Comedy Awards.

In the wake of the series the long-running disagreement between

Morris and Victor Lewis-Smith reignited. It was claimed that Lewis-Smith had complained to the controller of Radio 4 that Morris was being given more freedom than him to do pranks that pushed at BBC guidelines. Morris obligingly did his bit to keep the bad feeling festering: 'He's like an unofficial publicity agent who takes great pains to put my name in print whenever he can. It will run and run until he has a heart attack,' he said that summer, 'and falls flat on his fat face.'[5]

The mutual dislike had previously bubbled up into public view in *Time Out*'s letters page in late 1990 in a spat over who had originated comic broadcasting techniques and ideas. Lewis-Smith declared in one of the broadsides, 'It is an ineluctable fact of media life that for every Coke there is a Pepsi. While I am the first to admit that I am no Château Margaux Premier Cru, I like to think of Chris Morris as the Babycham to my Mateus Rosé.'[6]

'I object most strongly to Victor Lewis-Smith's recent use of the word "ineluctable",' began one 'Massingberd Stitt' from W1 the following week. 'Such magniloquent gasconism frankly raises the dander and my fellow symposiasts agree that this whimwham of an adjective sounds spoony and sticks in the craw like a probang.'[7] Matthew Bannister observed the skirmishing from a safe distance at the top of GLR. 'It definitely seemed like a passionate feud, six of one, half a dozen of the other,' he says now. Like others, he heard stories of Lewis-Smith scrawling Morris-unfriendly graffiti outside the station, but he had never seen it himself.

After *On the Hour*, Lewis-Smith said he was resigned to never receiving a sympathetic hearing from bosses. 'What's the point?' he said. 'You take a tape into somebody's office and say, "Listen to this – that man's a thief!" And they look at you and think, This is somebody with an obsession.' The *Guardian* featured the rivalry in its Feud's Corner column in June 1992.

But the arguments between the two were harmless by comparison with another, potentially more damaging, disagreement which was opening up closer to *On the Hour*'s home. The root of the problem was also partly what helped the show to be so remarkable – the collaborative, improvisational approach. Collectively, everyone did well, but individually it was harder to credit each contributor.

This was increasingly a worry for Stewart Lee and Richard Herring who, together with their formidable agent Jon Thoday, wanted to clarify credits. If the show went on tour, then they should be able to say how much they owned of such characters as Alan Partridge. The situation was further complicated by a personality clash between the pair and Patrick Marber, who had started to contribute his own material to the show. Yet over the summer the three were still getting on well enough for them to collaborate on what would be called the Dum Show. They took it to the Edinburgh Festival with Steve Coogan and fellow comedian Simon Munnery.

Morris, meanwhile, showed no more desire than he'd had in his early twenties to perform comedy live. While the others prepared to storm Scotland, he released a record of a few sketches on a *Select* music magazine freebie. He often included music parodies on his DJ shows, and among the offerings to the magazine's indie and alternative readership was an affectionate Pixies take-off – the incestuous tale of 'Motherbanger'. Although he always wrote the words and music himself for such items, they were often recorded in the studio of former Bristol University student Jonathan Whitehead. They had got to know each other better over the years and Morris had often stayed at his place in Shepherd's Bush when he'd been commuting from Bristol. Whitehead would work with him throughout the 1990s on the musical aspects of his shows.

Jonathan Whitehead had started his career harbouring a desire to be a serious composer, influenced by Stockhausen and John Cage, and also made an abortive attempt at establishing himself in the pop world. Realizing he was never going to write a chart-topper, Whitehead learned music production techniques and set about building a career in broadcast music. His background and training helped his role with Morris, assisting with the technical aspects of capturing the feel of a band. Just as it was all about close observation in Morris's news parodies, here it was all about the detail of the sound, referencing at least two or three songs. Morris didn't see a comic song as a quick filler. His songs sounded like something the target artist might do on a particularly demented day in the studio, suggesting their essence with little more than a brief sketch.

'Musically, they somehow got compressed,' explains Whitehead. 'There would never be a whole verse just to get it to a certain length. It was always cut up, so you had very fractured structures that were very compact, just to get across the maximum amount of gags in the shortest amount of time.' In 'Motherbanger' there was a brief 'Monkey Gone to Heaven' vocal breakdown: 'My mother gummed my weapon.' Like many of the bands Morris picked on, the Pixies were a real favourite of his and the affection helped to underpin the spoof with a sense of authenticity.

While *Select* was running Morris's work on its front cover, the Dum Show was making its way to Edinburgh, 'and therein begins the nightmare,' says Patrick Marber. 'There was a violent disagreement between me and Richard Herring. I thought he was a brilliant writer, but there was one sketch in which I thought Steve should play the part that Richard was playing. He got very upset, very angry with me, understandably, because it was hurtful, what I said, but I just felt it was true. I thought he was ruining his own sketch . . . Anyway, it all kicked off.'

The *Guardian* review was almost literally correct in observing of the show, 'Inside this imaginative yet fundamentally flawed showcase are two incisive writers (Richard Herring and Simon Munnery), a pair of adept stand-ups (Stewart Lee and Patrick Marber) and an amusing impressionist (Steve Coogan) all fighting each other to get out.[8] It didn't help, as far as Herring was concerned, that Marber spent the rest of his time directing Coogan's show *Steve Coogan in Character* with John Thomson. Coogan had a well-rehearsed show, designed to showcase his character work, which won that year's Perrier Award. Having struggled for so long to define himself as more than an impressionist, he had finally arrived.

Their colleague's success did nothing to dissipate the rancour between Marber and Herring and Lee. For a while Patrick Marber was a frequent target in their double act. 'I still see him every now and again,' says Herring now. 'He's not someone I have great affection for, but I don't hate him as much as we make out.'

Lee and Herring were still on good terms with Armando Iannucci and back in London got him to appear on their *Lionel Nimrod's Inexplicable World* that autumn. For his part, Iannucci enjoyed appearing in a show he wasn't writing, so he could just turn up and be funny, 'just the opposite of thinking about everything'. *On the Hour* had been such an intensive project that many of its participants went with relief to shows that lent themselves more to being performed than assembled. For Morris the reverse was true. He actively preferred to be away from it all in the studio. 'He enjoyed his writing and he does his stuff himself,' explains Iannucci, 'but it takes us to tell him that he's actually very good at all the voices and characters he does. He just feels that's something he does.' The GLR shows were all he needed.

Morris was absent from *Knowing Me, Knowing You . . . with Alan Partridge*, which began on Radio 4 in December 1992. Lee and Herring's falling out with Patrick Marber and the dispute over credits meant they weren't involved either. Yet it would be Alan more than anyone else who facilitated the team's crossover from admired cult comedy to mainstream success. Alan was put forward for his own series even before the TV version of *On the Hour.*

The tone of *Knowing Me . . .* was lighter than *On the Hour,* a welcome relief for its performers. If anything, the audience took the show more seriously than its creators, with several listeners assuming that the show was real. In the last episode, Patrick Marber's Lord Morgan of Glossop dies mid-interview, and the dismayed complainers included a headmaster of a public school. *Knowing Me, Knowing You* won Best Radio Comedy in the British Comedy Awards in 1993 and won a Sony award that same year. Of all the cast, Steve Coogan was the most obvious contender for stardom. *On the Hour*'s sports reporter had effortlessly passed his anchorman in the celebrity stakes – which suited them both fine.

Chris Morris was absorbed in *The Day Today* when he returned to GLR for six Saturdays from April 1993. Those shows – his last ever for the station – were his equivalent of the lightness of *Knowing Me, Knowing You.* He was confident and playful, displaying no apparent hint of effort in the endless stream of ideas and gags. There was plenty in the shows that would make it into Morris's 1994 series of Radio 1 shows, and there was also a precursor of the later *Blue Jam* series in the form of a monologue with a strange and desolate tone. The pieces were called Temporary Open Spaces and were read by Robert Katz. It was the start of an occasional writing collaboration that would last for years. Katz had come to Morris's attention through what he describes as a 'vaguely surrealist column' he wrote in London listings magazine *City Limits.* The two met through Jo Unwin, then sharing a house with Katz's girlfriend of the time. The stories they came up with had a distinct flavour that was unlike anything else Morris did.

They would be delivered in a flat tone, the backdrop London as an alien landscape peopled with heartless media drones and depressives seen through the sinking eyes of an everyman disassociated from everything he encounters, exploited by those he meets and adrift in the city. Robert Katz says that it was Morris who was interested in exploring the downbeat comedy of a 'fuzzy-headed' figure, someone running at a different speed from the world around him. The inspiration was 'partly the result of banging on my "fuzzy head" to see what thin noises might come out', says Katz, 'but also developed from one or two other bodies we stole from the morgue of real-life characters'. The GLR pieces were sculpted by Morris to bring out that quality of otherness: 'I seem to recall that Chris edited every intra-vocal breath out,' Katz recalls, 'so that there's a strange hiatus between each single word.' Morris had been thinking of a way in which to change the jaunty tempo of the GLR show, and Robert Katz fitted the bill to work with, although he downplays his contribution to the process. It was certainly an important shift in mood, flavouring much of what Morris would do towards the end of the 1990s with *Blue Jam* and its offshoots. In conversation by email, though, Katz is not unlike Morris himself, witty and friendly, but nevertheless guarded and considered in everything he discusses. He gradually opens up over time in a series of observations that are as thoughtful as they are frequently tangential, occasionally acerbic and entertainingly gnomic.

Emphasizing Morris's 'galaxy-sized mind', Katz says that he 'always had the vision and wrote and recorded the things to his satisfaction, and because he's a genius 99 per cent of that is perspiration. His, not mine. It's not false modesty; I was just thrilled to be able to do stuff with him.' And yet even in such casual correspondence, Katz has a precise and evocative style which could itself be straight out of a *Blue Jam* sketch. Asked if he agrees that something of the flavour of GLR's Temporary Open Spaces is at the core of the later shows, Katz says, 'I guess you could say the monologues in *Blue Jam* formed a centre, but only because that's where they physically are, in the middle of the shows, like a slow movement in a symphony, or a dead body lolling in the middle of a pond.' It's hard not to come away from a – typically oblique – email conversation with him without concluding that he was more central to the process than he admits.

Their work was going out on a station that was changing. For those who loved its bold remit and chaotic creativity, it wasn't for the better. Matthew Bannister had left GLR in 1991 to develop the BBC's royal charter renewal and Trevor Dann became the managing editor. But the BBC were determined to standardize regional stations and had enforced speech-only segments of the day.

Trevor Dann took redundancy in May 1993. It was the month in which Morris's last few shows were going out, as he and Armando Iannucci continued to work on *The Day Today* over the rest of the year. Dann knew full well what he was letting himself in for when he invited Morris to talk at his leaving do. 'I suppose you're all expecting something funny,' Morris said, 'but I don't do stand-up.' He played a pre-recorded phone call he had made to the director general of the BBC, John Birt. 'Could you take a message for him, please?' he said in Trevor Dann's distinctive Midlands tones. 'Could you tell him I think he's a big load of sloppery old bollocks.' The following day Dann had to make a conciliatory phone call to Birt's PA, who had been entirely convinced it was the genuine article.[9] There was a similarly painful call to Radio 1 assistant controller Chris Lycett, who greeted 'Trevor' with a matey 'Doctor Dann! How the hell are you?' But as 'Doctor' Dann bid ever more shamelessly for the inside track to becoming what he called a 'waggish' Radio 1 DJ, an increasingly unhappy Lycett attempted to shuffle out of the brittle conversation, which seemed for tortuous minutes to prefigure the classic desperate programme pitches of Alan Partridge's. At length Lycett clambered out. 'This isn't Trevor Dann, is it?' 'You may be clever,' said the counterfeit doctor over his victim's repeated demands to know who he's really talking to, 'but you're ugly.'

5

FACT x IMPORTANCE = NEWS

THE 1994 TRANSFER OF *ON THE HOUR* TO TELEVISION SHOULD have gone smoothly. The BBC had a proven hit on their hands, but BBC bureaucracy got in the way. They couldn't possibly allow Iannucci and Morris the same sort of control over the show when it left radio. It would be out of the question, the duo were told, that they could run their own programme when they had no experience of television. It didn't matter that much of the success of *On the Hour* had been down to their iron control – though as a concession, management told a distinctly unimpressed Armando Iannucci, he could have a script editing role. Morris and Iannucci decided they would rather take their show elsewhere than watch it slip away from them. It was a decision that the strengths of their partnership made far easier. 'I'm not sure that I would have said "no" if I hadn't been doing it with Chris,' says Iannucci. It was a risk, because although they knew they had a good and tested format, they couldn't be sure they would get someone interested to do it in the way they wanted. But if they were ever going to make the move away from the security of the BBC, now was the time. Chris Morris was only just thirty and neither of them yet had children.

But the hardest part of the decision for Armando Iannucci was leaving the organization he had worked for since university, where he had built a reputation as an excellent comedy producer. Now he was being effectively told that everything he did was somehow less accomplished because it was just radio and that television involved complexities that he just wouldn't be up to. It was a short-sighted attitude, but one that was then commonly held at the BBC about radio production. Iannucci pointed management at the example of Dan Patterson, who co-created *Whose Line Is It Anyway?* on BBC radio and then took it to Channel 4. 'Yeah,' came the dusty response that was a clincher in Iannucci's mind, 'but if you look at the lighting on some of those Channel 4 shows, it's not quite as good.'

He and Morris set out to find an independent production company that would let them work on the show on their own terms. Hat Trick, one of the biggest comedy producers, were one of the first they tried. They were welcoming but 'not quite right', says Iannucci. 'Didn't quite feel that we'd be completely left to do it the way we wanted to do.'

Talkback looked much more their kind of place. It had been founded by Mel Smith and Griff Rhys Jones while they were doing *Not the Nine o'Clock News* at the start of the 1980s, and when Morris and Iannucci arrived it was still a relatively small but inventive company. They put the creative goals of their producers first and worked back to make sure they could be realistically achieved. The company was headed by Peter Fincham, a Cambridge graduate and former musician who had joined Talkback in 1985 yet retained his enthusiasm for the creative aspects of the shows he oversaw. 'It was a really good camaraderie. I think Peter's very good at leaving people alone,' explains Nick Canner, a veteran of the company who was assigned to

The Day Today production team. 'People liked to work at Talkback because it's not like there's a David O. Selznick figure sending memos every day, saying, "I think that could've been funnier." Peter was very much a sort of hands-off figure: "You're a talented person – be talented!"' And somehow the Talkback 'vibes', adds Armando Iannucci, were right. They'd found an easy-going centre of excellence where talent was given space to thrive. By convention, companies controlling the entertainment business make impossible, soul-destroying demands of their stars – *The Day Today* creators would turn that truism around.

It was also the start of a long relationship between Morris and Talkback, which tailored their working practices to individual creative temperament. They realized he didn't need the safety net of a tight production contract – and that he wouldn't be constrained even if he had one – so there was never a formal agreement between them. They gave him an office away from their headquarters and the time to develop his ideas.

With production secured, the pilot of the new show was completed in January 1993, a year before the full series went out on the BBC. Iannucci and Morris reinvented everything, even the title. That they brought such a fine level of observation to both radio and then TV news journalism did make it seem as if they had it in for news as a concept, but Iannucci maintains it was not a vendetta. 'You do these things partly out of affection as well,' says Iannucci now. 'It was not saying, "All telly is bad and unless we change our habits British broadcasting is going to go down the pan."' Iannucci simply often found inspiration in politics and the media, though he had been the subject of enough interviews in which minor comments ended up being a sensational headline to feel a natural suspicion towards the media.

'You can see how artificial the process is,' he says. 'It's not that simple telling of reality. You realize how edited the news is.' As part of their research, he and Morris took a mini news-editing course organized by the BBC newsroom. The pair were given a story from the ongoing Bosnian War with four main pieces of information, which they had to set to rushes from BBC coverage of the conflict in the form of a two-minute piece with voiceover. As their allotted two hours came to a close, they realized they were without obvious footage to illustrate one of the key points of the package and they had to leave it out. It gave them a clear idea of how much news had to do with presentation and deadline. In the spring of 1994 Morris would write in his review of a war reporter's memoirs, 'Basically, news is glorified gossip. It is not the truth that makes a story news, but its entertainment value.'[1]

He and Iannucci were given a tour of the newsroom that same day by staff who expected to be quizzed by the comedians on what funny things happen in the studio, only to find themselves questioned closely on the technical aspects of making programmes and learning about how the designers and directors of the news did their jobs, an in-depth approach to research which Morris would always retain. Charlie Brooker, co-creator of *Nathan Barley*, remembers at least a full hour devoted to deciding the font that would most believably be used by *Sugar Ape*, the style bible for which journalist Dan Ashcroft writes.

For the writing of *The Day Today*, the idea had been to bring along the same people from the radio. Stewart Lee and Richard Herring were still concerned about how they might retain ownership of ideas that they co-created, but for a while it looked as if the dispute might be resolved. The pilot went ahead without them, but when a new front in the wrangling opened over a trivial sum for the commercial release of *On the Hour*, 'it was then beginning to stop things from happening,' says Iannucci. He refused the request and went through every tape in one long session, removing everything credited to the duo.

'God, I remember that night,' shudders Carol Smith, Armando's PA. 'I remember leaving him hunched over an editing block in the office and coming in the next morning and he was still there. And I said to him, "Oh, for God's sake! You're not still here?" And he slept on the floor in my office.' It was the end of any hopes that the pair might be in *The Day Today*. 'It wasn't personal,' says Herring now, 'and in the end I think it was the right thing for us. I think we would have got comfortable with *The Day Today* and we wouldn't have done our own stuff. I think it worked out for the best. But at the time I was really gutted. We might have ended up working on the various spin-off projects involving Coogan and Chris Morris.' Even without the benefit of being part of the transfer, they got their own television shows, *Fist of Fun* and *This Morning with Richard, Not Judy*, on BBC2, for which they acquired a devoted though small cult following. The BBC never really got wholeheartedly behind their material, and there was a sense of regret that ran throughout the team and into Talkback itself, where Sally Debonnaire, head of production, thought it was one of the major lost opportunities in comedy of that time.

The rest of the principal cast and crew were caught between feeling sympathy for the two and knowing that they had to get on with *The Day Today*. It put them all in a difficult position. 'It's something I chose not to follow too closely,' says David Schneider. 'I was friends with them all, really.' Iannucci was particularly apologetic. Everyone was trying to make their way, and the splits were partly a result of the immense pressure under which they all operated. 'You forget that everyone at the time was much younger and much more nervous and kind of energized,' says Iannucci. He remained on good terms with Herring and Lee, any residual bad feeling evaporating after the shared experience of an unsettling flight the three took from London to Glasgow. They hit turbulence, and Lee, who was sitting next to Iannucci, took the opportunity to say *The Day Today* episode wasn't worth bearing grudges over and, when they eventually landed safely, they all agreed they wouldn't have liked to have plunged screaming to the ground with an argument over writing credits still unresolved.

The greater demands of television meant that a far larger team needed to be recruited, including a director, though Morris and Iannucci had such a strong idea of how the show had to look that they were in some respects almost directing themselves. They would be involved in every shot, in Iannucci's words 'hovering around'.

Morris's GLR collaborator Robert Katz joined as a film researcher. 'I was an archive researcher at LWT when *The Day Today* started,' explains Katz, 'and Chris knew that and very punctiliously didn't interview me for the job. He left it to Armando and the charming late Susie Gautier-Smith [*The Day Today* programme associate who died in October 1996]. Armando's interview question was, "How would you illustrate a whale trapped in Harrods with footage?"'

New writers included Welsh comedian Peter Baynham, the most notable arrival as far as Chris Morris was concerned. The two would go on to become good friends, and Baynham would become his key co-writer as well as a performer in many of his shows, but to begin with Morris was not even convinced Iannucci was right in thinking they needed any new writers at all. Rapid-talking Baynham had long performed his material live but had come to Iannucci's attention through his work on numerous BBC programmes. He was like countless writers in having come up through shows such as *The News Huddlines* and *Week Ending*, though probably far fewer comics had also served, as he had, in the merchant navy and he was certainly unique among all in quitting the programme to write a sitcom based on his seagoing experiences. He was sufficiently convinced of his idea's potential to turn down an offer of work from Iannucci when the latter took over *Week Ending*. Two dead-end, nautically themed pilot episodes later and Baynham was amused and horrified in equal measure on hearing *On the Hour*. It sounded like the future. 'I thought I'd missed my opportunity. Bloody hell,' he says now, still sick at the memory. 'I scraped by for the next few months and as it happens I got a call anyway.' By then a script associate writing gags for *Friday Night with Wogan*, Baynham stayed up all night before the first meeting, excitedly thinking of ideas. He arrived to find a team who were all very comfortable with one another.

'Looking back, I was very glad not to know that at the time,' says Baynham. 'I went to this afternoon meeting and I threw in some idea about an infestation of horses on the London Underground and Chris laughed. It's an over-simplification, but that felt like it changed things.'

The other contributors were future *Father Ted* creators Graham Linehan and Arthur Mathews. They met at *Hot Press* magazine in Dublin, where Mathews was an art director and Linehan was a film reviewer. When Linehan moved to London to write for *Select*, Mathews followed to share a tiny flat in Bounds Green. They had no television – just a radio with patchy reception – but within a week they had tuned in to an episode of *On the Hour* and fell in love with it immediately. Listening to *On the Hour* brought back that intense feeling they had last experienced as kids discovering new bands for the first time. Linehan even listened to the show lying on the floor, just as he used to do with music when he was a teenager. It was after they got some sketches taken by Talkback that they got to meet the team. They were just a little bit in awe when their heroes appeared at the same company to start work on *The Day Today*, but not enough not to swiftly engineer an invitation to the writers' meetings, where they were terrified that they wouldn't measure up and didn't contribute a huge amount of material.

The pilot proved to be a clash of two cultures. Producers and a cast who were making their first steps in television and yet knew exactly what they wanted to achieve met established television folk who were used to doing the job in a certain way. The demanding process was made that much more complicated because of the straight approach required for the humour. Props were supplied by specialists in comedies when the show called for something more like a drama production approach. When the show needed a report from an American network, they wanted to use US-style recording equipment to capture the fuzzier broadcast quality. It all meant that everyone had to learn new ways of working. 'We were learning how to do telly and then how to undo telly for the programme,' says Iannucci. But the resulting programme was a success, very close to how the series would look. The cast, despite their relative youth, believably inhabited the shape their voices suggested on the radio. Character improvements required for the series were cosmetic. There was Morris's naturally curly hair, which bobbed around on his head in a way that was mesmerizingly independent of his own movements. When he had it slicked back for the series and adopted a more sober suited look, he would be sleeker and more menacing. Yet they all had an air of gravitas about them in the pilot that carried the inevitable moments of uncertainty in the performances. A few of the cast worried, needlessly, that Iannucci might prefer older performers, but they looked right in their television suits.

The pilot came in well over budget and rumours spread in the comedy industry that the team were somehow favourites of the BBC. In reality, though it was the higher end of the usual sketch show allowance, it wasn't excessive. It was just what they did with it that gave it its look. And they required a particularly flexible production crew who could interpret the very specific needs of the scripts. In the run-up to recording the main show, outside segments for which were shot in June and July 1993 and the studio work in October, those on the production side who hadn't adjusted to the new way of working were unsentimentally ditched. Among the replacements was production manager Alison MacPhail, or Ali, who came from the Jonathan Ross show *Saturday Zoo*, a programme she had found depressing and messy. She was disillusioned and close to leaving television altogether, but *The Day Today* proved to be exactly what she needed. She soon established a fearsome reputation for being able to get hold of anything for the show, no matter how mad or unlikely. She was impressive, funny, massively capable and, in not caring much whether she stayed in television, she was never in awe of the job or of the bright crowd she was working with. Seconded to Iannucci, it probably also helped that she was a fellow Scot. She didn't find it so easy to get on with Morris at first. He seemed removed and quiet, which she marked down as arrogance. She felt as if she were being tested. The uneasy initial period culminated in a bad-tempered exchange over nothing much, and she felt her honest and down-to-earth response won his respect. They established a bond that would see her continue to work with him right through to *Brass Eye*.

Morris and Iannucci themselves had surprisingly few arguments, given that they were in one another's company to the exclusion of any social life: 'It was probably eighteen months of solid fretting, hoping it wouldn't be a disaster,' says Iannucci. They worked jointly most of the time, though Iannucci, with the rest of the team, naturally leaned more towards the detail of performance and script while Morris immersed himself in the feel of the shows they were targeting and the technical aspects of production. Both were driven, but Iannucci tended to be less volatile than Morris, who could be quite maddening in his perfectionism. At one point in *The Day Today* production, convinced that he wasn't going to be able to realize the show in the way he wanted, he walked out after a row with Sally Debonnaire. He was back within a day and the details were soon forgotten. Long-time colleagues suspected his infrequent explosions were a way of giving himself time to think about how to solve specific problems.

One thing was clear to everyone at Talkback – both men pushed things as far as they could; it was part of the job for those who worked with them to work out what was up for negotiation and what was ring-fenced. One of their most demanding concepts was also on screen for the briefest time, a Graham Linehan and Arthur Mathews contribution about police dealing with noisy neighbours by releasing a tiger into the offenders' house. The production team put a huge amount of research into the realities of using a live tiger. It was risky and expensive, something that might have been dropped for an easier laugh. But the tiger, Talkback decided, would be something that the audience would remember and talk about. So the item was included in return for cutting back on some post-production work.

'The sketch that really sums *The Day Today* up is the tiger,' confirms Nick Canner. 'You would not believe the amount of work it took.' Few locations in London would deal with the risk of a live tiger – and when a council bottled out they ended up in Surrey in an army barracks. It took an entire day to film. One trained animal handler was hired to look after the tiger, while another looked after a gun that would be used in case the handler and his charge were to have a serious disagreement. The tiger was kept in a cage, with a second alongside in case it escaped from the first, but the results of such extra effort in *The Day Today* were so distinctive that everyone was willingly behind it.

The restriction of doing everything on camera meant there was less opportunity for improvising lines, but they kept the working process as close as possible to the open approach of the radio series. 'My memory is coming in with ideas which I'd been up all night thinking of,' says Peter Baynham. 'It was almost playing, coming up with the stupid headlines and the newspaper things.' Agrees Andrew Glover: 'I just thought that was the most fun you could have.' One of the few things that he worked on with Iannucci was suitable names for horses in Alan's sports reports. The original list of names was typed up and survives as an example of how even such a relatively minor element was reworked, the many names including Novelty Bobble, Different Types of Algebra, Astonishing Bomb Queen, Three Legs and I'm Yours, Back to the Drawing Board Lord Palmerston and Pah.

Anything that didn't work perfectly was ruthlessly excised. There was the time that Steve Coogan recorded a sports commentary and was improvising on Partridge being distracted from the sports action by advertising hoardings. He pointed out one for a computer he boasted he had bought. By coincidence the next ad happened to be for a credit card, 'and I used that to buy it,' he added. It was such a neat coincidence that he corpsed but, despite several additional takes, couldn't quite get it to sound as natural again and it was dropped.

Morris was more often around in the writing and improvisation phase than he had been in the radio show, partly because he couldn't work on his television material alone as he had on the radio. He would greet the cast with frequently bizarre concepts and start recording their responses. 'You had to be bold and just start talking, jump in without a net,' recalls Doon Mackichan. She and Rebecca Front say they felt it was 'liberating' to work on the range of roles they took in *The Day Today*. They could look completely silly in the report about the American condemned prisoner who elected to be executed on the toilet in homage to the way Elvis Presley died and then follow that by doing a comparatively straight report to camera. Rosie May's environment reports transferred from *On the Hour* with very little difference in style except for Front sporting a wispy new-age beard. 'Rosie May came fairly fully formed and scripted,' says Front. 'Barbara [Wintergreen, US correspondent], too, was scripted, but I knew how to play her from watching far too much CNN in hotel rooms . . . I'm a bit of a news junkie. I can claim credit for her trademark sign-off smirk, though, which started with me mugging at Armando when I thought we'd cut but we were still shooting.'

Mackichan's Collaterlie Sisters, icy and angular, spat out her financial news as if it were something half-cooked and gristly. 'When you watch the business news,' Morris later told journalist Simon Price, 'you always assume, oh, that's for the business community. But it would be great to find out that they didn't watch it either, but that it had a huge, vaguely new-age audience who liked the soothing, rhythmic effect of the numbers and that it eased distressed pets.'[2] She was a contrast to Dave Schneider's gently surreal weather presenter, his face floating across a map of the UK in different ways, in one report being fired around a weather pinball machine, as he intoned absurdist forecasts.

With Morris as the ringmaster for the bizarre collection of presenters, *The Day Today* was an only occasionally awkward blend of the savage and the absurd, Alan Partridge fumbling his brief or Morris humiliating guests such as the woman who has raised £1,500 for charity with her jam festival – 'You could make more money by sitting outside a Tube station with your hat on the ground even if you were twice as ugly as you are, which is very ugly indeed.'

The inventive mix of cruelty and wild stupidity put the show in a very English style of comedy. The novelist Jasper Fforde has pointed out *Diary of a Nobody* in this lineage, but he could equally well be talking about *The Day Today*. 'Pooter fits into the tradition of absurd humour that the British do so well, which started with Jonathan Swift and runs through Lewis Carroll and Edward Lear and is reflected much later on in Monty Python, the novels of Tom Sharpe and films like *The Wrong Trousers*. The satire [in the book] is cruel – but then a lot of comedy is cruel. You really squirm. But then the really great comics are not necessarily the people you always laugh at, but the people who make you think: Ooh, should I be laughing at that?'[3]

The Day Today's fantasies were framed in the serious news format. Morris's dazzling headlines were anchored by real footage – 'Headmaster suspended for using big-faced child as satellite dish', 'Bouncing elephantiasis woman destroys central Portsmouth'. Surviving scripts show that even the unused examples were strong – 'Major reacts after pony swallows cabinet' was one and there was the environment news – 'a large cloud of noise is threatening the north-east tonight. The noise is believed to have escaped from a chemical plant in Middlesborough and has now drifted as far south as Scarborough.' The studio looked believable, as if *The Day Today* existed within its own complete world, with mock trails for other programmes. There was a suggestion created of life off camera in the show's newsroom by the awkward flirting between Morris and travel news presenter Valerie Sinatra, moments that could have come directly from Morris's GLR show.

The force of his personality, which had been so apparent even on radio, was underlined by his commanding physical presence on camera, but the success of his presenter character lay fundamentally as much in what Morris wasn't. Not having wanted to pursue a career in comic arts, the power of his performance lay in him seeming to be a real newsman gone bad. He wasn't simply delivering jokes about news to highlight how funny he was, but rather seemed thrillingly as if he were deliberately sabotaging the medium, much as he'd done back at Bristol, and communicating the fun he'd always had with it to the viewer. It was the sense of easy confidence and understanding of the desperation to be seen as weighty by so many in journalism which made his appearance as mesmerizing as it was funny. He was doing the job he'd been trained for, but to excess, which was perhaps why, as Iannucci observed, he had to be reminded that he was actually good at doing other characters and styles of humour.

Following the pilot, Morris seemed to have calibrated his performance and he had become more intense in the way he played the presenter. His characterization took inspiration from many different sources: '[Michael Buerk is] like a priest and he pulls serious faces in a hammy way. It's like Russ Abbot saying to himself, "I know this can get a laugh,"' he said. 'Michael Buerk's probably saying in the newsroom, "I know this can get a tear . . ."'

'I've always found television news fantastically distracting because of people's mannerisms. If you're watching Peter Sissons, you're always thinking, Why's he got a nuclear missile up his arse? . . . Michael Buerk is pulling this po-faced, "Hey, we're all in church" act, Peter Snow is on fire.' And then there was the note-perfect Jeremy Paxman: 'Because I'm naturally a cruel bastard.'[4]

His other presenter characters were as carefully observed. Ted Maul had a subtle difference in voice which marked him out as a rougher version of Morris's main anchor, not quite as bright and slightly more old school and clubbable. He was one that Morris would come back to right through *Brass Eye*.

Other elements transferred from the radio series, often gaining in the process. Alan Partridge was increasingly confident, Coogan's live reports completely natural in their halting incompetence. Peter

O'Hanraha-hanrahan was a standout performance by Patrick Marber. Rather than simply be cowed by Morris's bullying, he was always argumentative and petulant when he knew he'd been caught out not having all the facts.

A spoof soap was set, on Doon Mackichan's suggestion, in a bureau de change. Iannucci was, says Patrick Marber, 'against us hamming it up. Of course, we do ham it up a bit. Compared to *The Office* it's primitive, but it's the beginning of that journey I think of doing it for real.' The authenticity was created by filming much more than was needed, rather than just scripting a few seconds to seem like an excerpt from a longer interview or scene. Just as he had for *On the Hour*, Iannucci assessed all the material before editing it down with the pace and fluidity of a real documentary. In the swimming pool documentary, a large number of characters were invented to approach Mackichan as the heroically unhelpful ticket clerk, and snatches from just a few were used in the final show.

Morris, meanwhile, did much of the work on the music in partnership with Jonathan Whitehead. In interview, Whitehead is a laidback and reflective voice who becomes precise and analytical only when he talks about his approach to music and how he and Morris took apart such staples as the *Newsnight* theme. They knew the history of their music, that *Newsnight* had been written by well-known movie and TV composer George Fenton. As they roamed around the news music landscape, picking over the major beasts of the genre, Whitehead noticed that they often had unexpectedly avant-garde roots. It was this that gave them their pomp and was a pretension that informed *The Day Today*. At Whitehead's Bayswater studio, he and Morris played around with ideas on keyboards.

'Gravitas,' muses Whitehead now, 'was a word bandied around *The Day Today* which I'd never really thought about before.' It was Morris who came up with the main four-note motif for the show.

Whitehead embellished it, made it lurch around disconcertingly in 7/8 and 8/8 time and created the associated programme stings. He also worked on incidental themes for the show and, as he had done on GLR, with helping Morris to produce musical parodies such as RokTV's Nirvana sanitary towel advert and George Formby as the real author of Dylan's 'Subterranean Homesick Blues'. Morris himself made a banjo sound by playing a guitar with a capo. 'It was the only time, really, that I've collaborated,' says Whitehead. 'I felt that I was doing something that required more time and effort than other jobs. Even though he would write bits of the songs and have them ready-made, there was still quite a lot of actual note-bashing to do. We were very closely involved in writing the music together. He'd come to the studio many times, which is completely unusual. I normally do it by myself.' And because they knew how each other worked, 'there was a chance to do something that wasn't so bland, something that might be noticed in some way'.

Every news show of the time employed computer graphics to heighten the drama of their stories – even when an illustration wasn't needed or relevant. All the channels competed madly with the most powerful processing systems to get the fanciest graphics. Using a funky three-dimensional image in a story was a guaranteed way to attract praise from a news editor, and the idea of using an illustration only to simplify a complicated concept was frequently lost in the rush to make sexy footage. The biggest constraint was the time it took to make smooth, broadcast-quality graphics. The brief for the on-screen graphics of *The Day Today* was to imagine what would happen if the wildest imaginings of the most megalomaniac editor were not constrained by the daily deadlines and budgets of a news show. *The Day Today* took five months to create a visual feast of overblown colour – graphs, illustrations and globes spinning dizzily. Eventually, computer power got to the point where any news show could do similar things on a daily basis, which then made it seem rather weirdly as if the real news had taken several years to look like *The Day Today*.

The design department of ITN, led by senior designers Richard Norley and Russell Hilliard, won the contract to do the graphics based on a pitch they did for what would become the story about dogs being used by the IRA as explosives. The graphics showed police spraying the dogs with a special sealant that contained the explosion within the animal and Hilliard and Norley cheerfully went over the top with the idea. They loved the whole idea of the show from the start, while immediately realizing it would be unlike anything they had done before. They laughed at the scripts, though sometimes a little nervously as they tried to work out how they were going to create a currency cat or a finance arse. The graphic look of the show was central, and they were part of the creative team rather than just being called in as an afterthought to prettify it. Morris and Iannucci briefed each design and returned graphics with detailed directions for improvement. The show meant long hours and many reworkings for Hilliard and Norley, who had to fit the work into a relatively small budget and around their day job at ITN. But, as enthused by the concept as everyone else, it was obvious to them that they were being stretched to do something special. They weren't able to realize every idea. Among the abandoned briefs was the world turning into a suit, the camera zooming out to reveal the jacket as the countries, with stitching as the coastline and the sea on the shirt. But what did get through was enough to win a BAFTA for Television Graphic Design in 1994, and it was also key in launching Hilliard and Norley with their own successful company making titles and graphics across a huge range of major entertainment shows.

Over the last few months of 1993 Morris sat in with editor Steve

Gandolfi to work on his tapes. Gandolfi says, 'And he had it all worked out. All the people – he knew what they all said, he edited it, but when we cut it, it didn't work. So we just went through every-thing and edited it.' Morris and Iannucci had very little padding in what they had produced, but it didn't make it any easier to fit together. 'It's like, when you watch Benny Hill, it's very simple,' says Gandolfi, 'and I'm sure that when they first started making it, every frame of it's perfect . . . but Chris; one thing was complicated, one was simple . . . the way it was all structured together. First couple of days were quite hard to understand, to get involved.' At one point it looked as if they couldn't possibly do it all by the end of the year. 'I remember, I was worried about Christmas,' says Gandolfi. 'When they were shooting the studio stuff, I was carrying on editing the other stuff. I was an absolute wreck.' Segments like RokTV – which might on other shows take a day to put together – were edited over a full week. When Morris spat out the words of rap parody 'Uzi Lover' at full pelt, Gandolfi had to work to get the sound to fit. 'The "cop/fuck/bitch/bang/motherfucker!" stuff I was synching. I was the one trying to get them in synch, it was so fast. His lips weren't in synch . . .'

Editing was completed by the end of November and the six episodes were broadcast between 19 January and 23 February 1994. The series was heralded by a press release promising the dawn of a bright age in news, saying that 'today's viewer must be able to "feel the reality of news" and will only do so if broadcast reality is assisted in a process called Ultranews'. Most of it was standard PR stuff, but buried among the biographies of the cast and principal crew were interesting embellishments to Morris's CV: 'In the eighties, numerous local radio stations found themselves unable to tolerate someone who would fill a news studio with helium seconds before a broadcast, resulting in the announcer reporting a motorway pile-up in the voice of a smurf. In 1990, Radio Bristol choked when Morris did a running commentary over a live news bulletin; later that year GLR decided that his vigorous pursuit of their brief "Get us into trouble" had put them in jeopardy – Morris left.' It was this press release that gave birth to so many of the myths and legends about Chris Morris. Even by his own lofty standards of misdirection, it was astonishing how full a life of their own these tales took on, repeated without comment in both friendly and critical press reports. Journalists swallowed the tales without blinking or thinking about how difficult it would be to fill a studio with helium without a newscaster knowing or, indeed, dying. But perhaps strangest of all was the way in which Morris's own friends and colleagues from those early days have come to accept them as if they were actual memories of the late 1980s and early 1990s, even though they didn't start to circulate until after *The Day Today* was broadcast in early 1994.

It was hardly as if stories needed to be invented to create more excitement about the show. A background buzz of interest in *The Day Today* had been building from the moment of its commissioning. As early as summer 1993 *The Times* said, 'Anything with Steve Coogan, Chris Morris, Rebecca Front and Armando Iannucci is worth cancelling a wedding for.'[5] The *Independent* did a feature they wanted to accompany with a group shot of the principals. Morris, already very careful in how he presented himself, didn't want to be photographed at all, and neither he nor Iannucci wanted to be seen as part of a ready-made troupe. Journalist Robert Hanks made it clear he found the reluctance to do regular publicity made them seem rather precious.

The interest they stirred was inevitable – a show about the media was always going to be watched closely by the media simply because it was about its favourite subject. Then there was the very specific fan base that *On the Hour* had won who would also be paying close attention. They were partly attracted to the show because it was so cleverly observed with the layers of subtle references which could be cherished and the numerous memorable lines to be savoured. It had attitude that you could line up with, and that made it something to be protective about, something to own. Fans were articulate, opinionated and media-literate. They would be waiting to see if the evocative world of *On the Hour* had sold out in an attempt to be a hit on TV. It all meant that the show itself then had not only to be good, but to be as good as everyone was saying it was going to be.

Right up to transmission, Morris and Iannucci debated whether or not they should do interviews to promote the programme, remaining unenthusiastic about the whole process. An unusually defensive Morris told *Time Out* just before the broadcast, 'We haven't got jokes that are just lines and it would be difficult to describe a lot of the characters in a sentence without blowing what happens on screen.' He didn't even seem entirely convinced the programme would work. 'There's a chance that people might find it all very clever but not at all amusing,' he said, adding with a little more confidence, 'I think we've got enough in there that's funny as well.'[6] Then the reviews came in and suggested that there might indeed be just enough to be thought of as funny.

'For once the waterfall of publicity preceding a new series is justified,' said Christopher Dunkley in the *Financial Times*,[7] setting the tone for much of the reaction. Even Victor Lewis-Smith was impressed: 'Unlike *KYTV* (which entirely lost its focus when it moved from radio), the team have successfully reassembled their current affairs parody in purely televisual terms, synthesizing elements of *Newsnight*, *Sky News* and US rolling news networks into a glorious fusion of inanity and insanity. On it went at breakneck speed, with not one weak link nor dud performance anywhere. Avoiding the obvious newsroom jokes and packing every second full of acute observation and sharp parody, Chris Morris, Armando Iannucci and the rest of the team have produced a brilliantly original show. Their radio origins reveal themselves continually in their distinguished use of sound. Current affairs broadcasting has taken itself far too seriously for far too long, regarding itself as beyond reproach, and it's high time that its pretensions were exposed.' He praised 'opening graphics so slick they put the genuine *Newsnight* titles to shame'.[8]

Talkback paid close attention to the reviews. Ratings didn't need to match the coverage as long as the reaction was good. *The Day Today* got between 2 and 2.7 million viewers, hardly a huge share, but all of those who saw it took it to their hearts in the way that fans had with *On the Hour*. Budding comedians were influenced by its approach, which, like some legendary rock gig that everyone later claims they were at, also helped to make its impact and reputation much bigger than its audience. Its originality and verve made everything else look dated. Journalist Hunter Davies thought the show was 'brilliant' and made the week's other offerings, such as *Wish You Were Here?*, *Holiday* and *Law and Disorder* (a new Penelope Keith show) look 'limp and laborious' by comparison – probably not the hardest thing for *The Day Today* to achieve, but a reminder of how unlike anything else the show was at the time.

The programme's newsreading targets were less fulsome in their praise. Only Michael Buerk admitted that it had been accurate. 'I'd love to say it was totally wide of the mark . . . but it wasn't,' he said. 'Bits of it were absolutely sublime. I was weeping with laughter at times. After a while, you wonder whether you oughtn't to be changing yourself to fit in better with their image of you, which was strange . . . After that 999 parody they did of me, I've burnt my trenchcoat.'[9]

Martyn Lewis was more typical, saying only he'd been out at a dinner during transmission. Alastair Stewart dismissed the show out of hand: 'The most charitable thing I can think of was that the graphics were very good. The whole thing had all the symptoms of an elongated two-minute sketch.'[10]

Jeremy Paxman said he had missed it because he was doing the real thing on Newsnight, but years later the show – or rather the excesses of news production it exposed – caught up with him. It was in 2007, when major broadcasters suffered a meltdown in public trust after a string of scandals involving everything from TV phone-in competitions being fiddled to footage being misleadingly edited, that Paxman gave the MacTaggart lecture at the Edinburgh television festival. His speech acknowledged that the all-consuming needs of news turned the media into what former Prime Minister Tony Blair called 'feral beasts'. But it sounded rather like he was describing an edition of The Day Today from thirteen years before: 'The problem is that all news programmes need to make noise,' he said. 'The need has got worse, the more crowded the market has become. We clamour for viewers' attention and a sort of expectation inflation sets in. So the pavement-standers in Downing Street or wherever must pretend to omniscience, even though they've spent so long on the end of a live-link that they've had no chance to discover anything much beyond where the nearest loo might be.' News, he said, 'doesn't really exist until there's a reporter there in flak jacket . . . The crisis of confidence in television reflects the crisis of trust in politics: the old "we know best" culture – in which producers affected a patrician concern to enlighten the poor dumb creatures who were their viewers – won't wash any more.'[11]

Would the industry have saved itself some heartache by paying closer attention when *The Day Today* first went out? As Armando Iannucci observed at the time, 'People who work in TV news will think it is a joke against the person working next to them, not against themselves.'[12] He might have been a bit too cynical. Craig Oliver, then a journalist and later editor of the BBC's *Six* and *Ten O'Clock News*, remembers that, egos aside, there was a certain amount of self-awareness created after the show. Newsroom colleagues noted the way the show had hit what he calls 'some of the occasional inherent pomposity and tendency to make the banal seem profound'. Like many in the industry, he still spots *The Day Today* moments in real news, citing a report about a massacre in America one Christmas in which the journalist says that people who 'should have been hearing "Jingle Bells" were instead hearing the jingle of shells'.

The majority of *The Day Today*'s audience were positive about the programme. About forty viewers complained each week, few of which Chris Morris took seriously. An exception concerned RokTV in which a skeleton swings from a rope with Morris's voiceover brightly explaining to a pastiche of Joy Division that he was the band's late singer Ian Curtis and he always watched the show. Curtis's widow Deborah wrote in to say their teenage daughter had been upset by the sketch. She had become a fan of the series and had convinced her mother to watch that episode with her. Morris was genuinely mortified and wrote a letter of apology.

It was a rare lapse for a show which had worked so well that even its makers thought they wouldn't be able to repeat it. And that they didn't really want to try. 'If you work really hard on something, there then comes that thought, God, do you want to do it all again?' says Armando Iannucci now. 'What would be achieved by doing it again? Would we just do more parody of the news? It's very much a slash-and-burn process.' He was relieved it had all gone well, though he had only vague memories of the show going out at the time, his son having been born the night after the first episode.

In the end there was only ever that one series and it was the last time they worked together as a group until they reunited for the DVD ten years later. 'Once you can operate the levers with 80 per cent degree of efficiency, then there's no point in doing it,' Chris Morris later observed. 'You should only do it if you think you're going to fail, otherwise the whole thing becomes depressingly routine.'[13]

The Day Today seemed to mark the last expression of a particularly creative and productive partnership – Morris and Iannucci – before the pair split to pursue their own projects, but it's not a description of events that either of them would recognize. 'We never really planned a big gap,' Iannucci explains now. 'We keep involving each other in our work and talk a lot about doing something together.' If they did become more peripheral features in one another's careers, it was because the likes of Alan Partridge and *Brass Eye* were so demanding that they could devour whole years of their lives at a gulp. But they haven't given up on the idea of another major collaboration. 'We meet regularly to think about something,' says Iannucci today, in a quick email sent in the smallest of gaps between promoting one project and starting production of another, adding distractedly, 'Don't know what yet . . .'

All in the core team had ended their association on good terms, and the various writers and performers would continue to work together in different permutations. Even Steven Wells, possibly the least involved in comedy in later years, did collaborate on one intriguing curio – never broadcast – with David Quantick and Chris Morris in the form of a radio play about a lighthouse and its crazy keeper. The lost piece, only dimly recalled now by its creators, featured seagulls attacking people in the water and a variety of characters annoying the keeper, who is made fun of by everyone, even dolphins – as everything in the piece has a voice. 'Chris tended to specialize in creatures of the sea,' says Quantick. 'He wrote the seagulls and the dolphins.' And he gave the gulls the kind of sarcastic, contemptuous voices their real-life cawing and crying suggest. The BBC turned it down at script stage.

But whether they went on to comedy, drama or journalism, all those who had been involved with *On the Hour* and *The Day Today* thought of the experience as formative. Patrick Marber sums it up: 'We all found our feet collectively as a group and all supported each other. It gave us all as individuals a lot of confidence to go out and make our own way in the world. It certainly gave me confidence to do that. I learned that your best work is done when you're not doing it for the audience, when you're not trying to please someone, when you're just trying to be true to the thing that you've invented. I learned that from Armando and Chris . . . I don't think I ever got that when I was a stand-up. It was very much, Well, if it works for the audience, that's good enough. But actually I realized that if you mine a more idiosyncratic and personal theme, then you might find something you didn't realize was there and you might find that others really enjoy because of the integrity.' And for their increasing base of fans, the quality of *On the Hour* and *The Day Today* meant that whatever else any of them did would be met with high expectations.

6

PUTTING A SPINE IN A BAP

AS *KNOWING ME, KNOWING YOU* WAS BEING PREPARED FOR television after *The Day Today*, a fax was sent from the Talkback production office to competitors Hat Trick: 'Most of your shows are shit.'

It was on non-headed paper and intended to be anonymous, but the fax machine automatically included the company number in the date stamp. And then the number was misdialled – so it never got to the opposition. As an exuberant, if ultimately fruitless, release of energy, though, the fax gave an accurate impression of the mental state of those who sent it. That was what being cooped up in a room with Alan Partridge for weeks did for you. Like Armando Iannucci and Steve Coogan himself, Patrick Marber was going a little strange at the time he scribbled the message. Iannucci says, 'It was one of those stupid things that people sometimes do when they're drunk, but this was more like tired.' News of the abortive stunt soon got around the rest of the team. 'Even when it was hubris, arrogance, wrong,' says Dave Schneider, 'I still admired that swashbuckling thing. The fact of sending it had that sense of, "Step aside, we've arrived."' It was also an acknowledgement of the pressures of expectation that came with success. 'We didn't realize that these things would have as high a profile as maybe they somehow acquired,' admits Iannucci.

To be part of *The Day Today* was to be part of the hottest group of comics around, or rather loose affiliation, as they still denied being a group. Chris Morris had been named Top TV Newcomer in the Comedy Awards of 1994, the same year that Steve Coogan was Top Male Performer and Best TV Personality, and Armando Iannucci was the only person ever to get a Special Award for Comedy. Almost anything they came up with would have been seriously considered for a series. Talkback was where it was all happening in the early 1990s. You could walk past its offices in Percy Street, between Tottenham Court Road and Charlotte Street, and, as one of Morris's colleagues did, witness Patrick Marber leaning out of the Partridge writing room to inform passers by in his best Peter O'Hanraha-hanrahan, 'We are the satirists of doom!'

Chris Morris's response to the success had been to move in precisely the opposite direction to all the noise. To the casual viewer of *The Day Today* it would seem as if the main presenter of the show had just disappeared – only those who shared his first love, radio, knew different. He did a series of interviews with Peter Cook that slipped out at the beginning of 1994 late in the evening on Radio 3, and later that year he took a slot on Radio 1 at 9 p.m. on Wednesdays. But the relative anonymity that all of that afforded him was crucial in later providing freedom to interview celebrities for *Brass Eye* without being noticed. And when that series was eventually transmitted three years later in 1997, its impact on those who had forgotten all about him would be that much greater for seeming to have come out of nowhere.

Morris and Iannucci had been such a tight team that it was only as they began to work on their own projects that it became possible to tell them apart. Iannucci's projects over the following years were characterized by reaching out to a much larger audience as if, as David Quantick archly observed, Morris played John Lennon to Iannucci's Paul McCartney. But it was always an arbitrary line – there was light-heartedness and outright silliness in Morris's humour, and Iannucci frequently displayed what his later producer Adam Tandy called an 'iron whimsy', as cruel as his colleague's but maybe more deceptively charming. And with Iannucci as producer, Partridge on television demonstrated that the attitude and the very detailed way of working that characterized *The Day Today* could make a mainstream hit without being bland.

The potential for the character's development had been obvious in *The Day Today*, which Lynne Truss observed was 'the making of Coogan, whose genius as the banal, dim and vainglorious Partridge is unmissable'.[1] Iannucci looks back on *Knowing Me . . .*, or rather the period of making it, with mixed feelings. Everything had been done at such a pace. The radio version of *Knowing Me . . .* was done at the same time as *The Day Today* pilot. And then the TV version followed straight on. 'I'm not entirely happy with it,' he says now.

Patrick Marber revealed, 'We wrote each of the television shows in blocks of six days, working day and night, living on takeaways, thinking we were going to explode. We had agreed a production schedule that was murderously difficult for us. We thought we were going to write the whole series in advance of making it, and of course we pissed about and didn't, so then we had to write it between shows. The whole series was an essay crisis.'[2] Morris turned up to the production one day with a large cake for everyone.

As with the schedule of the radio series, the real sense of imminent disaster only added to the sense that Alan himself could fall apart at any moment – which he did at the end of the Christmas special. It was that spectacular character disintegration over the series which made the show more than a chat-show spoof. The team had always thought of *Knowing Me, Knowing You* as a sitcom in the sense that Alan's character was revealed during the run.

Iannucci played with the sitcom format again when Alan returned in painfully reduced circumstances without his chat show in *I'm Alan Partridge*. Looking to develop the emotional resonance in the show, Iannucci checked out *The Day Today* contributors Arthur Mathews and Graham Linehan, who were making their own hit show with *Father Ted* and were rather flattered at the attention. 'I remember being surprised that he would ask us about anything,' says Mathews.

Having visited their set, Iannucci enclosed *I'm Alan Partridge* in four walls so the audience could only watch what was going on through monitors, explaining that the audience were to be 'eaves-dropping on something they weren't meant to see'.[3] Which was, in essence, Alan going down an emotional plughole, subsisting in his Norwich motel. It was all pretty grim stuff. Iannucci remembers looking at the characters and thinking, 'They're just a big bunch of losers, who've all gravitated towards each other and they're all keeping each other afloat.' Only the live audience kept the show from unbearable bleakness. Within the closed set they used hand-held cameras: 'You could see how cramped Alan's bedroom was because we could go right around him,' said Iannucci, 'but at the same time Steve could take the rhythm of his performance from the laughs that he was hearing.'[4]

Like so much of the best work of productions led by him and by Morris, the shows had a fluid, organic quality that refreshed the sitcom format. Both of them would amass huge amounts of material in the course of making programmes and threw out scenes that had taken months to develop if something funnier or a better direction was discovered in late rehearsals. The Partridge writers slowly teased out the plot and occasionally came up with 'Alanisms' on a range of topics which Iannucci compiled into what became a thick file. Actors would frequently arrive to find writers still working on the script for that day, but Iannucci and his team were good at handling chaos and Steve Coogan was always very sure of what would work for his character, so that somehow it came together. *I'm Alan Partridge* marked the height of popularity for the character.

Over the course of producing *The Day Today* and *Knowing Me, Knowing You*, Iannucci himself had felt an increasing urge to escape from the shadows. Steve Coogan and Chris Morris were such strong presences that much of the audience might well have thought the shows were all theirs: 'Some of it's inevitable anyway,' Iannucci says, 'and some of it at the time you get worked up about and then years later you think, I don't know what all that fuss was about. I can remember really genuinely feeling, I hope I don't get overlooked in all this given that I've spent the last eighteen months of my life devoted to it.'

In March 1994 he told the *Sunday Times*: 'I never set out to be a producer and I'd like to get out of it, really. I'm going to take maybe a year away from producing to concentrate on writing. Producing takes time. It can lead to me being frustrated because I feel that I'm not giving a hundred per cent to each project and it can also make the people I'm working with feel frustrated, so I'm trying to pare it down, not do two things at once.'[5] But it would always be hard to get away from something he was so suited for. He finally got to return to presenting with 1995's *Saturday Night Armistice*: 'I have an ego. I do like performing. I like hearing my voice,' Iannucci told *The Times*.[6] The show also featured old friends Peter Baynham and Dave Schneider, with writers including Graham Linehan and Arthur

Mathews suggesting ideas that Iannucci developed. The show was recorded the night before broadcast to get in topical news as well as pranks and more personal material.

'There are more traditional satirists like Rory Bremner who look at politics, and their agenda is set by the *Daily Telegraph*, the *Independent* or the *Sun*,' said Iannucci. 'We wanted to look at stuff beyond that – your day-to-day life, what it is like working in offices, the lottery phenomenon – things that are more the stuff of conversation at that time.'[7] The show moved to a Friday night for its second and third series, but the formula remained the same. The series producer was Sarah Smith, an old friend of Iannucci's from back when she'd been president of the Oxford Revue and her Small and Intimate female double act had performed with Iannucci and Andrew Glover's A Pair of Shorts. She moved into production, working in regional theatre for three years before joining BBC light entertainment, working with Iannucci again and later coming into Chris Morris's orbit.

'We were all part of the same gang, really,' says Smith. 'We were nicking each other's writers. I worked with Pete and Rich and Stew and so did Armando. We were across the corridor from one another.' She was also a master of detail and would regularly pull a couple of all-nighters just to edit everything together. When *Friday Night Armistice* took on politics, they hit New Labour as much as the Right, managing to attract complaints from both main parties, to Iannucci's pride. But although it took on current affairs, the show was always played with much less intensity than *The Day Today*. 'I think Chris thought it was rubbish, but there you go,' confesses Smith. 'I don't think he liked it very much. He saw it as much more lightweight. The whole idea of *Armistice* was to dress the political stuff up in a light entertainment format, and that was a deliberate decision. It was for an audience and had all sorts of different material, and I think Chris was more purist. That's just a difference of taste.'

Iannucci was not overconfident about his own abilities in front of the cameras: 'I am not comfortable in the limelight. It takes a bit of getting used to,' he said. 'But it makes a nice change working on television and hearing the reaction of a studio audience. I like my privacy. I enjoy performing, but I don't like the idea of becoming famous. I don't like what comes with it. I am the least cool person. I have only been to a few celebrity parties and left early because I was tired.'[8] But even he found himself in the tabloids in time, though it was for nothing more scandalous than being called the funniest man in Britain. In 1996 the *Mirror* made the rather weak observation that his 'name conjures up a wacky vision of a sharp-suited ice-cream seller', though readers were doubtless reassured to learn that, in reality, 'It belongs to a sharp-witted Glaswegian Italian who flogs laughter'.[9]

But if there were tabloid headlines that went unused by either Iannucci or Morris, Steve Coogan was ready to take them up. For a while he was rarely out of the press, displaying a difference in personality which his colleagues regarded with a kind of awe and incomprehension. Patrick Marber and he were in outlook the complete reverse of their colleagues: 'Were it not for the fact that he has this fantastic gift for comedy,' said Iannucci, 'Steve is fundamentally a guy who reads a lot of car magazines.'[10] He and Marber were the most visible, very close and very eager to get on. 'For a while it was kind of like a big brother/little brother relationship. I wouldn't do anything without asking Patrick what he thought,' said Coogan.[11] And when Iannucci was being pulled between the radio Alan and *The Day Today* pilot, it was Patrick Marber who guided his friend and acted as a champion of the potential of Partridge. But as Alan peaked, their partnership, too, was beginning to wind down. Steve Coogan looked to Hollywood, and Marber began to concentrate on writing drama. 'It's been a great luxury to be able to think, Oh, I can write on my own,' he said, 'because when you've written collaboratively, you start to wonder whether you can do it any other way. I'm saying what I want to say about the world directly rather than filtering it through one of Steve's characters, or one of my own.'[12] By February 1995 he was directing his first play, *Dealer's Choice*, at the National Theatre, whose Richard Eyre had been a fan of Alan Partridge and *The Day Today*. Eyre was interested in the transition Marber had made from comedy to drama. The play was first performed in the National's studio and then transferred to the Cottesloe.

'I know I couldn't have ever written a single play had I not done *On the Hour* and *The Day Today* and Alan Partridge,' says Marber. 'It was all stuff that built up some sense of self in the world and a kind of confidence and a sense of who I might be as a writer which was absolutely formative in my brain.' With *Dealer's Choice* Marber had developed the writing voice he had always wanted, and its arrival was singled out in the *Observer* as a theatrical highlight of the year: 'unbeatable ensemble acting' and a 'marvellous comedy debut'.[13] By the time of *I'm Alan Partridge*, Marber was too busy with his theatrical career to work on it for long. With Marber on his way out, Peter Baynham was drafted in on the writing side.

It was in *I'm Alan Partridge* that Morris at last made a guest appearance. Even then, Iannucci says, 'It took a little bit of persuading,' as Morris still wasn't sure he'd be good at acting. But by then his own mark had been made with the safe engineering of *Brass Eye* into the world, and he had been developing his own material and style through three years of intensive work, operating undercover for most of one of them.

7

WHY BOTHER?

THE RECORDING STUDIO IN WHICH PETER COOK AND CHRIS Morris sat was uncluttered. There were no scripts and no props, just the ever-present smog from Peter Cook's cheap cigarettes and a couple of mikes on the table. The tape machines ran continuously in the control room where the sound engineers monitored the recording and Peter Fincham gazed through the window at the men whose expressions remained composed no matter how absurd their conversation. But of the two it was Peter Cook who needed the reassurance of an audience, glancing occasionally through the window to where the engineers, lost in the stream of invention, needed the prompt to remember where they were and smile back their approval. Morris never looked up. Still weeks away from the broadcast of *The Day Today* and by comparison hardly known, he was assured and confident even when the infinitely more experienced older comic tried a verbal ambush, which was quite a lot of the time.

Why Bother? had been Peter Fincham's idea. Peter Cook played his established character, dissolute rogue Sir Arthur Streeb-Greebling, discussing his life over the course of five conversations. The series went out over consecutive evenings from 10 January 1994, each broadcast lasting about ten minutes. Fincham did some preparatory work with Cook and played Morris a tape of him with comedy producer John Lloyd. Following an initial lunch meeting, work began at Aquarium Studios in Primrose Hill, north London. Cook travelled the short distance from his home in Hampstead, arriving on the first day with the address scribbled on the cover of a copy of *Private Eye*. The studio was in a mews with enough room for Morris to park his old Merc. And then they just got on with it.

Accompanied by a supermarket bag of extra-strength lager, Cook 'proceeded to skip about mentally with the agility of a grasshopper', Morris later told the Peter Cook Appreciation Society. 'Really quite extraordinary.'[1] A pilot edition was recorded at the beginning of 1993, with a handful of others taking place towards the end of the year. The sessions were all held in the afternoons, each lasting a few hours, and Morris remembered them as 'very merry'.

It was all improvised, though one of the initial areas for discussion had been around since *On the Hour*. It was an idea that had been taken on a particularly circuitous route in Morris's imagination before finding its home in the third edition of *Why Bother?*, its journey providing an insight into how much development and reworking could go into Morris's comedy. Steven Wells and David Quantick had suggested that the discovery of the fossilized remains of Christ as a small child would make a good headline for the Christmas special, for which it was smartly vetoed by Armando Iannucci.

'You have to remember,' said Iannucci as he discussed it with Morris. 'I'm a guilty lapsed Catholic.'

'But so am I,' countered Morris.[2]

Carol Smith remembers the disagreement. 'Arm was adamant for it not happening – and not on Christmas morning!' she says. 'And I remember the two of them – and Chris is tall and Armando's quite tiny – and Chris would argue that black was white if he thought it would get him what he wanted. And in the end I remember Arm going, "Just *no*."' So Morris made it a festive headline of his own for his GLR Boxing Day show in 1991. And yet there was clearly potential in the concept that went unexploited in such a brief news story. Where could Sir Arthur take the suggestion?

'Now, in your address to the Royal Society tomorrow, you intend to reveal the fossilized remains of the infant Christ,' said Morris. 'How do you feel that will go down?' Such a question could be a good way of shutting down many an interview. But while there was a pause – just a slight one – Peter Cook almost immediately leaped back to suggest that Jesus was 'practising resurrection', dropping dead and bringing himself back to life. Morris complemented the suggestion with: 'A series of larvae?' And then the invention really began. Each attempt at coming back to life would take the young son of God about six months; Japanese companies were interested in miniaturizing Jesuses so that anyone who wanted to find Christ but hadn't got the time could get a real one posted through their letterbox. Predicting that the idea would lead to all sorts of BBC panics over blasphemy, Morris immediately decided, 'That's not going near anybody until seconds before transmission.'[3]

Peter Fincham was thinking along similar lines. 'I was listening to that going out on my car radio and thinking – I'll never work again. The duty log at the BBC will be overwhelmed because it's so blasphemous. But actually there were no complaints because I suspect hardly anyone heard it. It went out in a gap in the evening concert on Radio 3,' he told Cook's biographer Harry Thompson.[4] And finally Morris had found a setting in which the once rejected notion could at last grow and an interview partner who could take it in surprising directions.

Cook's attempts to go off at tangents throughout *Why Bother?* were relentless, but Morris was drawn neither into attempting to outdo his ingenuity nor into indulging it. He cut those segments dead, playing the deadpan, brusque interviewer throughout. Rather than attempting to create a comic persona to play off Cook, he was efficient, busy and professional, emphasizing his youth and vitality over Sir Arthur's declining powers. At times, Morris later said, he felt he was also interviewing Cook himself. And gradually a sort of narrative emerged, a sense of old Sir Arthur's wicked life.

Morris allowed Cook to invent the history through his responses but also threw out blunt lines as a challenge. It was clear that Cook was not in the best of health – one day he had come in late to the session with a massive bruise on his arm following a fall at his home. Another interviewer might not have drawn attention to the condition out of politeness and a sense of deference to an ailing comedy giant; Morris made it an integral part of the interview, with frank references to the imminence of Sir Arthur's death and the comic potential in the notion. 'We did remark that you were never sure if he was going to turn up,' Morris later said. 'He always did, but you always thought you might just as easily get a call saying, "Sorry, he's pegged it." Because a knock on the arm doesn't blow it up to the size of a leg unless the immune system is licking its wounds in its own corner.'[5] Cook, no stranger to finding comedy in the human weaknesses of others, recognized the technique with a jolt, but he seemed to enjoy being so fully engaged and having to include his own mortality as part of the humour.

Rather than record on digital tape, Morris preferred to use the studio's few remaining reel-to-reel machines to record and edit the hours of material. The engineers watched him hacking away at the analogue tape, quietly horrified by the knowledge that no back-up recording had been made, on his insistence. Morris began work as soon as each recording session finished in the back of the studio, immediately discarding what he didn't need on the floor around him. When he ran out of studio time, he took the tapes away to finish the edit.

'To some degree it's Chris Morris's construct . . . [He] turned often quite shapeless things into coherent pieces,' Peter Fincham later said.[6]

Each edition was shaped to focus on specific aspects of Sir Arthur's life and work, including his stint as a Japanese prisoner of war, when he collaborated with the enemy and made himself rich through getting his fellow prisoners to build a railway for their captors. By the final episode, an expansive Sir Arthur had moved on to casually discuss his crack use: 'The downside of this is you feel awful but the upside is you feel terrific.'

The final session was devoted to recording introductions to set up the subject of each programme, and it was the only time when Morris worked out in advance what was going to be said. He spent some of the time in the control room, directing Cook to record links that would connect the various edits into complete stories.

The shows were warmly received in the press. 'Peter Cook impersonated a mad old peer so persuasively,' said the *Guardian*, 'that without forewarning I might have been fooled.'[7]

It was a portrait that was as intimate and endearing as it was funny. And it felt true in the way that, rather than step around Peter Cook's ill health, Morris had insisted so much on making it part of the comedy. 'I like to meet somebody who treats me really badly,' as Cook remarked at one point. *Why Bother?* concluded with the Radio 3 announcer saying, 'Sir Arthur is not expected to live beyond May.' Though Morris and Cook had talked of working together again, the prognosis proved to be only a few months out. Peter Cook died in January 1995, barely a year after the original broadcast. If *Why Bother?* then became one of the last examples of Cook's vivid invention, it also showed him at his finest. Morris had elicited a classic performance and, though it's probably just a hopelessly romanticized notion that simply comes as a result of Cook's death, it seemed as if the broadcasts marked the stewardship of a certain kind of essentially English humour being passed down a generation.

Following *Why Bother?*, Morris jumped BBC networks later in 1994, landing in Radio 1 for a series that marked his first appearance on the station since his one-off Christmas 1990 show. Back then, Radio 1 had been a rather conservative broadcaster, sticking with music and formats that hadn't changed for years. But much had changed. Morris's GLR boss Matthew Bannister had taken over as Radio 1 controller. Before he'd even started the job in November 1993, old-timers Dave Lee Travis and Simon Bates resigned knowing, as everyone connected with the station did, that Bannister's arrival was another salvo in the long-running battle to modernize Radio 1. The station was about to be remodelled into a younger, fresher, more innovative place that was better able to handle the likes of Blur, Oasis and Pulp, the harbingers of a resurgent mid-1990s music scene. In 1995 Chris Evans followed Chris Morris on to Radio 1, as he had on GLR, and was soon a national star, the perfect mouthy foil for the new wave of similarly self-confident musicians.

Bannister's strategy for the station included putting comedy alongside the music. It was a timely idea. In selling out Wembley Arena in 1993, Rob Newman and David Baddiel had prompted suggestions that comedy was the new rock 'n' roll. The huge success of their generation of comics prompted greater interest in comedy throughout the country. And by the time it turned out that rock 'n' roll was the new rock 'n' roll, many acts would have been tried out on Radio 1 – with mixed results. Paul Merton, Angus Deayton and Lee and Herring were among those who had a Radio 1 slot, as did Armando Iannucci, his show including Dave Schneider, Peter Baynham and Rebecca Front. But the comedy was never fully integrated with the music. There was always a sense that the shows were made by comics who happened to be on a music station.

'Matthew Bannister fired me at GLR, so he knows what I'm made of,'[8] Morris declared at the start of 1994, which was at least half true. Bannister had left the station two years before Morris, but he did think of the GLR shows as a blueprint of how comedy on Radio 1 could be. But Morris's light-hearted warning also proved to be absolutely correct. Bannister now says that of everything he faced at Radio 1 – listeners being lost as they had over the changes at GLR, increasingly public spats with Chris Evans and the often furious criticism of the new set-up – Chris Morris was always his single biggest headache and had far from the largest audience. And yet despite all the trouble, he was managing to do something innovative that Bannister recognised.

Morris had usually worked his earlier DJ shows alone, but he had a small team on Radio 1. Producer Oliver Jones had been doing Danny Baker's *Radio 5 Live* show a couple of years earlier when he got Morris in to provide cover. 'I seem to remember in a rather pompous, self-important way that I urged people to get him,' says Jones. 'I certainly urged them to get him on Radio 5, but I must have said, "Look, if Chris ever comes to work at Radio 1 I want to work with him."' He'd played tapes of the show to his friend Rebecca Neale, a production assistant who offered to help out for free in the evenings on the Radio 1 show and was taken on for the whole run. Oliver Jones says, 'My job was to make sure that management didn't annoy Chris. Merely as a facilitator, mostly, and most producers in that kind of programme had a far more hands-on approach or would have to, and I kind of thought I'm not nearly as witty, not nearly as . . . I can't think as tangentially as Chris can.'

Morris had a regular foil for his most inventive material on the show in the form of Peter Baynham. After the initial meeting on *The Day Today* which had seemed to be so lacking in promise, the two had become friends and they created a succession of elaborate fantasies for the Radio 1 shows. Baynham would be deferential, frequently bullied and easily led, while Morris would deceive and hector him into getting in trouble, on the face of it a much less equal partnership than that which Morris had with Peter Cook, but no less hypnotic, and Baynham found it just as stimulating. Baynham and Morris gradually honed their material through informal chats which had a way of warping into disturbing imagery.

'It's very inspiring,' says Baynham of the creative process. 'Whenever I work with him, it makes my mind do that.' He always felt that he could suggest anything and Morris would never make him feel foolish. There was never the macho atmosphere around their meetings which he had found in other jobs. 'You get used to it,' he says, 'but I've never managed to develop a rhino hide when someone tells me something I've said is shit, but Chris doesn't do that.'

They had an easy bond together and a relaxed approach to working in Morris's office, retiring to the roof when the weather was good enough. Morris worked up the ideas later, pulling them together into more of a coherent form, and then they would go through them all again. 'One of my happiest times working on anything, to be honest,' Baynham revealed to the *Evening Standard*. 'I do feel I ought to describe his office as a secret underground cave with dead writers nailed to wooden boards. But in fact we . . . have very enjoyable, demented conversations.'

Morris reciprocated the compliment, calling Baynham 'the funniest person I know. He probably roars perfectly formed jokes in his sleep. He's an uncorkable geyser of nonsense, face bursting under the pressure of idiocy behind it. He's extremely willing to go all the way down a dark alley and come out with his head dirty.'[9]

In the show they would engage in what appeared to be unscripted DJ chatter that would quickly spin off into elaborate and highly polished comic riffs. On discussing a scientific report that had made the news by revealing that asteroids strike Jupiter with a force equal to 100,000 times that of a nuclear bomb, they agree that it's hard to imagine what that must be like. They decide to think of a way of expressing it that makes more sense and Morris creates an extraordinarily vivid scene:

> The best way to do it is to think of it in human terms. I mean, if you imagine an 18-year-old girl in the Fens towards the end of the last century and she's on the cusp of womanhood, yet retaining the natural beauty and God-given fragrance of Persephone. Her flaxen tresses are tugged playfully by the light June breeze which carries to us her coy, giggling, girly, gosling girl-giggles, like the sweetest mountain brook chattering over its pebbles. Imagine her standing on a bridge waiting for the 4.15 from Norwich. Blast of warning horn it comes. Girl body jump. Little child yet woman bump and splatter all over hot metal. Massive iron smash and pulp. Icky, ick it fly. Little brainy piece of purest teenage jelly meat flying across a whole field and landing on a squirrel's face.

Baynham would usually sit opposite Morris in the studio, much of the power of the sketches coming from the way they worked off one another. 'Watching him, his concentration and his . . . just kind of giving things a slight spin, just changing them very slightly and reacting with Peter Baynham or whatever,' says Jones, 'meant that you could have very different versions of sketches, and quite a lot of the time they would restage or he would take most of it from the first version and take a line or two from the second one and put them together.'

Often what seemed to be real in the show was entirely made up, and the most unlikely parts were happening for real. There was a sense of bogus authority the programme derived from masses of detailed research. Oliver remembers, 'Chris would basically contact us on Friday afternoon or . . . I mean, not contact us, not like *Charlie's Angels* – we didn't get an anonymous voice on a tape, but y'know – he would get in contact and particularly after the weekend he would say, "Can you get the following: a, b and c for me?" and quite a lot of the time we would have to go to media monitoring organizations or whatever in order to get things that he'd heard somewhere, God only knows where.'

The office fax machine buzzed ceaselessly with ideas for Rebecca Neale to research. She arrived in the mornings to find requests sent at an hour so early it strongly suggested Morris simply never slept. Each idea would become an area of specialization until they had wrung out every last detail and then he'd be off again, rushing to get into the next thing. 'The desire to be a comic is primarily a young man's thing which tends to be through by the time he's thirty,' said Morris, who turned thirty-two that summer. 'I try to keep ahead of it but it's a race because you're trying to keep yourself interested. Your biggest fear is being trapped with something you hate.'[10]

Rebecca Neale often only realized why she'd been asked to find some of the obscurer items if she later heard them used on the show. The request for taxidermists' numbers didn't make sense until she heard Baynham and Morris apparently discovering the cooling corpse of DJ Johnnie Walker in a neighbouring studio. The story was played out in real time over the course of the entire programme between records and included a genuine call to a shocked BBC security guard, squelching noises representing Walker's body being dragged between studios and a Morris-invented medical procedure involving Baynham scraping a hole into the back of Walker's neck and blowing into it while Morris moves the corpse's lips to allow him a ghastly croaked 'Goodbye' to his fans. Rebecca Neale's taxidermists pop up at the end when Morris phones to get them to agree to stuff a real human body as part of an exhibition about radio.

Morris happened to be leaving the Radio 1 building after that show went out just as the real Walker – still very much alive – was mounting his enormous motorbike. He didn't seem to have taken offence at the lengthy coverage of his demise or the inventive uses for his remains and as he roared off his only comment on the intricate drama came in the form of a yelled, 'Hey, Chris! You killed me!'

Peter Baynham called on the technique of seamlessly combining reality and comedy years later when he co-wrote the Oscar-nominated screenplay for the *Borat* movie. The Sacha Baron Cohen comedy came largely from the interaction between the crassness of the fictional Borat and the real world of his journey across America. 'That was the challenge of *Borat*,' says Baynham, 'to do a full-length feature version of that trick.'

For Baynham, the Radio 1 show was never more real than over late summer when the inspiration for one of their extended items came from his own life. He was overloaded with additional work for Lee and Herring's Radio 1 programmes and his one-man Edinburgh show. Prone to getting panicky and having tantrums under stress, Baynham decided with some reluctance that there was only one thing for it – he would have to drop his commitment to the Chris Morris show.

'I can't do it,' he blurted on the phone. 'Just give me a break next week, all right? I'm going mad. I'm really stressed out. Do the show with someone else.' He felt genuinely close to the edge and nervous about how his decision would be received, though Morris heard him out sympathetically. 'Let me think,' he mused at length. 'How can we use this?'

Baynham snapped, 'We can't use this! I'm going mad! I can't, I'm doing my show . . .' But Morris was convincing. By the end of the conversation, Baynham found it was he who was saying, 'All right, I'll tell you how we can use this. I'm going mad. I'm really going mad. I feel like I'm near to having a breakdown. Let's use that.'

So Baynham linked up from the BBC studios in Edinburgh the following week and Morris ridiculed his workload on air. It was exaggerated for comic effect, but underpinning it was a genuine sense of Baynham's own terror, which Morris tore into: 'Peter, you're a lazy sod . . . It's pathetic . . .' he sneered. 'You're a self-obsessed little Nazi . . . You little Nazi. It's about time you sorted your life out.' Baynham called him an old bastard, before disappearing off mike to sit on the floor repeating, 'The drawer's empty', while Morris phoned a BBC staff member in Edinburgh and ordered them up to the studio where they witnessed Baynham wailing and eventually running away. Discernible tension in the scene was layered with the real confusion of the BBC employee on discovering the gibbering Baynham.

Morris seemed genuinely curious to see how far Baynham would go in their exchanges, how far he could push it, but at the same time he didn't have an egotistical need to show he was in control, so what seemed like bullying on the show never – quite – crossed that line. Baynham even allowed his father to be brought into one episode. An elaborate fantasy, the background of which defies description, climaxed with Baynham and Morris kidnapping a baby and dressing it up as a fly by wrapping it in gaffer tape, attaching

CDs for wings, tea strainers bent back over the forehead for bulbous eyes and six spoons to make little fly legs. The sound of it flying with helium balloons floated across the stereo picture, accompanied by contented baby gurgling noises. With Peter out of the studio, Morris phoned up Baynham Snr to reveal confusing snippets of the lengthy story.

'Me and Peter, we've found him, you see.'

'Who?'

'Big spoon baby balloon.'

A few of Peter Baynham's friends were critical of him getting his father involved, but the phone call had been carefully worked out beforehand. 'I just loved the idea of him being not freaked out, but just totally bemused,' says Baynham, adding that he'd got to know Morris well enough by then to stipulate, 'Don't say anything that makes my dad think I've died.'

Paul Garner returned to work with Morris on the Radio 1 shows, though his partnership was based more around straightforward pranks rather than baroque comic fantasies. 'I was mainly the man out and about,' recalls Garner, 'suffering at the hands of the public.' But only because he and Morris set out to wind them up beyond endurance.

Since previously appearing with Morris on GLR, Garner's musical ambitions had taken a knocking. His band had been signed and then imploded, and he was beginning to think that maybe comedy could be his career. He was sent out to 'bother shops' – an activity that manifested itself in Morris ordering him to do things specifically designed to send their owners into a state of psychosis.

'Paul was some of the bits that made me laugh the most,' says Oliver Jones. 'Laugh out loud. With Chris I enjoyed it, obviously . . . but actually *spluttering* when you hear something happen . . .' Garner, a mobile phone clamped to his ear through which Morris barked instructions, would queue up in convenience stores to say 'thank you' twelve times at the till or insist that he be given different change, perhaps because the coins were 'sleepy' or they had 'a Harris' on them. All the time, buzzing on adrenalin, he would be giving Morris a breathless commentary on the deteriorating mood of the staff and an urgent account of how his subsequent escape was going, as if he were on a secret mission behind enemy lines rather than in the local corner store.

The final episode targeted a taxi, and Garner, pretending that he was taking one for the first time and that Morris was his father on the phone talking him through the process, recalls that he not only wore an anorak and clutched a bag of rubbish, but also covered himself with the entire contents of a large bottle of TCP, method pranking which was all the more admirable for being completely wasted on a radio audience. The taxi driver, however, was only too aware of his passenger's distinctive scent and so was already fairly enraged before Garner even started on a long list of annoying requests that resulted in him being dragged bodily from the cab as back at base Morris dissolved in laughter.

'The taxi journey as recorded,' remembers Oliver Jones, 'went out in the programme after we'd recorded it. So we used it almost imme-diately. I was almost breathless with that . . .'

'I've never listened back to it,' says Garner now. 'It just terrifies me. It's like Vietnam flashbacks that I have back to those days.' He and Morris never discussed Garner's missions beforehand or how they would progress. They frequently sound very much as if Morris is taking advantage of him. 'Of course he is. He did,' says Paul, 'and I let him. And that was why it was funny. It was weird for me because I've never been the fall guy in anything, but he is such a domineering figure.'

With Garner returned the public tannoy announcements from

GLR as he and Morris invented such passengers as Heidi Drargs-Queek and Miss D. Fäagen-Bazs to be paged at airport information desks. Towards the end of the run at Heathrow Garner called for Makölig Jezvahted and Levdarhöem Dabahzted. Returning for Steelaygot Maowenbach and Tuka Piziniztee, he was met by a grim-faced announcer with her colleagues standing in a line, arms folded, glaring. They had kept the first piece of paper he gave them and compared his handwriting with his second note. Busted. They claimed passengers had been offended and banned Garner from Heathrow. He drove straight to Gatwick to get them to read the last part of the message.

Having planned that the Radio 1 shows would lead to more commissions, Garner was also rather hoping for some kind of assistance from Morris in getting ahead in comedy. Rather than a nepotistic leg up, he received only the suggestion that he get a copy of *Ariel*, the BBC in-house magazine. Yet, says Garner now, 'It was probably the best thing he could have said to me.' He got it together himself to write for Radio 1 DJs who'd been impressed by Morris's show. And Morris did provide practical assistance, editing and advising on Garner's show reel as he developed his career.

Radio 1's *The Chris Morris Show* began its six-month run in June 1994. Promotion included an article in the *Radio Times*, who hoped it would be accompanied by a photograph of the star. The photographer was instructed to turn up at a certain platform at a particular time at Waterloo Station, displaying his camera prominently, so that Morris, his usual careless chic outfit topped by sunglasses and a black beret over his curls, was able to locate him. They chatted for a while before Morris abruptly broke off: 'I'm going to stop you there. This isn't what you think.' They were to meet an hour and a half later on Waterloo Bridge. 'Bring a ladder and your camera.'

It was almost lunchtime as the photographer struggled on to the bridge against the crowd of tourists and office workers. Morris explained that he never wanted to be seen: 'I'll go to the other end of the bridge and walk along with everyone else and you take pictures as I come along. But you must promise not to use any where you can recognize me.' They did about four takes before settling on an image of Waterloo Bridge which the *Radio Times* printed with a circle indicating where, if you peered very closely, you might just be able to make out a beret and a pair of sunglasses.

Morris also did an interview in the *Guardian* ahead of the programme. 'The whole point is that it's a music show with attitude.' He created the playlist 'according to tempo and feel rather than fashion. It's everything from utterly abrasive sounds to pop, from the Auteurs and the Pixies to Nik Kershaw, or even "Copacabana". Anti-snob, basically.'[11]

Oliver Jones made a few contributions to what was played. 'A lot of the time, we'd just chat afterwards and talk about records, because we'd go off for a drink after we'd recorded the programme,' he says. 'Chris just knows amazing things.' It wasn't just that an average programme might include Sly and the Family Stone or Gil Scott-Heron, but it could easily be one of their lesser-known tracks. 'He adores Sly Stone, not just Sly Stone the musician, but Sly Stone the lifestyle, the philosophy, all that kind of thing.

'It's like really good pirate stations – when you listen in to something and you hear an amazing track, and you think, These guys, they're not interested in what's going on commercially, they sort through some jumble sale, through hundreds of albums, and picked out some fantastic break . . . And that's what Chris is like.'

On relatively rare occasions he might even find he'd discovered a song Morris hadn't already heard of. 'The one thing I'm very proud of, which I always thought was a great record, was "Fisherman's Grotto" by Justin Warfield,' he says. It was a hip-hop track which had

Above: Chris Morris at Stonyhurst College on 17 December 1980 with friends Simon Armour (on guitar) and Paul O'Carroll

Below: The Exploding Hamsters on Anglia's *City Sounds* in July 1985. From left: Chris Morris on bass, singers Jane Reck and Mark Sendall, percussionist Jeff Lowrie, Shanti Paul Jayasinha on trumpet and John Telfer on saxophone

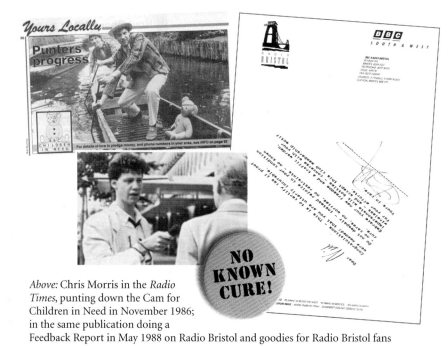

Above: Chris Morris in the *Radio Times*, punting down the Cam for Children in Need in November 1986; in the same publication doing a Feedback Report in May 1988 on Radio Bristol and goodies for Radio Bristol fans

Below: Taking the phones in the Radio Bristol studios

Above: Wayne Carr is interviewed at GLR for the *NME*

Right: Chris Morris in the *NME* in 1990, warning impressionable fans about hidden messages in pop records

Nirvana fan Chris Morris and Mercedes in June 1994, two months after the death of Kurt Cobain. 'Morris wanted to use the impact while it still counted, as I remember,' says *NME* photographer Stephen Sweet

Something approaching a publicity shot for *The Day Today* – blurred Morris with Dave Schneider, Patrick Marber, Rebecca Front, Doon Mackichan and Steve Coogan

Chris Morris at *The Day Today*'s portable keyboard

Above: Sports desk – with Alan Partridge (Steve Coogan)

Below: Peter O'Hanraha-hanrahan (Patrick Marber)

Barbara Wintergreen (Rebecca Front) for *CBN News*

Weather forecast with Sylvester Stewart (Dave Schneider)

Business news with Collaterlie Sisters (Doon Mackichan)

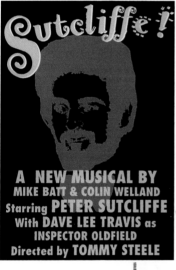

Above: Chris Morris in a typically illuminating photo-shoot

Left: A prop postcard for *Brass Eye*

Below: Apes & Music would later be better known as *Jam*

Apes & Music DAVID
Screening

Wednesday 14th July 99 from
7.30pm for 8.30pm screening

Upstairs Bar
Bricklayers Arms
31 Gresse Street
W1

RSVP   Alice & Philippa

Chris Morris in 2006

been released the previous year. 'I used to work in an office that belonged to another Radio 1 producer and they'd left behind a rack of records and CD singles and I put this thing on, and it was just extraordinary, such a walloping record. I do remember introducing that to Chris – it just comes on at a hundred miles an hour, wallop, all the things Chris loves . . .' On air, having been eloquent in sharing his passion for some track one minute, the next Morris played along with his guitar or keyboard on another song, wrecking it comically or augmenting it with his own riffs. 'Chris would sit in the DJ's position with his keyboard, which we'd always have to wire up,' says Oliver, 'and the studio managers always said, "That's unorthodox equipment, we're not meant to use that, how do we do that?" And I'd always say, "Look, it happens every week, please just put it in through, put it on one of Chris's faders, that's all I want you to do . . ." And every week they would complain about it.'

There were other features of the show which had become familiar parts of his routine over the years. The ever-rude kiddy's outing for younger listeners returned, and Bristol colleague Michael Alexander St John did a kind of sequel to his *No Known Cure* 'Ten Ideas to Change the World' with a take on the typical mid-1990s dance chart rundown. Acts included Discombobul-8 and 'Who's Operating Colin?', Burpmytosis with 'Brains of Chutney' and Oestrogen Blab Daddy's 'Bring Me a Chicken'.

Morris still refused to read out listener letters, and when he appeared to break the rule it was just to get in what turned out to be wild parodies of Our Tune-style record requests, proto-*Blue Jam* tragic stories of quivering love which always ended with the object of desire being pierced at a climactic moment by a spear of frozen waste dropped from a passing aeroplane. These epistolary mini-dramas were a favourite feature for Armando Iannucci.

Star interviews were a regular item, a testing ground for the *Brass*

Eye set-ups. Celebrities would be on their own in a studio and told that they were going to be interviewed down the line. Morris was actually in a neighbouring studio to preserve his anonymity, sometimes playing Wayne Carr and not exactly following the BBC rules which said that interview subjects had to be aware of the true purpose of their recording. Some material was taken out on review by management pre-broadcast when there wasn't evidence that Morris had told people he was recording, though the BBC always had a fairly strong feeling that very few of his assurances could be relied on. During an interview with Nick Ross, Morris explained that Keith Richards was next door promoting a Stones album and wanted a word. There were shuffling noises on the mike which sounded as if Morris was going out of the room to fetch the star. Ross was treated to Keef's thoughts on drug use among older people without once giving any indication that he had any idea it wasn't a genuine Stone he was talking to.

It was that kind of material which transformed the routine of BBC editorial meetings into surreal affairs in which Matthew Bannister's office had to pass judgements on such sounds as a kidnapped baby dressed up as a fly being floated out of a studio window and down to its mother on Oxford Street. Could the BBC open itself to charges of encouraging cruelty to children? Should it be transmitting that sort of thing? The answer with Chris Morris was often a seductive 'why not?'

Bannister was even persuaded that obituaries could be a suitable topic. Broadcast tributes were inevitably artificial constructs, prepared long in advance and regularly updated so that they were ready to go as soon as their subject did. Apparently spontaneous outpourings of emotion were pre-recorded and had to be remorselessly positive about the departed. The person delivering them might well be chosen because they could be relied on to give a good quote, whether or not they liked the subject or even knew them. There were some sound targets there, but Bannister was uncomfortable illustrating them with Michael Heseltine. Six weeks earlier, when Morris had been interviewed in *Time Out* to promote the first show, he'd given a broad hint at what was to come. 'Phone-ins will be on issues such as animals and justice and pregnant women in uniform,' he told Bruce Dessau, adding, 'I'm trying to get a direct line feed from Michael Heseltine's heart monitor. If there's anything dicky, I'll be first with the news.'[12] It wasn't so much that the Tory MP was very much alive that concerned Bannister, but that he'd survived a heart attack only a year earlier, which put him out of bounds and therefore intensely fascinating for Morris – Tarzan was untouchable, other than saying, 'If Michael Heseltine had died . . .' or 'If we were compiling an obituary . . .' Bannister knew that being told he had died was hardly the worst thing that Heseltine was likely to have heard about himself, but he didn't want the family to be upset.

Though Bannister or someone from his office would review the show before it went out, quite a lot of material was live and Morris always reworked and edited the shows to the last minute. Bannister remembers this meant he could drop in surprises which they might not have a chance to hear, 'thereby pushing us all into a kind of hysterical situation where we had to agree the material or we didn't and there would be no programme to go out'. Bannister listened to the 6 July show at 9 p.m. while driving home, and the first line was one he hadn't heard before.

'This is BBC Radio 1 FM and if there *is* any news on the death of Michael Heseltine in the next hour, we'll let you know,' said Morris.

'Very, very quickly, the studio telephone rang and it was News, trying to find out if there was something we knew that they didn't,' says Oliver Jones. 'And after that, it was a matter of fielding all the phone calls and explaining and all the rest of it.'

BBC News were on the phone to Bannister the moment he got through his front door, and calls continued to come in until late that evening. Recalling the tricky aftermath in interview, Bannister is characteristically good humoured and it's only at one point that his voice – his tones inflected with classic BBC warmth and measure – registers irritation. He disagrees rather pointedly with the suggestion that Morris only implied the death by saying 'if there is any news', observing sharply that none of the callers he fielded were in the mood to argue the semantics. Particularly not 10 Downing Street. That Morris wasn't making a serious attempt at a hoax became irrelevant in the storm that followed the broadcast, but there was only one occasion on which he explicitly said that Heseltine was dead, in the course of soliciting a tribute from 'close personal friend and colleague and bass player of The Jam, Bruce Foxton'. There could be few listeners who wouldn't have thought there was something odd about hearing the bassist asked for his reaction and giving a stunned 'Really?' while Morris adds with discernible glee: 'hit the ground screaming, yeah'. There had been enough clues in the first few minutes of the broadcast alone, including Toni Basil chanting 'Oh, Mickey, you're so fine'. But the nuances of what Morris did were of little consequence as Heseltine – quite possibly for the first time in his career – found himself the subject of sympathy and spirited defence in the press.

An inquiry was launched: 'Some of the pre-recorded material was heard in advance and some of it was not,' the BBC said carefully. 'That is the focus of the investigation.'[13]

Morris expressed surprise at the coverage and responded to the accusations of going too far: 'If I thought that, I wouldn't have done it. I'd do it again, only better.'[14] Matthew Bannister was at heart a fan, but he knew that he would have to be seen to be doing something. Not for the first or last time, he went to Morris's agent.

'Matthew used to go absolutely mental with me,' says Chiggy, 'if something had gone wrong. There would be a major kind of shouting.' But rarely did any action follow the bollocking – a feature of the telling off which Chiggy also recognized in Trevor Dann and others who were essentially Morris's champions. 'They're the people who've got a little bit of Chris in them,' she says. Even Morris, for all his Bannister baiting, admired him for having a 'miscreant child inside him'.[15]

After Heseltine, though, Bannister was pushed to hand out a more tangible punishment. With some irony, the moment he had to deliver it happened to fall when he was on a particularly dull BBC management away day, feeling like the corporate lackey Morris always accused him of being on such occasions because he knew it annoyed him. He had to tell Morris over the phone that he was suspended from Radio 1 for two weeks and all future shows were to be pre-recorded.

'He seemed kind of resigned to it,' says Matthew Bannister. 'He didn't strike me then as being angry about it. He seemed to understand what it was that I was doing and why I was doing it.' It was rather differently experienced in Morris's camp, remembers Rebecca Neale: 'Oh, Chris was furious that he wasn't live,' she says. 'He thought it was ridiculous and he was pissed off.'

Bannister had to write a letter of apology to Heseltine and the *Guardian* reported, '"Dead" Heseltine gets BBC apology after Radio 1 spoof backfires.'[16]

'Most of what I do isn't that troublesome,' Morris pointed out in an interview that marked his readmittance to Radio 1. 'It's just the one per cent. You don't set out to run over 160 sacred weasels one by one, otherwise you end up desperately trying to shock, like Richard Littlejohn. They know I'm contracted to Christmas, I want to carry on and so I wouldn't destroy my own rostrum. They probably sense that if I was forbidden to do something, a malevolent old man in my subconscious would goad me on to do it.'[17] The pre-recording made little material difference to the production of the show, which was recorded the night before broadcast so it could be vetted, but they did it as if it were still live. 'It would take about an hour and ten minutes to record an hour's programme,' explains Oliver, 'to allow Chris to restart a disc or whatever . . . We would race through.'

The new regime didn't guarantee the programme's safety, though it was only towards the very end of the run that an item caused offence again – and it would be one of the shortest clips, a spoof of celebrity endorsements which would be played as programme jingles. Morris scripted phrases that he deftly re-edited to make the stars say things they'd never intended.

'I'm Alice Cooper,' he got Alice Cooper to growl. 'Isn't Sybil Ruscoe a twat?'

'I'm Whigfield,' explained Whigfield, 'and I think Naomi Campbell has a gravel fanny disorder.' Paul Garner went out hunting celebrities at an event promisingly entitled Night of Two Hundred Stars. His first attempt failed when actor Robert Wagner quickly scanned through the phrases. He declined to read them. 'You're trying to get me to say I take coke,' the *Hart to Hart* man pointed out with some accuracy. With just 199 other stars to choose from, Garner zeroed in on Petula Clark. He improvised a few innocent lines that Morris later reordered into something far more suggestive that proved to be a cut-up too far. Clark sued the BBC over what the *Mail on Sunday* breathlessly reported was a 'sex tape'.

The series concluded on Boxing Day with a two-hour festive special, and the shows were never repeated. The Heseltine and Petula Clark moments provided the most publicity, but overall they were among the least creative examples of a series that was characterized by ambitious invention. Morris had fused music, humour and reality into scenarios that were often beautifully grotesque. Unfolding in the chat between records over the hour, the tales were like mini-concept albums, and their subject matter would have given the moral guardians of the press far greater concern than the fake obituaries if only they hadn't been so subtly introduced into the shows. But as skilfully as much of the material was often presented, there was also a strong current of basic delight in the tradition of smuggling rude stuff past the nation's moral guardians, back to the 1950s and 1960s when the BBC's list of proscribed phrases included 'winter draws on' and still further to the music-hall era when 'I sits among the cabbages and leeks' drew the attention of the censors. Morris was drawn to the instinctive, mischievous laugh. With Peter Baynham and Paul Garner by his side, he was able to cover all bases.

The shows also provided a useful signpost in their style to what Morris would later do with *Blue Jam* and in their choice of topics and celebrity interviews more immediately to what he was about to start working on for television. What became *Brass Eye* would prove tortuously difficult to create, a show that in many different ways should not have been filmable and was certainly not broadcastable.

8

BLATANTLY HIDING THE GROUND

THE CONCEPT BEHIND FEEDBACK REPORTS FORMED THE backbone of Chris Morris's shows from his first starring role in *No Known Cure* all the way to *Brass Eye*. Their mischievous blend of elaborate fabrication and mockery flavoured everything he did. He could tell with a glance on the street who would provide a good response to what he made sound like a pressing social question of the day without actually making the slightest bit of sense. When he gave the idea its first outing on television in an obscure and short-lived 1990 satellite TV show called *Up Yer News*, his high hit rate intrigued director Peter Kessler. He asked how Morris knew which member of the public would give the response he was looking for. 'Just stand and wait and watch,' Morris told him, 'and when the right one comes along, you know.' Kessler says, 'He was very, very insistent indeed about picking the right people to talk to . . . And he basically stepped out and went for the right people.'

'And if they're unknown, it moves the focus from the person being set up to what the fuck is being said,' Morris explained in

1994. 'Part of the point is the sheer randomness of those people – from vicars to builders. You're undermining any talking head on TV by showing them talking bollocks with apparent authority. And the whole of the media is a deception, everything that happens is a deception, cloaked in coded statements – a pay rise, a sacking, whatever. I can't stand that high-handed attitude that there's a proper way to behave. Everyone's fucking about. You're just displaying it.'[1]

Having refined his technique on the streets of Bristol and London, Morris used it in his celebrity interviews. Of everything he did, they attracted the most attention, whether praise or criticism. They were an exposure of sloppy thinking and self-promotion. Or they were cruel and cheap. His anger was scouring. Or he was a misanthrope who preyed mercilessly on those who gave their time to talk to him. Morris saw the set-up as very straightforward: 'In everything I do there are enough clues, you're challenging the situation to collapse by getting stupider. They're given a fair chance to say "fuck off"', he said.[2] Few people did so at the time, although famous victims used their access to the media to say it loudly and publicly after they saw the shows go out. Accusations of unfairness dominated the headlines, obscuring what made his verbal traps so effective – their lining of rich and imaginative detail.

Virtually every premise Morris offered had at least one element in it that looked as if it might be true. And that was generally good enough for most people to overlook the fact that his questions were nothing more than gateways to a mad world – albeit one with its own internal and consistent logic. The breathtaking aspect of the interviews was the readiness with which people stepped into the alternate existence with him. His fierce criticism and satire on the media and its audience were the most discussed aspects of his work, but they would surely have been unremittingly bleak had it not been for the colourful absurdities he created in his least celebrated role – that of accomplished storyteller.

He had identified the way in which people can be susceptible to a mutant folklore, that they could be convinced to accept almost anything as long as it confirmed the long-held suspicions they'd always had about the way things were. His experience in local radio had taught him that even less encouragement was needed to get people to expound on big social issues, the instinctive collective fear that barbarians are around the corner. Morris was sparing in his suggestions, and respondents enthusiastically filled in the rest for him, condemning 'gut festivals' or the cruelty of 'hinges on dogs'.

One couple expressed horror on his radio show about 'this so-called fashion for blatantly hiding the ground', and they were typical of his respondents. There was an easy laugh to be had at their expense, but what made the interview so memorable was how far they travelled down the rabbit-hole with Morris. He engaged with them sympathetically throughout and allowed their personalities to come through, she forthright, he slightly reserved. They need no prompting to declare it is kids who hide the ground. Somewhere in the murky confusion kicked up by Morris was a tethered sliver of a solid concept, unspoken, that even if the yobs who populate news headlines weren't really out there hiding the ground, you felt sure they would if they could. And that was almost enough to make it true.

'Let me put to you, at least in the mind, in this rather grim scenario,' Morris asks them in Michael Buerk mode, 'you open the front door, the ground's been blatantly hidden . . . What could happen to you?'

Understanding exactly where he's leading, she responds, 'We should perish, shouldn't we?'

'Rather horribly,' confirms Morris.

'Yeah.'

Peter Kessler describes the quality that Morris was looking for in members of the public as that of 'being vague enough in their mind to answer in the right way', an echo of Robert Katz's description of their monologue characters of GLR and *Blue Jam* as 'fuzzy-headed'. Both the interviews and the stories explore in their different ways the arbitrary way reassuring smears of sense and logic are imposed on the terror and chaos of life and how easily that layer can be revealed to be a fiction. Few props were required for the feedback reports. The set-ups were more elaborate in *Brass Eye*, but basically Morris needed little more than the fig leaf of a microphone, a pleasant speaking voice and the natural presence which meant he could hold his subject through a mixture of willpower and sheer height. He exploited the natural willingness that people have to help and to feel useful, despite not knowing anything of what it is they're talking about. His credibility was rarely questioned, no matter how far he pushed it, playing with accents and delivery, even emphasizing words with a little bleat – nothing broke the spell. The power of the pieces was all verbal, and no concessions were made to the visual format when they appeared on *The Day Today* as Speak Your Brains. Morris was always almost out of sight, or half visible from behind, always suited, occasional bow tie glimpsed. He seemed very reassuring.

Celebrities were no more resistant to the lure of his convincing storytelling. Gary Numan appeared on one of the Radio 1 shows to condemn fox-hunting, and Morris mentioned that his call would help provide protective clothing for foxes. Immediately, Numan switched from taciturn rock star to a delighted innocent, though he says he's never heard of such fox-wear. Morris has a ready explanation – safety material as worn by chainsaw operators. But how do you get foxes to wear it? Morris likens the process to trout tickling –

hunt saboteurs move in a circular fashion around the fox, so it can't tell where they're coming from. Numan audibly brightens at this notion, and there is something endearingly playful in the way he seems to have ended up in a better place at the end of his call, surrounded by bright-eyed fox cubs in sunlit meadows, gambolling safely in their extra-small-size Kevlar jackets.

Morris called on a seemingly limitless supply of such vivid imagery to slather his work in thick pseudo-authenticity. His scripted scenes were equally rich. In 1997's *Brass Eye* there is the staged 'modern drugs party' which he wanders through, spilling out in a minute enough substance-abuse gags to keep most other shows going for a series. As he delivers his apocalyptic summary of drug-fuelled mid-1990s decadence you might even miss the final throwaway bilingual pun, 'This decade is not so much the neinties as the Ja danketies', if you were concentrating on the special effect of Morris being rolled up into a syringe and injected through the top of the screen into the next scene.

Even those ideas that came from contributors and colleagues rather than from Morris himself were, as writer Jane Bussmann points out of *Brass Eye*, all filtered through him so that however disparate the suggestions, they had a focus, what she calls a 'clarity of voice, it has a loud voice. That's the reason it stays good.' He was open to inspiration from anywhere, though it was also true that there were certain areas that he would frequently revisit. When Peter Baynham had had to prove himself in his first *The Day Today* meeting, he had no way of knowing he'd done himself a great favour with his outbreak of horses on the London Tube. Zoology graduate Morris had long been obsessed with the comic potential of animals, particularly 'the horse' as slang for heroin. Bovine comedy was another fascination – spherical cows regularly rolled over his horizon, and in his brief guest appearance on *I'm Alan*

Partridge Morris's character is farmer Peter Baxendale-Thomas, furious at the inane slurs Partridge has made on the conditions in which he keeps his cattle. 'This is exactly the sort of rubbish you came up with the other day,' he says, 'when you talked about putting a spine in a bap.'

In *Blue Jam*, freed from the frameworks of interviews and parodies, Morris whispered his nightmare confirmation of the world being much stranger than it appears to be directly into the listener's ear, giving his favourite preoccupations their fullest expression. Lions were set free in the suburbs by unconcerned residents. Neighbours fell out over the nuisance of a pet giant living in the garden. The quality of being 'vague enough in the mind' that Morris had used in Feedback Reports was taken to its furthest reaches: the unlikely notions that he once got real people to comment on could be performed by the characters in his sketches. The lines dividing what for them was real, what was imagined and what was a strong belief became ever more blurred until they disappeared entirely into the exploration of the powerful and persuasive imagery conjured by depression, illness and mortality. And for the GPs' son the essential unreliability of figures of authority was characterized by regular consultations with a doctor whose 'What seems to be the problem?' presaged a diagnosis as sympathetic as it was complete nonsense.

The subtle skill that Morris showed in storytelling went entirely unappreciated by the celebrities he caught out. But their fury and sense of humiliation in some ways provided their own tribute to the strength of his stories. He didn't hide behind a comic personality they could say they had felt they had to indulge. It was essentially his words and his lightning responses, leaving them raw and exposed from the mental equivalent of an abrasive rub-down with a wire brush. Very few celebrities would look back fondly on their experience.

It was a contrast to the traditions of satire. Public figures lampooned on *Spitting Image* were said eventually to have asked if they could have their puppets to keep at home. Back in the 1960s Prime Minister Harold Macmillan regarded his tormentors with a tolerance that bordered on affection. At the height of the Cuban missile crisis in 1962, President Kennedy asked him whether he thought the US should invade and Macmillan stalled for time. He later confided to his diary that but for the deadly seriousness of the situation the dialogue sounded 'just like a revue called *Beyond the Fringe* which takes off the leading politicians'.[3] There was no such cosiness with Morris. Even given the years that have passed since *Brass Eye*, no celebrity who had been successfully taken in would be interviewed for this book.

On occasion, Chris Morris's supporters would invoke the name of Jonathan Swift in the press in defence of what he did, but if this was intended to reassure those who were already feeling foolish, it had the opposite effect. It invited the response that Swift's subjects were more worthy, more appropriate, and that his style was better formed – altogether more acceptable. It seemed a rather pointless argument on both sides which didn't go much further than to note that other people had done satire, too – Morris's work by its nature would never be justified in terms of earlier writers. It had to stand on its own merits in the context of its own times. A more useful comparison to be made between the two as writers was in their lithe use of language and their ability to make scenes of fantasy live in the head as if they were real. And those were qualities that were more impressive and, in the end, made for more durable work than even the most fearless satire.

9

NOT SO MUCH THE NEINTIES
AS THE JA DANKETIES

IN THE 1990S CHANNEL 4 BECAME ACCUSTOMED TO BEING accused by middle England of defending the indefensible. Minorities, sexuality and explicit foreign films (flagged up on screen with a red triangle) were served up with a teasingly obnoxious side order of *The Word* to earn boss Michael Grade the title of Britain's 'pornographer-in-chief' in the *Daily Mail*. When *Brass Eye* began in 1997, the press needed little prompting to step up and take their partners for the Channel 4 moral-outrage two-step. Yet *Brass Eye* was different – though even its most outspoken critics didn't seem to realize why. They hadn't noticed that they didn't need to construct an argument for the prosecution. The show simply broke the broadcasting code. Programme-makers were not permitted to mislead interviewees for entertainment. Channel 4 knew it when they commissioned it. Talkback knew it when they made it. And Chris Morris knew it when he conceived it. *Brass Eye* was his first solo TV show – and it really shouldn't have been allowed.

Only news and current affairs could deceive interviewees and even then only if their makers could show it was part of an investigation in the public interest. The options in entertainment were much more limited. It was OK to set people up as long as your presenter confessed at the conclusion – what was called doing a reveal. Even then, you had to get people to sign a release form for the footage. Morris's typically ingenious way around this was to prove that there was a public interest in exposing the way in which celebrities attached the respect and reputation of their names to anything that would get them on the television. In other words, there was no reason why a comedy couldn't adopt the justification used by undercover journalism. Every aspect of the *Brass Eye* campaigns would be as ridiculous as possible and vulnerable to exposure by the most rudimentary checking. If a celebrity still willingly appeared on the show, they'd only have themselves to blame. That would – he hoped – provide the defence, albeit retrospectively. It was a high-risk strategy.

'That was the rule: the letters we sent out, the letterheads, everything was stupid,' said Morris.[1] The tools of the deception were all shown on screen – the badly designed press releases of the bogus organizations, their T-shirts and coffee mugs with their inept logos. Even the names of *Brass Eye*'s campaigns were in themselves clues – Free the United Kingdom from Drugs and British Opposition to Metabolically Bisturbile Drugs (FUKD and BOMBD). Its letterhead featured a huge syringe skewering three unhappy cartoon figures, the last of which was a glum little skeleton.

The letters were packed with spurious jargon – more clues – such as 'zoochosis' as an explanation for the plight of Karla the elephant, which had wedged her trunk up her own bottom. Morris was, he told colleagues, being generous to his interviewees by giving them the chance to read about what they were getting themselves into. They had more time to reverse out than was allowed by most prank shows. 'Chris asked me how many people I thought genuinely gave consent,' says controller of Channel 4 legal compliance Prash Naik of other shows. 'They approach subjects on camera as soon as they've revealed. Some of those people feel under pressure to say "yes", to appear to have a sense of humour.'

And the logical conclusion – at least for Morris – was that his set-ups were more honest in that he didn't even ask permission. It would be argued instead that appearing on camera implied consent for broadcast. Only those interviews conducted in studio discussions had release forms, and even those said only that they would be used in an unspecified late-night Channel 4 show.

The case for justifying the show, if defence itself was impossible, was built slowly over the months of the show's production. The question was: would it be convincing enough? They would know only when the series was broadcast.

It was a long time coming. The pilot was begun in early 1995, just after the conclusion of Morris's Radio 1 shows, and absolute secrecy about the true nature of the show would have to be preserved for almost two years. Most importantly, the crew had to avoid interviewees making a connection between the various campaigning organizations and Talkback. For the most part, they were successful, after an initial hiccup involving the Kray twins. The pilot was then in the early stages of production for the BBC under the name *Torque TV*. Much of the material in the show formed the later Animals episode. As Morris had previously explored in his Radio 1 shows, it was a subject that could be relied on to make anyone go gooey and drop their guard – even Reggie Kray. From the phone on his landing in Maidstone Prison, he recorded his support for WOFDCAP (World Organization for Decreasing Captive Animal Problems), incorporating AAAAAAAZ (Against Animal Anger and Autocausal Abuse Atrocities in Zoos). Morris told him he wasn't sounding the 'aaa's long enough. He got him to repeat it again and again, Kray preparing with wheezy deep breaths.

Late the following afternoon, researcher Andrew Newman opened the door at Talkback's office in their Percy Street house to a large gentleman from the Krays' organization. The man was holding the letter Reggie had received from WOFDCAP and was very angry. 'I seem to remember him having a baseball bat,' says Newman, 'but that might be just embellishing the story.' He pretended he'd not heard of the campaign or of Andrew Dean, the pseudonym under which he worked. Talkback's receptionist had gone home and there was nobody to pick up calls. 'If I ring this fucking number,' his visitor roared, the letter in one hand and Newman in the other, 'will your fucking phone ring? Because if it does, I'm going to break your fucking head.' Newman assured him it wouldn't as well as he could while being pinned against the wall, waiting uncomfortably for the switchboard to light up his desperate lie. Another member of the production crew came downstairs and disappeared into the back office, where Morris and a few others stayed rather than riding out to rescue Newman. Whether distracted by the interruption or having concluded, correctly, that frighteners had adequately been applied, the visitor left, warning, 'And remember there are three Kray brothers – and only one of them's dead. Do you know what I'm saying?'

It was a mystery how the Krays found Talkback. Morris's own office had been given as the correspondence address, but only Talkback's number was on the letterhead. It shouldn't have been possible to find the production office from that – apart from anything else, directory enquiries weren't supposed to give out addresses from phone numbers. The reach of the Krays was evidently still rather impressive. Morris and Newman came back later in the evening to move sensitive material out of the building, and everyone made a mental note to run the campaigns out of an entirely separate location when it came to making the full series. Always assuming, of course, that it was commissioned. It hardly felt like an act of overconfidence to think that it would be. BBC2 had provided funding for a very strong pilot, and the channel's controller, Michael Jackson, had overseen *The Day Today* and *Knowing Me, Knowing You*. And he did admire the pilot when it was completed late in autumn 1995. But admiration wasn't the same as commissioning. Jackson quickly came to the conclusion that the BBC wouldn't be able to support the celebrity interviews and the treatment of the subject matter.

Torque TV co-producer Duncan Gray says, 'We were utterly shocked when Michael Jackson turned it down. We couldn't believe it. This is the man who'd done *The Day Today*. How could he turn that down?' Peter Fincham was the angriest of anyone. It was the BBC's public funding system which allowed people like Morris to develop his work in all its complexity. The corporation should have been his spiritual home. More practically, the pilot had been stamped rejected – and many, including some of the crew, thought that would be fatal. But Talkback weren't ready to give up. While Fincham, Morris and Chiggy acted quickly to open up negotiations with Channel 4, Talkback's head of production, Sally Debonnaire, took on the complicated and time-consuming work of buying back the footage – all owned by the BBC – at under the cost price to ensure the pilot remained intact.

Peter Fincham spoke to Seamus Cassidy, a senior commissioning editor at Channel 4 who was immediately intrigued – not least because, like everyone in the industry, he wanted to know what Morris would do next. Cassidy knew people who worked on the show but, sworn to secrecy by Morris, they had said nothing of what they were up to. They didn't even discuss the project with other colleagues at Talkback – even Fincham preferred not to be told the details of what they were up to. The intrigue and mystery added to the appeal of the show and, in real terms, the effect of the BBC's rejection was negligible – if anything, it helped. Channel 4 liked the idea of poaching talent that the BBC couldn't handle. It was more than enough to ensure that they would at least give the pilot a watch.

For Cassidy on a personal level, *Torque TV* came at a point when he had become disillusioned with Channel 4 and had all but decided he was going to leave. But then he saw this show. It was like nothing he had ever encountered. He still vividly remembers taking it home and watching it with his girlfriend one evening. Neither of them could quite work out how *Torque TV* could have been made with its deceptions, its focus and originality. They ended up both laughing and gasping at the same time, howling together helplessly. The programme was compulsive, 'almost narcotic', he says, faith in television and Channel 4 restored. The feeling was shared throughout Channel 4, up to John Willis, director of television. *Torque TV* – eventually renamed *Brass Eye* – had come home.

Michael Grade approved of the decision to acquire *Brass Eye* in a broad sense but wasn't directly involved in the production process. While he declined to be interviewed for this book, colleagues at Channel 4 say that his awareness of the show would have been limited to a belief that he had got something like *The Day Today II*. And it was true to say that *Brass Eye* shared the same news-parodying DNA. But Morris was busy making a new mutant strain out of it, and by the time Grade realized the true nature of what was lumbering around in the Talkback laboratory, the *Daily Mail* would already be handing out free pitchforks and lighted torches and pointing the way to his office.

'*Brass Eye* was scarier [than *The Day Today*],' confirmed writer

David Quantick. 'It would be, "We're doing this thing about a priest wanking himself to death." You'd go, "OK – Armando's not here, is he, Chris? It's just you, isn't it?"'[2]

Recording of *Brass Eye* took place over 1996. Complete secrecy had been restored after the Krays interlude, and Morris himself anyway always maintained the lowest public profile he could get away with, something that was reflected in the quiet family existence he led, a marked contrast to the daily pressures of *Brass Eye*. By the time production started, he had been settled for a number of years with Jo Unwin, the actress and performer who had made such an impression on him when he had been in Edinburgh playing bass on the Footlights tour back in 1984. When Morris moved from Bristol to London on a permanent basis, she was sharing a place in Holland Park with Caroline Leddy and Jonathan Whitehead. On hearing that Jo and Chris had got together, Bristol friends immediately recalled The Millies in Edinburgh. 'Oh, my God! He's going out with Cat Woman,' Hugh Levinson said with some admiration to Jonathan Maitland.

The couple went on to make their home in south London, where they would have two boys. It was a comfortable existence, but not showy, completely out of any celebrity spotlight, and they had a low-key marriage many years later. Morris kept up with his old circle of friends and interests that continued to include a passion for cricket.

He never showed interest in corporate work or adverts, though he did confess to one friend that thinking about the sums he'd been offered for commercials and the difference it could make to family life, he'd had the odd night that, if not exactly sleepless, was at least slightly disturbed. But he never seriously wavered in his opposition, and requests to do ads virtually dried up entirely when agencies at length realized that his management company would always turn them down. Not only that, but they would be warned as a matter of course that PBJ lawyers would be watching with interest to see if an advert would appear based on Morris's work without his involvement. It left him free to spend much of 1996 in varying shades of lunatic undercover disguises as *Brass Eye* interviewers, reporters and characters – everywhere but nowhere.

He kept up as much of a normal routine as the workload allowed. Friends recall that he remained very caring and was always closely interested in whatever they were doing. He carried on the same kind of intense conversations and debates as he always had, an experience which, as Jonathan Maitland remembers, was for others 'like being interviewed to go into university'. The reputation that continued to build around him, says Maitland, 'didn't even register. He would genuinely spend as long talking to the sound technician in the corner as anyone else.' His thoughtful attitude was summed up for production manager Ali MacPhail on one of the rare occasions when he had been at an award ceremony. Armando Iannucci had just made a speech in which he thanked her. The next recipient remarked that he would thank his production manager, but he wasn't sleeping with her. MacPhail was furious at the false implication, and Iannucci's wife Rachael was loading a glass with red wine to chuck over the culprit. Morris was the one who talked them both down.

And yet he could also be both energetic and loud – not least in the check shirts he favoured and anything with a leopard-skin print on black. He would regularly hold meetings in coffee bars or restaurants, sushi being a favourite, and he was often on health kicks. The old Mercedes had at last died, but he regularly used public transport or cycled to Soho. His kit would be familiar to anyone who saw his performance as Denholm Reynholm, stridently promoting less stress through fitness to his long-suffering employees in 2005's *The*

IT Crowd. Reynholm's alarmingly tight-fitting outfit might have been a disturbing vision of Lycra bondage by way of *Tron* costume, but Morris's own commuting gear was not so different, topped off with a pair of distractingly oversized goggles. Both Reynholm and Morris clearly relished the disconcerting effect their appearance could have, but the on-screen caricature belied a personal warmth to Morris that he never allowed to show through in his work. The creativity he put into his friendships was typified by his startling Christmas cards, which are mentioned in interviews by almost all of his close friends and colleagues with something approaching reverence.

For years, from his early days in radio onwards, he had sent his own designs that incorporated metal and wood, sometimes barbed wire and even bone. They included a fly on a fob in a test tube of formaldehyde (Sally Debonnaire muses in a Morris-like fashion on its meaning, 'Maybe it buzzed itself to death?'), a container with yellow liquid on one side with some dirt on the other (and the message 'Piss 'n' earth'), a sculpted skull and blocks of wood with wire on them. The cards were, says Graham Linehan, a particularly personal gesture, something that could have looked positively threatening if you didn't know their sender. They seemed to be an expression of creativity for its own sake, worlds away from the increasingly single-minded focus that would characterize *Brass Eye*. That came from somewhere completely different, according to Matthew Bannister. 'He's on a one-man mission to expose the hypocrisy of the media. That is his moral crusade,' he says. 'It's an act, but the reason comes from the core of his being.' Doon Mackichan, who joined Morris from *The Day Today* for a few appearances in *Brass Eye*, feels that his aims were more general, that his motivation came from whatever was in the air that needed cutting down to size. And writer David Quantick similarly says, 'Chris's thing is that he seems to me to be really outraged that the world is not the way it should be.'

Brass Eye explored that sense of outrage by taking six perennial favourite documentary subjects – the sort of topics that were just too difficult to cover in thirty minutes but which the media regularly tried to simplify to the point where they didn't make any sense at all: Animals, Drugs, Science, Sex, Crime and Decline. 'You haven't got a clue, have you?' Morris admonished the viewer from his position behind the sickbed of British culture in Decline, 'but you will do – if you watch for thirty minutes.' Was the decline of morals in the country irreversible – the country's 'The-moral-mometer' reading just two morals per head – or was everything just great? Was science good or bad? These questions would be asked repeatedly throughout the show in varying ways as if there were some actual progress in answering them. Test tubes were shown in a courtroom to illustrate the trial of Science, 'accused of going too far; of befouling, pollutement and the intoxifaction of men's minds . . .' There was a relentless rhythm to the shows, punctuated by the questions, without the respite that *The Day Today* had in the shape of its soap *The Bureau* and its mini-documentaries on the office and the swimming pool. At the end of each edition, Morris would curtly summarize the big issue before dismissing the viewer, but not the vague sense of disquiet that the constant interrogation of the show created.

The big themes provided rich inspiration for the show's material which, when it didn't come from Morris himself, was the result of sessions with Peter Baynham, shared with Armando Iannucci's *Armistice* over the summer. 'I find that writing is definitely made easier by having meetings with people,' said Morris, 'because you say things that you didn't know you thought . . . In my experience anyway, if you sit and strain away at a blank sheet of paper on a desk, you know, you can get things out, but the type of things that come out are different from the sort of things you almost accidentally say.'[3] There were also Monday-morning writing meetings with a wider circle. There was no set method for coming up with material. Peter Baynham particularly remembers being in a vague, hungover state the Saturday morning after they'd been to a Talkback party. It informed the way in which he and Morris were talking about an idea for a fox-hunting sequence in what would be Animals. At one point Morris suggested his pro-hunt spokesman might comment, 'They say it's cruel, but they wouldn't say that if . . .' Baynham added woozily '. . . if it was a little four-legged car . . .' and Morris finished '. . . full of chips.' And that was the defence his character used.

The other writers worked primarily to provide initial ideas. Graham Linehan and Arthur Mathews came having evolved their own way of working in *Father Ted*, where they would write a couple of pages each, editing the other's work as they went along. They settled into Morris's looser way of talking around subjects, their suggestions including Egyptian pyramids being revealed as the ears of giant underground cat statues.

David Quantick had been working with writing partner Jane Bussmann when he was alerted to the existence of the new Chris Morris project. He brought Bussmann along. She had got into comedy after failing all her exams before university and had worked for Talkback and the BBC. Sharp and energetic, she had a filthy laugh and filthier sense of humour. The duo fitted in well. In the *Brass Eye* sessions, she recalls, she and Quantick wrote some material about a US army health film on gonorrhoea just to 'out-disgusting each other with stuff coming out of your cock'. She was the only female writer on *Brass Eye*, but as with Doon Mackichan and Rebecca Front performing in *On the Hour*, there wasn't any partic-ular significance to a writer's gender. It wasn't the sort of show where there were female gags to be written and, referring to the general lack of women in comedy, she pragmatically describes her presence as over-representative if anything. She wouldn't have had a female perspective to write from even if it had been required: 'I never have had,' she says now, 'which is the reason I can write comedy, I think.' But she did come to the sessions with some expectations of what the experience would be like, having been a fan of *The Day Today*: 'Obviously, Chris is an amazing individual, so I always thought, Fucking hell, I wonder what he's doing next? Everyone was in awe of Chris because he can say what he wants . . .'

It made writing for *Brass Eye* a liberating experience. 'Nobody ever got the impression that he had to change what he was saying or kiss up or try and schmooze any of those cunts in commissioning. Chris was a bastion of free speech. From the outset he seemed to bypass all the haggling and explaining process when you have to say why people would like your stuff and then it becomes shit because you have to change it.'

When she and Quantick contributed material – such as the miraculous vision of the Virgin Mary driving a car – it would be taken on by Linehan and Mathews and refined further by Morris. 'What you were doing basically was you were having the world's greatest pub conversation,' reflects Bussmann now. 'The process generally involved making each other laugh for long periods of time. She cites the discussion of how Victorians might have courted, something which didn't make it into the show. They riffed on gentlemen wearing stovepipe hats which would rotate at the object of their desire to show a zoetrope – except instead of the classic scene of horses jumping it would be people having sex. Even at the early writing stage, it was clear the series would be special. 'I just remember thinking, It's like some fucking summit in space,' says Bussmann. 'It's a period in history you can actually look around and think, This is fucking amazing and I hope I remember every moment.'

Radio 1 contributor Paul Garner also got a few pieces in and played a couple of parts, and – as ever – Morris gave him the jobs that most involved potential physical harm. He was to illustrate fear of science by jumping out at people on the street with a big sign saying 'Technology'. Each take Morris managed to cue him as a particularly bad-tempered commuter walked by.

After *The Word* was finally axed, several members of its production crew joined *Brass Eye*, including Andrew Newman. *The Word* shared with Morris's show a casual disregard for its medium, and Newman had worked on the prank set-ups which required a certain amount of ruthless character to carry out. He specialized in getting *Brass Eye*'s celebrities to do the interviews. Production manager Ali MacPhail returned from *The Day Today* to work with Morris again. Caroline Leddy had arrived at Talkback after working in BBC radio. She liaised closely between Morris and Channel 4, a job which became more tricky as the relationship deteriorated alarmingly towards transmission.

They had a fairly healthy budget to work with, particularly in terms of comedy production, but there was so much going on in *Brass Eye* that it was swiftly swallowed by a large cast, location shoots, elaborate sets and the secret office for the campaigns. The amount of time and money Talkback spent on Morris's projects would always far outweigh any tangible financial benefit, but the company knew they were powerful shows whose importance wasn't easy to price. Morris would go over budget in every series he made, and nobody liked to tackle him about it, partly because he could be ferocious in defending something he felt was integral to a show and partly because he was usually right.

When Talkback did have to step in, it would usually be Sally Debonnaire who was tasked with telling him to stop spending. Peter Fincham tended to avoid battles with Morris if he could, although he did offer the team a kind of back-up support on occasion. During the making of the *Special* in 2001, he wrote a stern memo to Morris on the subject. And asked Philippa Catt, who looked after day-to-day production, to hand it on. Later that day she and Morris were riding to a shoot with director Tristram Shapeero. Morris read the note as they set off and immediately ordered the car to pull over. He jumped out, grabbed his coat and bag from the back of the car and told them, 'I may or may not be there this afternoon,' before slamming the boot shut and striding off up Berwick Street. Shapeero and Catt looked at each other and wondered what they would say to the rest of the crew. They arrived at the location to find Morris apologetic and having got there before them by public transport.

Money seemed to have no further meaning to Morris other than getting as much of it as possible up on the screen. He was entirely unconcerned about making it for himself, to the point that a despairing Chiggy virtually had to do aspects of deals for him behind his back to ensure that he didn't negotiate his cut away entirely in return for a bit of extra filming – while simultaneously trying to get Peter Fincham's executive producer fee diverted to production. And during the making of the *Special*, he hit on the idea of getting the crew to use his house as a location base for a Brixton shoot. About twenty of them turned up, and production coordinator Holly Sait had the distinct impression that Jo Unwin, at home with the two young boys, hadn't quite been briefed on their arrival.

Everyone was expected to help save where they could so that ever more footage could be shot. Crew checked out locations by public transport – when Morris received the memo from Fincham they'd all been sitting in Tristram Shapeero's own car rather than a taxi – and during shoots for the original series Ali MacPhail, who lived near Morris in south London, remembers that he regularly hitched a lift back with her. Enjoying a good gossip, he relied on her to fill him in on any production crew scandal on the way. It was about his only distraction as he absorbed himself in the technicalities of production.

When he wasn't involved in battles about budgets, Morris's charm and humour meant that the crew worked far harder than they might normally – without that goodwill, a show with the complexity of *Brass Eye* just wouldn't have happened, no matter how much cash was poured in. More than anything, the ambition and boldness of the concept made everyone care about the show. 'He's hard work in terms of you've got to be prepared to put the work in,' says Armando Iannucci, 'but it's always very rewarding. It does sort the men out from the boys. Because some people just want to do what you normally do for a show and don't want the hassle. You find that he raises the quality threshold of anything you do. It makes you ask if something is good enough and if it's not, then don't do it. But it is hard, it's very hard. It's just sheer, gruelling, hard toil.'

Ali MacPhail likens Morris to a general leading from the front. When he marched smartly down the corridors at Channel 4, curly hair billowing, people would actually get out of his way. But then there was the weekend she had flu and he came over. By the time she had made it to the front door, he'd gone, leaving a little bag with a lemon, a jar of honey, a small bottle of whisky and a get-well note.

Charlie Brooker is one of those who saw a different Morris in production – his personality shifted into a grave and reflective mode, dwelling on everything that might go wrong. And the job was made trickier still for those around him because Morris actively enjoyed catching people out. You had to back up what you were saying and not waffle. He wasn't looking to be surrounded by sycophants, and there was never any point in putting your point over half-heartedly. It was always good to take notes in production meetings with him, though you could never be sure whether he'd test you out because he was trying out every option or just because he wanted to see what you knew. There was a sketch in his later series *Jam* involving a television filled with lizards. What, he asked art director Dick Lunn, was the 'operating temperature' of a lizard? Having done a special project on lizards as part of his zoology degree, he probably knew more than most.

Just as on the Radio 1 shows, the production office fax machine whirred late into the night. Sally Debonnaire also received calls after hours, but more usually from tearful crew members for whom the constant demands had become too much. She acted as unofficial mentor– a role she would reprise in his other programmes – talking them down with ideas they might suggest to him for how things could be more reasonably accomplished.

Veterans of *The Day Today* had an idea of what to expect. Graphic designers Russell Hilliard and Richard Norley had left ITN by then and were building their company Jump. Money was tight and they used their old employer's equipment during downtime. Their work was a key element of *Brass Eye*, which was designed to operate in a graphical environment that was rarely static, the viewer continually dropped in and out of reports which were framed in boxes popping up and down at speed. It was as if the documentary were the entire world and, having made you dizzy with confusion, *Brass Eye* held out its hand to be your only guide. The effects were complicated and, at the point of exhaustion, Jump eventually had to beg Morris to prioritize. He made an attempt – sort of – by faxing over a list of effects numbered by importance. The first was marked top priority. So were all the others.

Composer Jonathan Whitehead had initial idea sessions with Morris, after which he was largely left alone to produce the incidental music. He wrote to the completed graphics sequences in the shows to effectively suggest mayhem, panic and life-threatening urgency. Then the two of them refined or reworked the music – generally making it more rather than less overcooked. Briefed to write a main theme with the heartbeat of the inexorable progress of 'Montagues and Capulets' from Prokofiev's *Romeo and Juliet*, Whitehead's production indicated how clever the show thought it was with a shifting time signature. Just as the ad break started, a brief excerpt would be repeated over Jump's rushing graphics disappearing into a perspective point, giving an effective feeling of falling into a bottomless chasm with the brass section from an orchestra.

Actors were drafted into *Brass Eye* at an early stage to make even the briefest part seem believable. 'Often things are best when they're thrown at you and you have no time to prepare,' says Doon Mackichan. 'So Chris would often just say he wanted to do a particular character and would talk. And then I would go away and have time to come back with some ideas.' There were often new bits of script to be learned at short notice or props were changed at the last minute. 'You just don't take it personally,' she says, recalling the moments she grabbed to learn words while simultaneously feeding her baby in the dressing room. 'It's the people who think they're geniuses who actually don't come up to scratch when they tell you to do things. That's when your hackles get up. Chris can kind of get away with murder.'

It was a restless approach Chris shared with his brother Tom. Then at the Battersea Arts Centre, Tom Morris had been in experimental theatre for most of his career. Composer Adrian Sutton worked with both of them: 'Tom, in particular, during theatre shows is always very infectiously enthusiastic about trying things out,' Sutton says. 'You just can't help but want to please them because they're just so gracious and lovely about it.'

Not all the cast came to *Brass Eye* with experience of how Morris did things. New faces included Kevin Eldon, Mark Heap and David Cann, all of whom worked so well with Morris's meandering approach that they became a core part of his unofficial repertory company for both *Blue Jam* and *Jam*. 'Work-wise it's rewarding being asked to contribute to the process,' says Eldon, 'and the preparation that's gone into is a marked contrast to how TV works mostly; you don't get directed. You don't rehearse.' Both Heap and Eldon had an understated way of approaching their parts which gave even the most extreme scenario a sense of realism. They had a quality of stillness which bordered on the eerie, suggesting a sense of otherness to even the most ordinary character. Their deceptive normality was matched by David Cann's startlingly reassuring figures of authority. But *Brass Eye* was most strongly associated with Morris's anchorman – bullying, sneering, Paxmanning. Its strength made it easy to overlook the twenty or so other characters he played over the course of the series. But while his scripted parts were mostly reporters, so essentially men all doing the same job, Morris lightly suggested individuality with a skilful touch which never allowed characters to obscure the jokes in the stories they reported. Ted Maul was an old favourite from *The Day Today*, still blazered and not quite able to hide his inferiority fears about his provincial roots. Austen Tasseltine was geeky and not as clever as he thought he was. Alabaster Codify was more occasional, a US reporter with the full permatan and gleaming teeth which made him seem much more of a developed character than his brief screen time suggested.

Others made up an array of varied experts and witnesses for each topic. A baseball cap and wrap-around clear glasses marked out earnest anti-drugs campaigner Lemuel Webb as overanxious to appear to be seen as cool by the kids he's trying to warn off drugs. Showing them a jar containing the bloody contents of a coke-head's sneeze, he thinks he's impressing them in saying, 'That man is lying on his back thinking, Where in shitting crikey is my nose?' For Captain Clyde Jackson, Morris wore blue contacts with a jet-black centre and a thin moustache to create a modern borstal psycho-governor, demanding of a prisoner, 'Where's your self-re-cocking-spect?' It was the sparklingly demented dialogue more than the subtle characterization which stayed in the mind, but each episode was scattered with those tight cameos. Greasy US talk-show host Chuck Fadanoid talked glibly about priests with guns and – strictly just an impersonation of Jarvis Cocker but as rounded as Morris's radio Keith Richards – there was Purves Grundy, lead singer with Blouse.

Brass Eye was solid enough to pass for a documentary strand in its own right rather than trying to take off any one programme in particular. It had the feel of current affairs as macho eventing with bold and elegant editing and its emotive presentation of the big issues. The realistic presentation of the show supported its stylized dialogue and wilder invention – in a report on a detention camp, it's somehow not surprising when one of the inmates is caught out during a regular dormitory inspection for not having polished a large brass moustache hidden behind a noticeboard. And as Gina McKee's Libby Shuss concludes the scene with a voiceover explaining that the inmates will then have to strip their beds, bury the blankets and dig them up to sleep in them 'all earthy', the sense of indefinable menace is carried by the realization of the staging.

Throughout the series, even those props and situations which appeared fleetingly were sourced and worked to look authentic. In the sketch about Shaftesbury's Jam, the company which allows drugs in its production meetings, the drugs drew praise in an article by Will Self: 'Not only were all the paraphernalia and substances depicted with uncanny accuracy rare on television, but the reactions of the drugged executives were entirely credible.' The marketing manager falls out of the boardroom as the voiceover intones, 'Soon he will learn to maintain his levels.' Will Self commented, 'Maybe he will, but I doubt Chris Morris ever will. Put starkly, this man genuinely knows no limits.'[4]

It was an assessment that was most apparent in *Brass Eye*'s interaction with the real world. Morris had little time for other comic interviewers of the time like Mrs Merton, who appeared to mock their subjects. 'So easily assimilated,' he said of Caroline Aherne's character. 'People know how to play her, they just get their best grin on and come out stinking of roses.' And the same was true of *Have I Got News For You*: 'It's the biggest warm handshake, glass of sherry, pat on the back, pair of fluffy slippers to the Establishment you could possibly dream up. It becomes mere court jester tittle-tattle which has no bite whatsoever.'[5]

Morris was prepared to put himself in situations of real physical risk in his interviews. For the Drugs episode, he bothered west London drug dealers, dropping extracts from his mission into the programme as if part of a real investigation. That casually professional approach, using just snippets, combined with his supernatural confidence meant there was no indication in the final sketch of the very real fear that the crew had for his safety.

Researchers Rob Moore and Andrew Newman had selected All Saints Road after a reconnaissance mission which was successful in every respect, except that on closer examination their test purchase turned out to be nothing more potent than wood shavings. On the night of filming, the team gathered in Peter Fincham's house nearby. Morris was relaxed, sitting with a cup of coffee, chatting and watching the telly. The crew mothered him anxiously, saying he would get cold and be stabbed. Ali MacPhail talked him into wearing a padded jacket for protection.

Morris was first driven down the road a number of times looking for likely characters. Once he was on All Saints Road itself he was covered by a film crew in a flat overlooking the road, while Andrew Newman was installed in the back of a van filming on a digital camera on the opposite side. There was no police back-up. The crew were in radio contact, and Morris was wired for sound but would have been hard to reach if anything went wrong. When one of the dealers took him down a side alley, everyone held their breath as the sound cut and Morris disappeared from view for a while.

His dominating attitude was the most effective defence – he dodged ahead of his quarry all the time, as if he were cutting off their way of escape while blitzing them with a stream of entirely made-up drug terms – 'triple sod', 'yellow bentines' and 'clarky cat' – and demanding to know if one dealer is the 'boz boz'. Clearly angered yet strangely weary, the dealer eventually says, 'My friend, please leave us alone.' It was almost as if there had been a physical confrontation which Morris had won, yet it was all aggressive word-play. Not that it all went his way. Remembering how the researchers had been ripped off, Morris hectored the dealer, 'Last time I came here a friend of mine just got triple-jacked over the steeple hammer and jessop, jessop, jessop, jessop, jessop. It's not wood, right?' The dealer was clearly not completely cowed by Morris's stream of non-sense. Despite his angry, 'This is not wood, man,' *Brass Eye* had once again bought shavings.

Reconvening back at Peter Fincham's house, the rest of the crew were fizzing with nervous excitement and yet Morris remained as calm as he appeared on screen. If you were concentrating on his mental agility, you might even miss his deceptive physical tough-ness entirely. But it had been part of Morris as early as his days on Andy's Records, when lugging heavy boxes of records around had been as important to the job as knowing music. It was always there, just under the surface, even in the celebrity interviews, alongside the psychological power play – it was as if he exercised an almost tangible control over his guests while simultaneously signalling huge amusement to the audience. Morris told Armando Iannucci that he struggled not to corpse, but it was sometimes visible – when he played a pretentious music critic asking one-hit wonder Jas Mann from Babylon Zoo, 'What is your song? Is that like an audible sound or just like a bubble of oxygen?' he had to choke back a laugh.

Morris seemed to be energized by those celebrity interviews, which the *Brass Eye* team called hits, but for the other crew members there was just sweaty, prickly fear in setting them up. It wasn't quite so bad when they were doing interviews in the familiar surroundings of a studio. They used ITN with a production secretary who had worked on Radio 4 news shows to reassure subjects. But location shooting was a miserable experience if Morris didn't go along, as everyone else was left with the worries that he just didn't seem to have – about how unconvincing they felt they were. Once the interview was confirmed and set up, Morris would think about questions and guidelines and fax them as late as the morning of the shoot. The crew would have time only to look them over as they sat in their taxi on the way to the hit.

For the 2001 *Special*, DJ Neil Fox was approached to assert that paedophiles have more in common genetically with crabs than with humans, and the crew had to get him to back it up by smashing a crab to pieces on camera. The runner on the show, James Serafinowicz, recalls going to Billingsgate Market to procure a genuine crab and, as he shivered among the ranks of early-morning stalls, the pseudo-science of *Brass Eye* seemed as if it would never convince. And yet DJ 'Dr' Fox did what he was asked to do. 'There's no real evidence for it,' he said of the genetic assertion, 'but it is scientific fact.'

The interviews were recorded months ahead of broadcast, and the worst thing for the crew was the fear that they would be the ones who said something which made a celebrity go to the press and ruin the whole concept. 'Those were horrible. I couldn't handle that at all, the going to the hits,' says Tristram Shapeero. 'It felt like your whole world was going to end.'

Remembering the experience of the Krays during the shooting of the pilot, Andrew Newman and Rob Moore hired an anonymous serviced office off Leicester Square for the main series under the guise of being telemarketers. The front organization of each show had its own phone line, post office box and headed paper. Some campaigns were given a veneer of authority with specially shot film shown to the victims, such as the grainy footage of the cow in Animals being rounded up and fired out of a metal tube in Libya (a stretch of land under the A40 Westway in west London stood in for the Middle East).

No celebrity was off-limits and, although there was little sympathy for media veterans like Noel Edmonds or Bernard Ingham, some of the production staff felt a bit of a pang about certain much-loved figures like Claire Rayner or kindly Richard Briers. But Morris accepted no pleas for mercy on the grounds of twinkly national treasuredom. Everyone who was willing to speak up for something that didn't exist was fair game as far as he was concerned.

It was usually only Andrew Newman and a camera operator who went to the hits so that it seemed as if they were working with limited resources like a real campaigning organization. Though they sometimes filmed the preamble to an interview, there was no covert recording and they were careful not to slip into breaking the law by passing themselves off as a charity. Rather than telling outright lies to the targets, much of what was revealed about what was going to happen with the filmed material was more or less true – in welcoming new inmates to prison, as Tommy Vance did for the Key 2000 spoof Home Office video, he was told his footage was to be shown to as many young people as possible and hopefully would be given airtime on Channel 4, possibly in some late-night slot – 'We told them as much as we could,' says Newman.

Only very few followed up their interviews and even then only in a very basic way, in one case calling the fake office to check on Gita, one of the teens affected by 'heavy electricity' falling out of domestic power lines. Had she really been squashed to just eight inches? A simple, solemn confirmation by the researcher was all the reassurance required.

Morris was insistent on the same level of quality control in the hits as in the rest of the show, which meant on occasion redoing the shoot, despite the even greater fear of the crew in getting someone to say the same nonsense twice. One team had got Sebastian Coe in the Houses of Parliament for the *Special*, but Morris decided that the eyeline of the sporting peer, who read his words off cue cards, was wrong. The next day they got into the imposing Conservative Party headquarters, the grand surroundings making them feel particularly fraudulent. But Coe again held up the pictures of Hall and Oates treated to look like police shots, once more said the images were of a paedophile before and after changing his appearance and again that he 'holds a low-status job in the American music market'.

Not all hits worked. There was the celebrity gangster who seemed so frightening that crew members won't go on the record about him even now. And Welsh Tory MP Nigel Evans had an interview that became too farcical when Morris hit on the idea of introducing black powder into Evans's make-up. Ali MacPhail pretended to be a make-up artist and applied black powder to Evans as he sweated under the hot lights. Inevitably, he spotted particles coming off his face and asked if he had any marks, but Morris had become determined to continue and point-blank denied the evidence with a politely puzzled expression. Evans called over Ali MacPhail who, had there been an award for least convincing make-up artist in an interview, would have won it for steadfastly claiming she didn't have a mirror in the make-up box. So the MP said he would just go to the bathroom. Morris got Newman and Moore in the production gallery to race Evans to the studio toilets and jam the doors shut from the inside. Evans returned – fairly good-humouredly – and the interview was abandoned.

Other celebrities were asked to give reactions to *Brass Eye*'s brief news stories. It created further potential for secrets to be revealed months before the scheduled transmission start date of that November. Bernard Ingham's segment in Drugs was shot at the *Daily Express* offices, and he later showed the paper's news desk one of *Brass Eye*'s fake foreign articles on cake. A very enthusiastic *Express* crime reporter phoned the Leicester Square office and suddenly FUKD and BOMBD were placed in the awkward position of being anti-drugs campaigners who seemingly didn't want any publicity. Yet somehow secrecy was maintained almost to the end, by which point the threat came not from an external source, but from Channel 4 itself. Just days before transmission, the broadcaster abruptly lost its nerve over the more contentious material in *Brass Eye* and pulled the programme.

It wasn't as if they had only just become aware at that late stage of what was in the show. Channel 4's legal team had been working with Morris from the start to meet the many challenges in getting it out. For Prash Naik, controller of legal compliance, it was better to be in at the beginning of something like *Brass Eye* than doing a last-minute, messy round of cutting, re-editing, blurring images or bleeping out words.

He took on both the scripted elements and the hits, balancing the show's content with regulatory requirements for libel, contempt and taste and decency. Young and informal, he was a good match for Morris. Rather than telling him what wasn't possible, he and Jan Tomalin, head of legal and compliance, knew the grey areas in programming regulations and were enthusiastic about trying to get as much as possible on air. And they loved the show.

It was anticipated that the most difficult element would be the interviews with politicians. The channel had just had to apologize to Harrow MP Jerry Hayes – who had also been caught on Chris Morris's Radio 1 show – because he had been filmed for campaigning comedian Mark Thomas's *Comedy Product* in early 1996 in an eight-foot inflatable penis costume without being told it was for a humour show.

Prash Naik worked closely with Morris to build the case for *Brass Eye* being in the public interest. MPs had parliamentary researchers who could have checked out the bona fides of campaign organizations – Basildon MP David Amess had his with him during his Drugs interview that summer. During the interview, the MP himself added a new element by offering without prompting to submit a written question about cake in the Houses of Parliament. It was naturally irresistible for Morris, despite the additional risk of discovery, and the official parliamentary record *Hansard* registered the government's response for posterity: 'We are not aware of any reports of misuse in the United Kingdom of the substance known as "cake" but the advisory council nevertheless has under review the question whether this and a number of similar substances should be brought within the scope of the 1971 Act.'[6] They tantalizingly didn't say what the 'similar substances' were, and a request under the Freedom of Information Act to the Home Office in the course of writing this book prompted the disappointing news that accompanying briefing papers for questions are always destroyed after two years.

Though the scripted parts of the show weren't as legally troublesome as the interviews, almost every episode involved subjects being treated in a way that could breach parts of the broadcasting code. The general defence for the whole series was to be that it built the outrage over the course of the episodes and was a satirical treatment of the often arbitrary reasoning for taboos in the media.

The toughest edition to sort out was Sex, where almost every scene had something to worry a regulator. It opens with Morris simulating intercourse as the camera pans back to show he's on a monitor being watched by a fully dressed version of himself, turning to do the introduction while the sex continues vigorously behind him. The studio audience debate section of the programme features a character Morris criticizes for having 'bad AIDS' – having caught it from a boyfriend – rather than 'good AIDS', which he says you get innocently through blood transfusions. The audience back Morris as he demands the man is removed from the studio.

The uncomfortable atmosphere in the studio was more than matched by the response of many at Channel 4 in the debate with a 12-year-old character called Judy Lehewuttwhohen, who is introduced as having been abused from the age of nine by her uncle. Morris questions her with agonizingly slow and quiet prurience. 'If you fall over in the snow do you make a couple of bumps?' he asks. 'Probably do, don't you?'

The sketch was one that Morris discussed with Chiggy, who had been half-expecting the call. He phoned so rarely during production time that she rather suspected that he guessed she would be as uncomfortable with certain sketches as Channel 4 and just wanted to rehearse the argument he would later have. Sometimes the broadcaster would have already been in contact. 'Chris and I had these pointless, circular conversations,' says Chiggy. 'If I agreed with them, that would set him off on a major rant . . . Sometimes you get into those arguments with him and he can way outwit anybody, as far as I can see. He can create any argument for the most ludicrous suggestion and in the end – and I'm sure he does this on purpose – you become quite emotional about it. You descend into these increasingly plaintive responses like, "I don't know why I think that! I just *do*!" It's a feeling, not an argument. But it's what informs a lot of people's reactions.'

There were also sketches which it always seemed were never going to get through, and some both on Morris's side and at Channel 4 thought that he put them up to be sacrifices to make other things look acceptable. An advert for a board game called Horrorcaust – based on the Holocaust – seemed particularly unlikely to make it. But if anything was designed to be expendable, Morris would never admit as much to anyone at the channel in their regular battles. Enthusiastic as Prash Naik was about the show, he grew to dread the daily calls about a programme which had begun to take over his working life. Morris had familiarized himself with the ITC code,[7] as every programme-maker was supposed to but not all did in practice, and he had also identified loopholes and worked out how to circumvent restrictions. Naik would frequently seek the advice of Jan Tomalin, and they would endeavour to find a creative way around the code only to find that Morris had thrown another tricky problem their way. The two never actually fell out, though there were plenty of heated conversations – literally, at one point.

'He actually said to me, "If you don't let me do this, I'm going to burn all my rushes. I'm not going to deliver. I will destroy everything." And it's the only time I've ever thought, You're mad enough to do that,' Naik says, adding thoughtfully: 'I don't actually think now that he would have.'

It seemed that nothing sapped Morris's energy. The daily grind of living didn't seem to affect him. Even when his home suffered from subsidence in the 1990s, he took on and won a fierce battle with the insurers. It was as if he didn't see the same obstacles that affected other people. Back in 1993, when he and Armando Iannucci went to see *Reservoir Dogs* in the cinema, they found it sold out. Morris immediately went to the nearest phone box and, says Iannucci, 'just spun some yarn and wouldn't stop and eventually – and I've no idea how they did it – we were shown into the cinema and given two seats'.

Yet even Morris began to betray a sign of the colossal battering he was taking towards the end of *Brass Eye*, though it took the eye of the make-up artist to spot it. When they shot more material for Animals to augment the *Torque TV* pilot and had to apply make-up to match him to how he'd looked the previous year, he was candidly informed he looked 'fucked'.

The last of the cuts and changes were eventually agreed – and despite everything they were in the end relatively minor. It looked as if the show would meet its scheduled transmission dates. And then Michael Grade became interested in the content of the programmes.

10

BRASS EYE

BY LATE 1996 EVERY INSTINCT IN CHANNEL 4'S PRESS OFFICE was keenly attuned to giving *Brass Eye* a major push. They wanted to offer the star to the press for interviews and profiles and circulate clips. But *Brass Eye*'s profile was to be kept deliberately low. It had even been suggested that Talkback handle the publicity themselves. Realizing that this would effectively be giving Chris Morris complete control of Channel 4's public relations, the station promptly suggested it might be better if the show were taken in-house. Senior press officer Greg Day was used to working with comedians and on entertainment shows which had always been promoted in a very straightforward way. It wasn't long before he found himself working against everything he knew as a PR for *Brass Eye*. He was never able to contact anyone on the show apart from Morris himself, who allowed him to release just a trickle of information into the void. The press, like the celebrity interviewees, were told only that the show was a 'factual entertainment' which was 'looking at topical issues in an entertaining way'. The press office was instructed to admit if directly asked that Chris Morris was behind the show. Nobody did, and his identity was revealed only two weeks before broadcast. For someone whose job was to make a big fuss of things, it was agony for Greg Day. Morris supplied only non-attributable quotes for the press. Sometimes he would give enough juicy facts to start a story and then get Day to promise to call back – but never actually do so. Journalists excitedly invented the rest of the story for themselves.

'I can say to you it was the right time for that series,' says Day. 'There is no way that the Channel 4 press office would ever do now what I did then.' Day had to consciously stop himself from giving more information. 'As an in-house PR there is a part of you that is trained to be corporate, and I got very upset about it, but I found myself being a much better liar and manipulator than I thought I could be,' he says.

It took three weeks to get a press release for the overall series that both he and Morris could agree on. When he was forbidden to release a couple of pages of the show's highlights, Day said issuing only the couple of paragraphs that Morris wanted would look strange coming as an official release from Channel 4. Morris retorted that in that case he should issue it without the broadcaster's logo. The deadlock was eventually resolved with a reluctant compromise of half a page. 'He just wrote it,' says Day, 'and I took out the expletives.' Day was frustrated and felt undermined by Morris, and thought he was crippling his own show.

But elsewhere in Channel 4, the fears about the show's content that were coming to crisis point would prove far more dangerous for its existence than arguments over headed paper. It was a reflection of the character of the publicity campaign that when the news broke that the show had been postponed, many assumed the announcement was just phase II of the anti-PR PR master plan. The show had been trailed on Channel 4 by then, and the week's listings magazines had already highlighted it for 19 November. 'Is Chris Morris too hot to handle?' asked Bruce Dessau presciently in his *Time Out* preview.[1]

Conspiracy theories circulated among Morris's base of fans on the internet about the official line from Channel 4, that more time was needed to be sure that everything complied with regulations. But prosaic though the explanation was, senior management at the broadcaster were still concerned about certain sketches. In the end, the series was referred up to Michael Grade and the effect was catastrophic. It was the first time he had become properly involved, and he reignited the debate over many sketches, instigating another set of changes with the lawyers. Morris was faced with beginning the negotiation process all over again.

'Right up until the end,' says Seamus Cassidy, 'Chris was gentlemanly, courteous and reasonable.' The end was in sight. With the reports of the postponement had come rumblings from David Amess and Sir Graham Bright, the MPs who had been featured in the Drugs episode. They got together with Home Office Minister Tom Sackville, who had been involved in drafting an answer to David Amess's question on cake, to condemn the show for wasting taxpayers' parliamentary money.

And it wasn't just the MPs' interviews that were under threat. Other celebrity names began to appear in the press, and Michael Grade suggested revisiting all of the hits. Morris's gentlemanly reason went up in a sheet of incandescent rage. 'Grade was just looking for an easy life and a knighthood, and he didn't want to have the cigar swatted from his mouth by some blowsy celeb,' he later said. 'He called me into his office and offered me a drink in a showbizmatey kind of way and said, "Look, all we have to do is ask permission [for the interviews]." My argument was that wouldn't work. The whole point was that the hoax wasn't bulletproof. It was quite brittle.' He refused to make any more changes. Grade told him, he later claimed, that great though the series was it would never go out: 'I really spent three days thinking about very little else than what great pleasure, what absolutely total pleasure it would give me really to kill somebody. I've never felt that before. But I could imagine every aspect of killing somebody and but for the fact that the opportunity didn't present itself . . .'[2]

The channel's regular editorial meeting was the most popular event in the company the week that the *Brass Eye* question was debated. They were turning people away. Executives, commissioning editors and their deputies jammed themselves into the room, with the majority – though not everyone – in favour of the show. Strong support was expressed by John Willis and Seamus Cassidy. Caroline Leddy from Talkback lobbied hard on Morris's behalf. 'It began to turn Michael's views,' said Willis later.[3] *Brass Eye* went to the heart of what Channel 4 meant for the station staff – whichever side they were on. But there was still much to be done to convince a boss who had become reluctant about the show as a concept and about Chris Morris in particular.

'Why on earth was I keen to buy trouble by giving him a slot on Channel 4?' Grade later asked readers of his autobiography. 'Why do people become lion-tamers or swallow razor-blades for a living? I recognized a rare talent and felt that Channel 4 had a libertarian tradition that ought to be able to accommodate Chris Morris's satire – though, as with lion-taming, the cardinal rule would have to be: never take your eyes off the beast.'[4]

The *Guardian* reported no fewer than 112 websites discussing *Brass Eye*, and journalist Jim White wondered at the source of their information: 'You could imagine Morris at its centre, firing off the email, relishing the opportunity to drop a few pearls of misinformation into the public domain, undermining and sabotaging, while all the time maintaining his anonymity.'[5] It couldn't have been further from the truth. The mood in Morris's camp was despondent at the way in which his innovative PR campaign had descended into a shouting match.

'After spending a year of our lives and £1 million,' Peter Fincham told the *Guardian* on 25 November, 'we are very keen that this thing be shown. I can assure you this is not a stunt.'[6]

On the Hour and *The Day Today* writer Steven Wells ranted splendidly in his *NME* column against the 'bottle job over *Brass Eye* . . . Having seen previews of the series, *Brass Eye* is great and utterly moral comedy. Its "postponement" is nothing other than an act of spit-licking corporate cowardice. You DESERVE to see this programme. Are you pissed off yet? Are you going to do something about it?' He gave the Channel 4 number and instructed, 'Give them hell.'[7] Morris happened to run into Wells some months later and asked with some amazement what he'd written, saying readers had flooded Channel 4 with calls.

Emotions were running just as high within the station itself. Seamus Cassidy was among those who maintained that the second round of cuts was unnecessary. And eventually the tireless campaign mounted by champions of *Brass Eye* paid off, with Grade persuaded by the arguments and undimmed passion for the series. It was rescheduled for the new year.

The battle might have been won, but it had exhausted everyone. Cassidy, all the enthusiasm he'd had when he'd first saw *Torque TV* lost, soon quit the channel. Michael Grade himself abruptly announced his departure from Channel 4. Having timed the statement two days before rescheduled *Brass Eye* began its run on 29 January 1997, it was widely questioned whether the series had been a factor in his decision.

The new transmission date placed *Brass Eye* at the start of an election year which was anticipated to mark the end of almost two decades of Conservative rule. There was a sense of imminent change in the country which seemed to fit with a show as sharp, clever and knowing as *Brass Eye*. Morris might not have been party political, but targeting the self-satisfied and the hypocritical seemed to fit in very well with the mood of the times. The Tories were seen as burned-out history, stale and stodgy, and their replacements were younger and smarter and promised to create a fairer society. Morris himself would have been the last to claim to be part of any of that – only months later he dismissed New Labour as 'hopelessly cosmetic'.[8] But for those watching the show who could barely remember a time without the Tories, there were eerie parallels between *Brass Eye*'s celebrities prepared to say anything as long as they got on television and the Tories hanging on desperately to power having lost their majority of one seat in Parliament. Incompetence and sleaze coloured the perception of Major's last days. It was only the previous September that the 'cash for questions' affair climaxed when MP Neil Hamilton and lobbyist Ian Greer dropped their libel actions against the *Guardian*. Their reasoning was that they could not afford to continue with the case, but the damage to the Tories' image had been done – they were seen as the party who could be paid to take issues to Parliament. Overdosing on too much cake somehow went well with fat-cat Conservatives.

Brass Eye was smart, subtle and innovative and tackled the big social issues that seemed to be natural New Labour areas. The party also understood the media and how to manipulate it. Watching *Brass Eye* it seemed as though not only would the Conservatives disapprove, but they probably wouldn't even grasp what it was about. Tony Blair and his band of idealistic young hopefuls gave every impression they would be instinctively more in favour of the liberal arts and – something that, if nothing else, the controversy over the *Special* would prove to be wrong in almost every respect – would encourage such daring programming. Being a fan of *Brass Eye* in such heady times wasn't quite a political gesture – but it did feel like being part of something momentous.

The sense of imminent change in the early months of 1997 was matched by a cultural renewal which even America noticed. *Vanity Fair* ran its 'London swings again' cover story that March. By the summer the phenomenon even had a name – Cool Britannia. Its glory shone on both the youthful incoming political establishment and the artistic community, the Young British Artists who understood the media and were outspoken and amusing and produced art that didn't necessarily want to be liked or categorized, but demanded a response. Alongside them was the resurgent music industry, with Brit Pop artists playful and innovative and as hungry for success as the YBAs. Grouped together by the media, all those artists were inevitably disparate, but they shared a refreshing cynicism allied to genuine exuberance and creative energy. *Brass Eye* was as bold, looked as finely crafted and sounded as sharp as anything else that defined the times. You instinctively felt watching *Brass Eye* that like so much of the best that was happening at that time, it couldn't have come from any other country and that it had a creator who was operating on full power. The country was waking up, and *Brass Eye* was in the middle of it.

The first episode, Animals, had an audience of about a million that January. Its impact had been muted by the extensive coverage of the postponement, and suspicion lingered that the series was more hype than anything else, but it was well received in the *Guardian* and the *Financial Times*. A letter in the *Daily Mail* protested about the filth of the show. Cosmo Landesman in the *Sunday Times* thought that Morris was part of the Jeremy Beadle generation, that his duping was smug humour that flattered an audience into thinking they wouldn't fall for such media tricks.

What *Brass Eye* really needed more than anything, to paraphrase Ted Maul, was a shot in the arm from celebrities. And that was exactly what it got a week later, after the broadcast of Drugs. Noel Edmonds, having read out the ingredients of cake and explained how 'it stimulates the part of the brain known as Shatner's Bassoon', realized he'd been set up and issued a furious 400-word denunciation. It was intended to damage the show but actually did more than anything else to convince journalists that *Brass Eye* wasn't just full of stunts hatched by Talkback and Channel 4 with everyone in on the joke. Suddenly there was the proof that the near cancellation had been for real. Celebrities really had no idea that the campaigns weren't authentic. And Noel Edmonds, the man behind the Gotcha! prank, hadn't seen the funny side.

Chris Morris made no response to any of the stories in the press. He deliberately refrained from being drawn into justifying his shows which he wanted viewers to judge on their own merits. Channel 4 were left to draft statements in defence of his series.

Viewers were as polarized as the press. For fans, watching *Brass Eye* could be more like the feeling of passionate engagement you might get with a favourite and formative band. It was something to take to your heart for being its own entire world; it credited the viewer with intelligence and it was startling in its approach to celebrity. *Brass Eye* inspired a fierce devotion or an equally strong sense that comedy shouldn't be doing that sort of thing – a view encapsulated by the *Daily Mail*, which launched its first attack on Morris on 7 February.

The hostile press searched for scandal without success and settled on claiming that he was a tyrant on set. The *Sunday Times* said it was clear that Morris 'hated something'. His birthmark and acne were cited and compared with Dudley Moore's club foot: 'Morris, how-ever, had a comfortable background,'[9] they said, something that went to the heart of the moralizing. Morris's real crime for many commentators was to betray his class. His parents, as country doc-tors, were the very people who kept Middle England alive, who had given him a privileged education. Here he was, letting light in on the media existence he should have been celebrating.

Libby Purves wrote that *Brass Eye* had gone too far and thought that the show lacked the art of a scripted and performed parody such as *Knowing Me, Knowing You*. She claimed that getting real celebrities in had to be easier and therefore less worthwhile. Writing in *The Times* in response the following week, Michael Grade said that if people 'exercise proper caution in future before allowing themselves to be used in this way, then Chris Morris . . . has performed a public service'.[10] He might have added that it wasn't impossible for celebrities to guess the interviews were set-ups.

Astrologer Russell Grant immediately realized there was some-thing amiss in Morris's unwelcoming style, the weird little goatee he wore and the questions which sounded ridiculous. He went into what he calls 'outré camp' mode and the interview was never used.

'They should really [spot that it's a gag],' said Morris years later, 'because . . . there's no fun really in so perfectly mimicking reality that you pass off something that's made up that might as well be real. Whereas if all the labels on it are saying, "This is fucking non-sense," then you've got a gap to play with.'[11]

Some *Brass Eye* interviewees said that they were too busy to check their appointments. Laurence Llewelyn-Bowen was booked on the *Special* by his office and was caught alone early one morning when the crew turned up. He had no idea who they were, but he knew who they weren't – polite, suited and deferential, they were the opposite of the scruffy, overfamiliar campaign workers he was used to. They set up a monitor on which they showed what they claimed was police footage of paedophiles on Tottenham Court Road which was clearly ludicrous, and Llewelyn-Bowen guessed they were filming his reaction to it live so he couldn't claim they later cut away to a different piece of film. He came up with some polite excuse to get rid of them.

But as *Brass Eye* was being broadcast, the only voices heard were from those who had been taken in and were angry about it. The production team had expected as much and knew there was little they could do about what people said outside the show. Internally, security remained very tight to the end of the run. Though when information did finally leak, it concerned the single most contentious sketch in the series – *Sutcliffe! The Musical.*

The life of the Yorkshire Ripper was brought to the stage in the last edition, Decline, with the claim that he was to appear as himself on day release from prison. The sketch featured a montage of songs from a rehearsal of the musical, concluding with him singing that he's 'very truly sorry'. Celebrity comment was elicited from racing commentator John McCririck, who seemed less angry at the concept of the musical than at a comment by Morris which reveals the killer has an agent, bellowing, 'His agent! What a game!'

Grade had been unhappy about *Sutcliffe!* even when the series was initially postponed in November: 'Because of victims' families and so on, I just felt it crossed a line that I didn't feel was defensible,' he said.[12] John Willis felt personally involved in that he had made an award-winning documentary about the relatives, but he, Prash Naik and Jan Tomalin knew it was one of Morris's ring-fenced sketches and were resigned to having to defend it. Before the press got hold of the story, there was little public objection to the concept of *Sutcliffe!* The crew booked advertising space on one of the neon billboards of

Piccadilly Lights without comment either on the name Peter Sutcliffe or the title of the musical flashing up in front of thousands of tourists and commuters. Andrew Newman tried to stir up reaction from the reliably outspoken phone-in audience of talk radio station LBC. He called in posing as a member of the public who had heard about the show and condemned it, but nobody else followed him up.

An audience was rounded up from the streets around Wimbledon Theatre to be filmed watching the rehearsal sequence of the sketch, and it was from one of those members of the public that the leak came. Someone tipped off *Daily Mail* media correspondent Alison Boshoff, who swiftly called Channel 4 to ask if it was true that they were making the life of the Yorkshire Ripper into a musical comedy.

Back in the Channel 4 press office, Greg Day had by then been totally won around to Morris's way of doing PR. Having thought that Morris was sabotaging his own show, he'd seen how the seemingly counter-intuitive approach had if anything created more interest in the press. But he didn't think he could handle the *Mail*'s story in the same way. 'That was a stage where I had to deal with it with Michael Grade,' he says. 'I couldn't go to Chris.' A response was agreed within Channel 4. They would confirm what Boshoff already knew but give away nothing more. 'But that affirmation was because it was good for the channel,' says Day. 'We couldn't be seen as a channel to be so ignorant that we didn't know about that.'

Discussing the show later in a PR trade magazine article, he referred to the Wimbledon leak as the only 'blip' in an otherwise successful campaign. But that particular blip came only halfway through *Brass Eye*'s run. There was a lot of *Mail* froth that could be brought up in the remaining few weeks before Decline was due to go out, and the paper was never knowingly underfrothed at the best of times.

Boshoff's article included MPs and 'television watchdogs' – in the self-appointed shape of the Mary Whitehouse-founded National Viewers and Listeners Association – condemning *Sutcliffe!* as 'sick and tasteless'. The article recounted the offending piece in that weirdly detailed way the *Mail* often used with Morris's work – like someone disgusted by the antics of their neighbours, but poking their binoculars through the net curtains for fear of missing a second of the upset.

Ironically, Morris's sketch wasn't that far removed in tone from the *Mail*'s favoured editorial position. *Sutcliffe!* made a parallel with the ageing gangsters who appeared on chat shows to discuss their murderous careers, were celebrated in film and wrote best-selling autobiographies. Extraordinarily violent men such as Frankie Fraser became folk heroes, and this was still a year before the genre got a further shot of glamour in the shape of *Lock, Stock and Two Smoking Barrels*. Morris was only asking, as the *Mail* itself did on a daily basis, what British society was coming to. It was the media's appetite for criminal tragedy which was the subject and the defence that Channel 4 had prepared in anticipation of an investigation by the ITC. But the *Mail* was not in the mood for arguing those kind of nuances. It was busy with the next day's article, which coincided with Sex. 'Is this the most hated man in Britain?' it instead asked of Morris. The paper had become determined to get *Sutcliffe!* out of *Brass Eye*. Michael Grade flew to Los Angeles the following week, and the very next day Channel 4 reported a call from the paper threatening them with the ITC. As Grade feared, families of those murdered by Sutcliffe were brought into the protests, which put him in the position of having to say that it would be included against their wishes. The channel also started to receive calls from celebrities who said they wouldn't work with them if it were to be broadcast. It began to feel as if Channel 4 were under siege, and by no means everyone sided with Chris Morris. 'It was a general feeling that the channel was allowing one person to upset an awful lot of other people,' says Greg Day.

Peter Fincham was called into the increasingly tense discussions between Morris, Prash Naik and Michael Grade. Just as in November, the channel's nerve held until the last couple of days before transmission. And it was again Grade himself who made the final decision – *Sutcliffe! The Musical* was to be cut from Decline. Morris argued for it into the day of transmission and right through that afternoon, but to no effect. He had to acknowledge defeat but – as Channel 4 were nervously aware – he also still kept the programme itself.

During the run of Radio 1 shows, Morris had held on to his tapes until beyond the last possible moment that anyone might reasonably expect to get away with it before transmission, and he did the same with *Brass Eye*, delivering the masters for each show as little as two hours before broadcast. Channel 4 had become used to being on standby to give the programmes a thorough check, knowing that at the best of times he could be relied on to sneak in something forbidden. 'He tinkers,' says Prash Naik. 'That's what Chris does.' Naik and commissioning editor Katie Taylor, having been instructed by John Willis to review the master, waited patiently and braced themselves for a major tinkering. It was Caroline Leddy who made the hand delivery from Morris in his post-production bunker. Naik and Taylor soon discovered what had been changed. *Sutcliffe!* had been replaced with a black hole in the middle of the tape. Thinking they had got away lightly, the pair had the section quickly removed and the show was passed for broadcast with minutes to spare.

Decline was a powerful conclusion to the series. The pre-title sequence opened under a flyover in black and white where cardboard cut-out citizens had been positioned in the rubbish and rubble. Voiceovers gibbered inanely, representing a society in melt-down, before the scene jumped to Morris in a comfortable house as the head of a happy family, all laughing slightly too loudly to illustrate a society in which nothing could be better. There was the human-sized model of Britain in its sickbed, animated so it was breathing shallowly – until Morris shot it to put it out of its misery. And a pastiche of Pulp came in the shape of 'Me Oh Myra', a love song to moors murderer Hindley. All before the end of part one. Even the cut to the commercial break itself was a fake, inter-rupted by a Channel 4 newsflash on the apparent shooting of Clive Anderson by Noel Edmonds, complete with grainy images of the alleged killer gesturing from the window of his mansion. The sequence prompted complaints from viewers who claimed to have been fooled, having perhaps missed the generous moustache mod-elled by Gina McKee as the reporter. Decline was one of the finest editions of the series.

The success was matched by the relief everyone at Channel 4 felt that it was all over. The following night there was to be a celebratory dinner for all involved at the broadcaster and Talkback. But that morning there was disturbing news of a posting on a *Brass Eye* fan website. It indicated a specific point in Decline – not just a scene, but a precise moment, a single frame. If you pressed pause there, you would see a caption. 'Grade is a cunt.'

Surely not, everyone at the station thought. They told themselves that a screen grab of the offending insert was a fake. But then the ITC called John Willis with the same tale, closely followed by the tabloids and *Time Out*, which had been given the story by a known Chris Morris sympathizer, journalist Simon Price.

John Willis asked Prash Naik and Katie Taylor to review the trans-mission master. Armed with the timecodes leaked to a number of websites, they quickly located the sequence but there were no offending words immediately visible. After persevering and slowing down the sequence frame by frame, they found the message. They briefly wondered if, having cleared the show for broadcast, they would have to resign. The *Sutcliffe!* substitution had simply been a diversion. While they were all looking at the blank space, something much worse had been inserted elsewhere. A classic sleight of hand. But after the initial, sickening lurch, Naik and Taylor knew they couldn't really be held responsible. It would have been impossible to see a single frame without being told precisely where it was. Even then the words were partly camouflaged by having been superimposed over an existing scene rather than inserted as a caption. But they were there.

The end-of-series dinner was cancelled.

'I have a fairly thick skin,' Grade later wrote, 'but I developed serious sense-of-humour failure with Chris Morris.'[13] Channel 4 quickly announced an enquiry into the circumstances.

'He weaves reality like a spell and turns everything into ironic media language,' an exasperated Channel 4 press office told the *Independent*. 'Although the series has finished now, he won't go away. He seems to lurk in the air.'[14] With Morris not returning Channel 4's calls, Chiggy was asked to get a response out of him. 'That wasn't you, was it?'

'No,' he said.

She recalls that she called Channel 4 back: 'Like a real idiot, I went, "That can't have been Chris."'

Talkback were responsible for the delivery of the programme, and Peter Fincham received letters from Channel 4 solicitors threatening action 'and worse'.[15] He was himself annoyed with Morris, albeit fleetingly and – like so many of Morris's managers – more as something he had to do in his official capacity. Others who had been more directly involved with the show were angrier.

'It was a very dark day,' says Sally Debonnaire, 'because we just thought we'd finished and we'd worked through every last difficult thing and I was certainly breathing a sigh of relief, thinking, I don't believe we've got this to air. I don't believe we've done it. Feeling really exhausted and elated and just sort of bewildered by the hours spent on what felt like getting every last sentence through. And then for that to happen . . .' Bluntly telling Morris he'd turned on everyone after they'd been dedicated to the production for months, she made a resolution never to do anything like *Brass Eye* again with him – though she had long relented by the time of the *Special*. She found it hard to stay angry at Chris Morris for long.

'It just takes hours out of your day that you hadn't planned to spend dealing with very cross people,' says Chiggy. 'It doesn't happen that often.' It was a reaction typical of Morris's friends and colleagues, none of whom were critical of him when recalling the incident. They seemed to accept that it came out of frustration with how *Sutcliffe!* had been sacrificed rather than egotistical reasons. And yet there was something in the nuclear nature of Morris's explosion which went beyond reluctance to compromise and connected directly to his early radio days at Radio Cambridgeshire when he'd left his colleague to get on with interviewing boring old ladies on her own. That unswerving resolve which he had undoubtedly needed to get his shows as good as they were did, when unchecked, veer towards outbursts of petulance.

Channel 4, and Michael Grade in particular, had run out of patience. They were aware that the only other person with access to the master tape that night was the editor, and they threatened to go after him if Morris didn't make a confession. This was a challenge that Morris couldn't avoid. And once his initial fury had subsided, he showed no sign of wanting to preserve his anonymity and make his point at the expense of the editor. Morris officially took responsibility for inserting the frame, and Talkback agreed a deal with Channel 4 in which he was effectively banned from working with the broadcaster for the immediate future.

The stunt quickly became part of *Brass Eye* lore for fans. The series had in any case been packed with fleeting gags which rewarded those who were quick on the video pause button. The Grade caption was absorbed as another example of a treat for the sharp-eyed. As Armando Iannucci observes of the shows from the safety of some distance: 'You just don't know what attitude it's [*Brass Eye*] going to strike. It is genuinely unpredictable. And part of the unpredictability is the level to which he will take it. And Chris has always been that one to take things to a level that you didn't realize you could take it.'

The pressure on Morris around *Sutcliffe!* continued to tell. In the weekend following the broadcast of Decline, Will Self wrote in the *Observer*: 'About halfway through Wednesday night's final episode of *Brass Eye*, it began to occur to me that Chris Morris might possibly be God.' The article appeared as Morris was being threatened with legal action by Channel 4, and it was a measure of the level of suspicion at which he was operating that he initially thought he was himself being hoaxed by Self's mordant tone: 'The idea of a Morrisian deity is appealing for a number of reasons: it explains why there is little real justice to be had for the poor and the oppressed and it provides a convincing explanation for why public life in this country is dominated by talented mediocrities . . . Coming to *Brass Eye* was witnessing that most unusual and remarkable of phenomena: an artist who has grown and reached the height of his powers.'[16] The Royal Television Society Awards agreed. In spring 1998 Morris won Top TV Performance of the Year.

There was still one more battle for *Brass Eye* to fight, but at least it was one that had been long predicted. A complaint had been made to the ITC by the MPs featured in the Drugs episode. Graham Linehan remembers Morris telling him he had phoned David Amess pretending to be Piers Morgan in order to find out if he intended to sue. Amess not only shared his plans but was sufficiently convinced by Morris's impersonation to round off the conversation by asking who he thought would win the general election that month. Morris improvised some likely Morgan-esque banter on the subject.

On 19 May the ITC ruled that the MPs had been misled over format, subject and purpose and, as expected, the robust defence of public interest offered by Prash Naik and Jan Tomalin was not allowed under the code. Both complaints were upheld and Sir Graham Bright's contribution was removed from further broadcasts, though the ITC also ruled that the show was 'in general amusing and innovative'. Channel 4 believed that the adjudications helpfully acknowledged, for the first time, tacit approval for the use of a public interest defence in entertainment programmes of a similar sort and some months later lobbied successfully for the ITC code to be revised to allow such set-ups (an amendment affectionately known in the station's legal department as the 'Brass Eye clause').[17]

In some ways the clause made it harder for programme-makers. Producers might once have subtly misled subjects about certain aspects of how they were going to appear, but after Morris had exposed the most intimate parts of celebrities' media transactions for the public to point and laugh at, anyone else had to make very sure they could comprehensively defend any deception.

Brass Eye's Andrew Newman went on to develop the 11 O'Clock Show, where Sacha Baron Cohen, advised by Prash Naik, developed Ali G off the back of the changed code. Newman applied Brass Eye tricks and methods to Ali's celebrity interviews, though he recalls that the production team had to explain a little more of what was happening post-*Brass Eye*. He was later a consultant on *Borat* the movie. Ali G's target was media vanity but, while Prash Naik's advice was that the new public interest test might be met, it was also heading into uncharted broadcasting territory. Its overwhelming success led to further amendment of the code after lobbying by Channel 4, and Baron Cohen was able to do further set-ups – though had it not been for *Brass Eye* neither Ali G nor similar programmes would have seen the light of day.

Brass Eye had an equally formative influence on the production of serious documentaries. 'The parody was so brilliantly close to reality at times it was painful,' acknowledges Dorothy Byrne, Channel 4's head of news and current affairs. It's a view held by many in the industry, if one on which few others are prepared to be quoted. Byrne notes how journalists suddenly became much more self-aware and naturalistic in their delivery and the presentation of shows was toned down as a direct result of Morris's series. Rather than being heralded by a great fanfare of a theme, investigative strands such as *Dispatches* now shuffle sheepishly into living rooms with little more than an embarrassed cough. Being 'too Chris Morris' remains shorthand for a very particular sort of criticism in news studios. *On the Hour* and *The Day Today* had begun the process of observation, but after *Brass Eye*, says Byrne, 'there was no going back. It really hit people in the face.'

More immediately, the series established Chris Morris as a contemporary satirist, though he was never at ease with the term. Towards the end of 1997, as part of the promotion for *Blue Jam*, Morris touched on the subject in interview with Simon Price for the *Melody Maker*. 'Satire is essentially a conservative form,' he said. 'As soon as you stand up in front of an audience, you're immediately relying on the consent of more than half the audience which neuters the whole exercise. If you look at *Private Eye*, which is the most prominent satirical organ in this country, it's little more than a more intelligent and witty version of saying, "Whatever next . . .?" Anyway, I've never really thought of what I do as satire. I think of it as opening my mouth before I can shut it. What I do is rooted in . . . intense stupidity.'[18]

For Morris there seemed to be something dismissive in the term satirist, as if it suggested taking the moral high ground over being funny and made him safer through explanation. The fire of *Brass Eye* was as much to do with a deep questioning that showed the influence of the rigour of Jesuit teaching. It was something that Iannucci describes as, 'that kind of: "Well, you say that, but let's just examine what you've just said to make sure that it stands up and isn't just nonsense."' That Morris had produced something with wider resonance was for him secondary to making people laugh. 'If you make a joke in an area which is for some reason – normally random – out of bounds, then you might find something out, you might put your finger on something,' said Morris later. 'But it's a matter of finding yourself in that area rather than setting out to cause trouble.'[19] Once there, Morris roamed those areas with agility and tenacity until he had it all mapped out with terrifying clarity. It was that disquieting energy that seemed to characterize his humour, something which his brother Tom identifies as an 'extraordinarily self-contained approach and process'.

Tom says he regards the discussion of the 'slightly transgressive element' within Morris's work as something of a distraction, explaining with distinctive Morris eloquence, 'I regard Chris as an artist of astonishing ability, clarity and single-mindedness in a way that I'm not in any sense. The strength required for him to define his creative practice both in terms of what it was and where and how it was made is truly inspiring to me and I think anyone else. The fact that you really can be, and he has continued to be, completely uncompromising in his selection of material, the way he has approached the dramatic language of it in whatever form and the way in which he has insisted, in an industry in which it is famously impossible to insist on the terms within which you can carry out your work, he has absolutely done that. It's extraordinary. It requires a much stronger force field around his creative process than I have and actually than almost anyone else I know has.' In taking subjects for comedy of which others were wary, Morris had discovered a painful kind of honesty through techniques that seemed to owe as much to the traditions of investigative journalism as humour.

Morris's force field was depleted at the end of *Brass Eye*. He typically fell into something of a slump after finishing off a major project, when there was nothing left to do but pick over the parts of the show that might have been done better and wonder where the next idea would come from. As the torture of the process was forgotten, he would become increasingly absorbed in the next thing. But *Brass Eye* had been a particularly gruelling experience. It had, he told the *Guardian*, 'exhausted my appetite for discovering people's tolerance for talking nonsense'. And the constant fighting in getting *Brass Eye* out and keeping it intact had been worse than anything he'd known: 'No doubt getting to the end, where you've been forced to be a sort of surrogate lawyer, well, that's the most creatively stifling thing you could possibly do.'[20]

Radio seemed like an appealing place in which to get back to work in a more immediately creative way. He returned to Radio 1 free of the constraints of creating accurate parody with what would become *Blue Jam*, late at night, approaching delirium, something of a reflection of how Morris himself was feeling: 'It was so singular and it came from a mood, quite a desolate mood. I had this misty, autumnal, boggy mood anyway, so I just went with that.'[21]

11

NOW, WHAT SEEMS TO BE THE PROBLEM?

CHRIS MORRIS AND MATTHEW BANNISTER MET BY CHANCE on a Soho street in early 1997. It was the first time they'd seen one another since Morris's Radio 1 series in late 1994, but they hardly needed to ask what each other had been up to in the intervening time, both having in their own way reached a certain level of public notoriety. The coverage of *Brass Eye*'s controversies had familiarized even *Daily Mail* readers with Morris, though that was largely limited to disapproving of him as a concept. Bannister's ruthless remodelling of Radio 1, undertaken with fellow former GLR manager Trevor Dann, had been played out on the front pages to pantomime boos and hisses as the nation's favourite DJs quit or were abruptly removed to make way for a new generation who were less predictable and whose record collections hadn't stopped in 1985.

Comedy on Radio 1 had not fared so well since Morris and Bannister had last worked together. It had only been Morris who had managed to combine humour and music with the fluidity that

Bannister had wanted to bring to the station. The comic presenter experiment had been shelved. And people had stopped saying comedy was the new rock 'n' roll. But Bannister was nevertheless intrigued to hear that Morris was thinking of following up *Brass Eye* with a return to radio. 'I've been working on a programme which is sort of like the nightmares you have when you fall asleep listening to the BBC World Service,' Morris explained.

He had a similar idea back in the GLR days, when BBC2 still closed down for the night with the picture fading and a long tone playing for those still dozing in front of their TV. It was then that Morris imagined a sinister voice enquiring, 'Are you still out there? Let's have a little story . . .' To deliver it, Morris enlisted his childhood favourite, former Bonzo Dog Band singer and artist Vivian Stanshall. Morris had seen him perform live and thought his rich, sepulchral tones would be perfect drifting unannounced into the half-dream state of the audience. But the recording session didn't quite work out the way they planned.

Morris smuggled them both into GLR late one night, Stanshall late in his career and fragile. As they approached the studio, Morris accidentally let go of the heavy studio doors. It was, he says, an anxious moment: 'Fuck, I nearly killed a legend,' he remembers thinking at the time. When they came to record, Stanshall, then in one of his attempts at sobriety, seemed to be lacking in confidence. Morris later had his part re-recorded, but the BBC were sufficiently unimpressed not to acknowledge receipt of the resulting tape.

What became *Blue Jam* was in some ways a development of that indefinable sense of being awake when you should have long been asleep. 'It's going to be a spooky-woozy kind of thing,'[1] Morris later wrote to a cast member. The exact shape would only emerge from experimentation in the studio, but Bannister instinctively felt that Radio 1 should be supporting it. He waived the ban on comedy just for Morris's new show. It was to start broadcasting in November 1997.

Blue Jam bypassed the rational mind of the day to speak directly to the nearly unconscious, as music and humour oozed together, grotesque concepts surfacing into the slick and away almost before your mind had a chance to register them. It was also Morris's creative response to being what a colleague describes as 'deeply, deeply terrified by the dark'. If *Brass Eye* loudly cracks open the brightly lit armour of professional life, *Blue Jam* examines in microscopic detail what happens at the most disorienting time possible, when defences are at their thinnest and even the familiar seems distorted, sinister – and hopeless.

The programme seemed unlike anything else around, to have come fully formed from nowhere, though the basic elements were exactly those that Morris had developed over his years in radio. The difference was he had freed them from the traditional hand-holding of the audience which he'd found so agonizing in his early career. *Blue Jam* had eliminated news, weather, jingles to remind you whose show it was and where you were listening to it, trails and chat. Listener interaction, always minimal with Morris, had also gone completely. What remained was comedy linked by DJ'ing without the admin. Morris drew fully on his wide-ranging taste in music to create a playlist that leaned towards the more interesting areas of dance and electronic music at a tempo that suited the lateness of the hour.

Warp Records tracks featured regularly, which wasn't that surprising. There was a more than superficial similarity between Morris and the artists on the pioneering label. The likes of Aphex Twin, Plaid and Squarepusher were as accomplished in the use of their technology as they were in writing – and as a breed they were also artists with a reputation for being obsessive, experimental, uncompromising and reclusive. Many at Warp itself were confirmed fans of

Chris Morris, among them Greg Eden, whose roles for the small and tight-knit company included business, internet and A&R. He followed *Blue Jam*'s broadcast with interest, and when one of Morris's team phoned for a CD he took the opportunity to arrange a meeting. What started as informal chats about music would become a long and productive relationship between Warp and Morris.

More like the work of a cross between the kind of cutting-edge electronic music producer who might be on Warp and a club DJ than a traditional radio show, *Blue Jam* was an uninterrupted, hour-long mix of music, fracturing and dissolving into sketches. The comedy developed from the style Morris performed with Peter Baynham in the 1994 shows. Updating the cut-up celebrity quotes of the earlier series, *Blue Jam* had subversive jingles in the form of vivid mini-stories. 'I can see Steve Lamacq as a frail old man in a wheelchair,' says a computerized voice, 'trying to shake hands with an elephant.' Other Radio 1 DJs would be caught in their jingle just at the moment of committing a, usually unmourned, suicide.

And Michael Alexander St John was another old friend who returned to deliver a round-up of club culture, lending his unmistakable regal solemnity to Morris's nonsense genres and hot venues. *Blue Jam* provided their last opportunity to work together, as St John died in August 2002 aged sixty-six, but his delight in the material was evident as his resonant voice lent credibility to such top-ten dance hits as Gloop Mongy Mong's 'Fat Bleeping Bitch'.

Having removed all the unnecessary explanatory parts of traditional music and comedy shows, the elements that remained were completely reconstituted through Morris's enthusiastic use of the computerized audio processing which had come to dominate music production: 'You can mix music until it's coming out of every pore of your body,' he later said. 'You can do things that were unimagin-able on tape. It seems to be a fantastic opportunity for people to do funny things in a new way.'[2]

Manipulating audio on screen had become as easy as word-processing text. You highlighted sections of sound and applied effects such as time-stretching – altering length without changing the pitch – something that Fatboy Slim was just over a year away from having a huge hit by doing with 'Rockafeller Skank'. In the late 1990s, you would scarcely be able to go in a club or turn on the radio without hearing songs made almost entirely of simple words and musical phrases repeated, filtered and stretched. *Blue Jam* seemed at once to be at home in the scene, part medicated dance mix and part original, innovative electronic creation, but it also stood on its own ground, luring loved-up clubbers on to its pitch-black dance floor late on Radio 1 and then brutalizing them.

Morris needed more than a conventional post-production facility to get to the innards of *Blue Jam* and give them a visceral twist. It was via a friend of Caroline Leddy, then just a few months from leaving Talkback to become a commissioning editor at Channel 4, that he was introduced to Natural Sound in Soho and Adrian Sutton. Born in 1967, Sutton was a classical musician with a music degree from Goldsmiths, University of London. He had just the sort of background that Morris was looking for, having been a lecturer in computing and electo-acoustics in music. He had covered everything from synthesizers to using computers to manipulate sound directly. Sutton had also edited *PC Direct* magazine before becoming an adviser on the technical aspects of producing music for adverts. At Natural Sound he started writing music full-time, and he was as enthusiastic about audio experimentation as Morris.

Together they worked on *Blue Jam* for some three or four months.

Morris came in twice a week for three-hour sessions, when they pushed the capabilities of the equipment more as if they were an updated version of Pink Floyd mid-1970s, creating some exotic genre-defying concept album rather than a radio comedy series. They built up layers of sounds until the whole audio picture was in a state of constant dreamy shift. Voices in the foreground were contrasted with sparkles of filtered sound mixed back to create a sense of distance. Jingles were created from scratch, and Morris also sequenced his playlist mix into a seamless whole in the studio.

But even Natural Sound's state-of-the-art equipment had trouble keeping up with what Sutton calls Morris's 'firehose of ideas'. He was used to the days of analogue, when he could instantly hear the results of his edits once he'd spliced the tape together. You could accomplish far more elaborate effects with a computer, but they would often sit there for a frustratingly long time, whirring away as they applied the complicated calculations necessary to alter each selected portion of audio. And Morris was keen to try out alternatives, each of which would have to be saved separately on disk by Sutton. When they'd done them all he'd have to go back and locate Morris's preferred take. It was a laborious process, one big experiment, and the results would be as much of a surprise to *Blue Jam*'s cast as it would to their audience: 'Until the pilot I didn't know what it was going to be like. Then it all made sense,' said actor Amelia Bullmore. 'During the recording he was telling us to become more detached, more stoned, slower, dreamier. He obviously had a rhythm in his mind. He had a pulse. After that it made sense. It was thrilling to hear it. I had never heard anything like it on radio. I had never been in a mood for an hour. Clearly in his head he was mixing it.'[3]

Bullmore and the rest of the cast of *Blue Jam* had come together when Morris directed the pilot episode of Graham Linehan and

Arthur Mathews' sketch show *Big Train* that summer. She and Kevin Eldon and Mark Heap had also been in *Brass Eye*, but in *Big Train*, alongside Simon Pegg and Julia Davis, they gelled into a tight unit who could react plausibly to each other in comic situations where there were often no conventional set-ups and punchlines. For the show's creators, it was an approach to writing that went all the way back to *The Day Today*: 'We were huge fans of Chris and Armando,' says Mathews. 'The idea is stupid, but it's played really straight.'

Linehan adds: 'We just were wondering if the effect of that would be one that would eventually make you just get the giggles.' He introduced Simon Pegg to the show after seeing him do stand-up, but otherwise Morris brought everyone on board. He was able to spot and develop a particular ability in an actor in audition – sometimes a character might end up being created around it. Rather than simply doing read-throughs and discussing the back story of a role, Morris often used the casting sessions to suggest something completely unexpected. When it later came to *Nathan Barley*, Charlie Brooker remembers Morris working up such scenarios as one in which the actor had to agree warmly and sincerely with whatever Morris said, which turned out to be a series of increasingly appalling statements. On occasion Morris's auditions grew into new comic situations which would later be used in the show itself.

Morris also started to work with new crew members on *Big Train*, some of whom would go on to work on *Jam* and the *Brass Eye Special*. The show was produced by Talkback, where Morris's appointment in his first role as director generated a faint odour of foreboding. With *Brass Eye* still fresh in their memory, they imagined long and arduous days of filming in which only tiny amounts of footage would be completed. But, directing for someone else as a favour, Morris seemed to delight in not having to fight for everything and was content to bring all of his considerable natural enthusiasm behind the camera as well as a sensitivity in the way in which he elicited performances. And his first stint at directing would be useful experience for him when he later decided to make his own version of a sketch show with the television version of *Blue Jam*.

It wouldn't always be so easy for Morris to step back when he worked on other people's projects. When playing Denholm Reynholm in the later Graham Linehan show *The IT Crowd*, he would be doing his usual debating and questioning of everything, whereas Linehan was ready to leave jokes as they were without examining them for clues to the characters. It wasn't made any easier for Linehan having taken on board Kevin Eldon's description of Morris as 'officer class'. Denholm was killed off early in the second series of *The IT Crowd* when Morris was too busy to come back for the full run, though Linehan confided in him that he'd also found doing the first series with him hard work. It was clear when he returned for the spectacular suicide of Denholm that opened the second series that Morris had taken all the concerns on board and unplugged his brain entirely from creative concerns. He swiftly and brilliantly rattled through his lines – though when it came for Denholm to jump out of the window at the back of the set, just a few feet off the studio floor, Morris still asked the art director if they could build it higher to make it look like he was really plunging. No, he was told, health and safety wouldn't allow it. Denholm proved such a favourite that Linehan brought him back to provide a malign ghostly influence in the third series.

Simon Pegg was the only member of the *Big Train* cast not to join *Blue Jam*, and David Cann, who had provided such congenial figures of authority in *Brass Eye*, augmented the line-up as sessions began in the grubby basement at Talkback. Morris returned to the instant creativity of radio with a small cast who knew each other well and could develop their roles. The only other staff were a studio manager and Rebecca Neale, returning from Morris's Radio 1 shows as production assistant.

Morris would shout out suggestions as they worked; there was no fixed way of producing the sketches. Sometimes they veered wildly from the script for hours, sometimes they would nail it as written. The tape ran all the while and the performances were carefully logged and script changes noted so that Morris could find his way when he took the recordings away for reworking.

It was later rumoured that the show's mood had been conjured by recording in the small hours, but though taping might run late, the sessions were in regular time, and rather than being infused with dread purpose they were frequently broken up by outbreaks of hysteria. It was sometimes apparent in the show – particularly in the 'Bad Sex' series of sketches in which lovers engage in increasingly bizarre pillow talk with laughter never far from the actors' voices, Kevin Eldon and Julia Davis particularly prone to cracking up. The crew would also have to stifle giggles or quickly look away from the actors while the tape was running. The genuine sense of enjoyment gave the performances an energetic life that made them far funnier and if anything contributed more to *Blue Jam*'s disturbing quality than if the cast had deliberately set out to do weird and shocking. Though some critics would accuse the show of setting out to break taboos simply for the sake of it. 'It just seems like the laziest criticism,' says Peter Baynham, who was again Morris's main writing partner. It was more, he says, that they 'allowed' themselves freedom to go where they wanted.

The writing meetings were as loosely structured as the recordings. It helped, Morris explained to the *Guardian*, to 'evolve things casually. It proceeds almost like a conversation.'[4] Most of the supporting writing team, largely unchanged from *Brass Eye*, were as enthusiastic as the cast about the creative possibilities that this offered. David Quantick and Jane Bussmann were relatively fresh from the heady live chaos of *The Election Night Armistice* with Armando Iannucci. They had also appeared on the show, Quantick causing some slight awkwardness for Iannucci and producer Sarah Smith when he said something to the effect that they were 'spurting the jism of news over the hard stomach of fact'. He and Jane Bussmann took the *Blue Jam* 'woozy' briefing to mean it would be trippy, that you wouldn't be sure of what you'd heard, and set about coming up with the nastiest ideas they could, concentrating on relationships going bad. The writing meetings were as lively as the recording sessions, on occasion continuing at the upstairs bar of the John Snow pub in Soho late into the night with Baynham, Quantick and Bussmann joined by fellow comic Peter Serafinowicz and later *Blue Jam* cast member Sally Phillips.

Graham Linehan found the writing brief less inspiring. Preparing to direct the first series of *Big Train*, which would go out a year later, he nevertheless contributed material throughout *Blue Jam* and *Jam*, including some fine moments such as a sketch for the TV version written with Arthur Mathews in which Mark Heap's mumbling, embarrassed security guard never quite manages to warn the staff of an office against leaving for the evening via an open lift shaft. But while he shared Quantick and Bussmann's analysis that the show would have a hallucinatory feel, for him it was a 'bad trip' that Morris was making in which people were given moral dilemmas with increasingly bleak resolutions.

For the listener, it was partly that complexity which could make the show such a rich and resonant experience, particularly in the monologues. They came from Morris's writing partnership with Robert Katz, and the longer form of the stories gave them the space to develop character in a way Morris hadn't done before.

The pair evolved the monologues from the Temporary Open Spaces pieces on GLR, with a flavour of Morris's fictional listener letters of the Radio 1 show. The media remained a target for Morris, though here it was accompanied by an exploration of depression. The flat-voiced narrator of the monologues seems once to have been a member of London cliques whose fringes he now haunts, a medicated observer of their absurdities. Each story stood alone, though they were characterized by invariably climaxing in a finale of humiliating slapstick for the narrator while all around him narcissistic dregs of the more vapid reaches of the creative industries climb over one another in ceaseless comic efforts to be top dog.

In their way, the monologues became as much a trademark of *Blue Jam* as Morris's anchorman had been in *Brass Eye* and *The Day Today* – and went on to be the inspiration for later work for both Morris and Katz, the latter taking a show to Edinburgh where he performed alongside his wife's sister, Sarah Parkinson. He based his segment of their *Unfucked* on the narrator character. Director Paul Merton was married to Parkinson, who died in 2003.

Morris himself appeared in relatively few other *Blue Jam* sketches, apart from the introductions that set the tone with disorienting scenarios that embraced the humiliated, the lost, the suicidal and the abjectly confused . . . 'Then welcome . . . in *Blue Jam*.'

David Cann's deranged doctor was one of few regular characters, subjecting his credulous patients to degrading examinations. Most other characters crept in and out just once, often in a haunted kind of mini-documentary format, like the landlord who explains how he once evicted a tenant by creeping into her room when she was asleep and, like an amalgam of figures of horror from Edgar Allan Poe to Struwwelpeter, 'I tiptoed to the bottom of her bed and I lifted up her bedclothes and took out a scalpel – a very sharp scalpel; I used to be a medical student – and I *slivered* the thinnest possible layer of skin from the bottom of her foot and it just came away like a sort of silk insole and I took it out and I put it under a shrub', without her waking. He repeats the process nightly until 'she wasn't there at all'. The slum landlord of nightmare.

The lateness of the hour prompted characters to confessionals of self-inflicted suffering – the woman who brushes her teeth until the gums are so raw she faints, and the man who has deliberately amputated both his legs so his girlfriend has to do everything for him. 'They're trapped in a mutual loathing, but it works,' explained Morris, 'they've reached a symbiosis where they both get something from it.'[5] But however visceral each set-up, the characters invariably met them with a very English equanimity – a composure not always matched by BBC management on hearing the sketches. But Matthew Bannister of all people had known from the start that a certain number of moments of unease came with Chris Morris territory. He seemed to welcome the way in which Morris's presence caused a slight warping in the fabric of life at the BBC.

'You couldn't put your finger on it,' he says now, laughing, 'but almost everything in it was deeply disturbing. There was a question of whether or not you wanted to disturb people to that extent. And sometimes you couldn't even articulate why it was you were worried about it. Almost everything had some kind of question in it.'

For his part, Morris said that his return to Radio 1 had been greeted with some suspicion: 'It was enshrined officially as a kind of abuse relationship.'[6] There were many long discussions between Morris and Bannister over such issues as the number of times 'fuck' was allowed per broadcast. Bannister became managing director of BBC Radio in addition to his other work and nevertheless took the time to count all the instances from one episode. The majority were said to have contributed to the pace and rhythm, and those that seemed to be in there to offend – suspected of being deliberate Morris sacrificial fodder – came out.

'I think to a certain extent if you're a pompous BBC manager, you're fair game,' says Bannister. 'Sometimes he forced me to confront some of my lazy preconceptions about what was acceptable in broadcasting. I found it rather exhilarating actually to be able to debate it with somebody who is deeply intelligent, cares passionately about it, but who could drag you into a slightly parallel universe where you suddenly found you'd gone mad. That was where it got a bit scary, when you found yourself agreeing with points that he'd made, which you knew in your saner moments were absolutely weird and you shouldn't have agreed with them.' Each of Morris's managers seemed to have their own way of dealing with him, and his strategy for coping with what he called Morris's 'attempt to make me look like a lily-livered BBC poltroon' was to make a creative case – to say that something was not funny rather than being against policy. But when it came to the Archbishop of Canterbury, negotiations broke down.

Morris had re-edited the words of the Archbishop at the funeral of Princess Diana in September 1997: 'We give thanks to God for those maimed through the evil of Mother Teresa,' the sermon begins over a trip-hop instrumental backing track. It hardly formed the most challenging material Morris had ever come up with, and the technique itself was one he'd used to the same effect on countless occasions. The cut words were worked into the beats, and there was a sense of silliness – 'Lord of landmines' – which if anything was light relief in the context of a show where elsewhere, to take just one example, listeners met parents who'd always felt their daughter was a 45-year-old man trapped in the body of a 4-year-old girl and so have had her suitably fitted with the correct vintage 'penis and testicle glands'.

But the show was due to go out in December 1997. Prime Minister Tony Blair had only just anointed Diana the people's princess. Mountains of flowers left by her distraught admirers outside the palaces had scarcely had the chance to rot. It wasn't, as Matthew Bannister pointedly observes, 'any old Archbishop of Canterbury speech'. Which only made Morris more determined to include it. No compromise was reached after lengthy phone discussions, and the two arranged a meeting with Peter Fincham at which Bannister asked what he was supposed to say if it went out and he then had to pick up the phone to a wrathful Archbishop of Canterbury. It was intended as a rhetorical question, but not only did Morris tell him, he went away and drafted a written response for the Archbishop. It was convincingly detailed, it was brilliantly argued, it was irrefutable – and quite beside the point as far as Matthew Bannister was concerned. His office had no wish to field the sort of calls that had come after the Heseltine obituary. The decision was final. Morris smuggled it in anyway.

The studio engineer on the night duly faded the programme down at the offending point and substituted an edition of the show from earlier in the run. But as a fan of Morris he deliberately took so long to make the switch that most of the re-edited speech was broadcast. If George Carey tuned in, he made no comment. And Matthew Bannister himself, recalling the episode in interview, appears even years on to be unaware that it went out. 'I hope not,' he says now. 'I think he might have put it back in, but I mean . . . I'm not sure . . . I don't believe that the Archbishop was ever transmitted. I think we'd have heard about that. I really don't believe that.'

But it was easy for anyone to miss *Blue Jam*. The lateness of its slot made sure of that. 'I seriously did want it to go out at three in the morning,' Morris told the *Guardian*. 'I thought that was about the latest time of day that could be late without being early. It's a sort of autumnal, middle-of-the-night show. You need to be as far from light as possible.'[7]

Radio 1 had wanted it to go out when there would be more listeners awake to hear what had been an unusually expensive and time-consuming production. It was known that listener figures went up at about 10 p.m. as people were on their way to bed, but in the end the compromise was settled on midnight, by which time the listener numbers were negligible. There was also little publicity. Morris came up with the idea of doing a photo shoot under water (even though, Rebecca Neale later learned from his partner Jo, he wasn't actually a great fan of swimming) and was captured in startling blue on blue, his eyes suffused with an eerie glow and his hair billowing around him. The show was given a preview playback at Tom Morris's Battersea Arts Centre. *Blue Jam* was placed in its natural environment as Chris played it back to an audience who lay down in a completely blacked-out auditorium. There were no preview recordings issued to the press, and the series slipped out barely noticed in mid-November while everyone's attention was on Steve Coogan's motel-dwelling agonies in the first series of *I'm Alan Partridge*. Only Radio 1's introductory warning of strong language and material that some might find offensive gave any indication of what lay ahead.

The anonymity that *Brass Eye* hadn't achieved was part of the joy of *Blue Jam*, the potential for it to be discovered accidentally by the sleepless looking for something soothing. Which might have been the best way to encounter it. If you were looking for the thing that Chris Morris did next after *Brass Eye*, you might be trying to work out the whys of the show and where it fitted in too much to let it wash over you in its peculiar way. But when it permeated a fitful consciousness, it could be a genuine and joyful surprise.

It was something entirely of itself, an extraordinarily original achievement. And Morris's obvious love of radio allowed *Blue Jam* to reach some surprisingly warm places. The freedom of the humour credited the audience with intelligence, dispensing with self-censoring and trusting they would instinctively feel a structure to the show and follow *Blue Jam* as it led with the loping rhythms of Morris's musical set, matched by the hushed voices of the cast, into the wilder territories of late-night emotional wonkiness. Matthew Bannister says, 'It was a leap forward in the use of radio as a medium.' He felt it was a world that was almost palpable, 'a deeply disturbing and upsetting world. It was a very exciting thing to hear.' In the press, the *Daily Telegraph* heard the sound of 'rage in a bottle corked with savage melancholy, bobbing on sound waves'. While for Tracey Macleod in the *Mail on Sunday*, '"Sketches" seems an inadequate word for what fell somewhere between comedy, art and audience abuse'. Discussing Morris's description of the show as 'ambient stupid', she wrote: 'that only goes some way towards conveying the richness of the world he has created, as imaginatively complete and distinctive as Viv Stanshall's *Rawlinson End*.'[8]

There were to be two further series of Sony Award-winning *Blue Jam* and each had six episodes. The second series started in March 1998, just three months after the first, and John Peel was among those who played trailers for it in his own programme. 'Twice I have been so startled by what I have heard,' he wrote, 'that I failed to start the following record on time.'[9] Towards the end of the run, Sally Phillips joined the cast which was augmented by Phil Cornwell and Lewis Macleod when the third series broadcast the following January. The concept of the show itself lived on and would prove appropriately conducive to mutating – into print, CD and much later film. It also transferred to television for one series on Channel 4.

Having forgiven him for his Grade-bothering incident, the station had been hoping that Morris would do a second series of *Brass Eye*, though he never seriously entertained that possibility himself. He was, however, already thinking about doing a one-off special, which was still two years away when work started on *Jam* in early 1999. Morris had a much easier working relationship over the course of the series with Channel 4's new boss, Michael Jackson – the man who had turned down *Brass Eye* for BBC2 – than he'd ever had with Michael Grade. The station had become the natural home for Morris that the BBC had once been, with other allies including Caroline Leddy and *Brass Eye* researcher Andrew Newman, who, like Leddy, had also moved into commissioning and would later become head of comedy and entertainment.

Many existing *Blue Jam* sketches were transferred with the new material supplied by the same pool of writers. The principal cast was largely unchanged and looked as deceptively ordinary as they had sounded on the radio. David Cann inhabited his characters with the cardigan-cosy plausibility of his *Brass Eye* performances. And Kevin Eldon and Mark Heap performed a weirdly symbiotic routine in many of their joint sketches, as if they were sharing a yet more unsavoury joke that they kept from the audience. The female roles were just as strong, giving Julia Davis and Amelia Bullmore a rare opportunity in comedy for women to do as much weird as the men and to join in with that trademark *Jam* smile that spoke of perverse secretiveness.

Morris himself again made relatively few appearances, and the monologues didn't make the transition, though co-author Robert Katz could be glimpsed in one of the introductory sequences, waking in a playground with a mouth full of (live) flies to the sound of children chanting 'maggot mouth'. It was those 'Welcome in *Jam*' segments in which Morris's presence was most commanding and unnerving. Otherwise, lacking the DJ element of the Radio 1 incarnation, *Jam* was more of a recognizable sketch show, at least in its basic elements, if not in the way they were put together.

The relatively brisk gestation of the *Big Train* pilot was a distant memory, as it was back to a *Brass Eye* standard of schedule that stretched over a year, with attendant fraught phone calls between Talkback and Morris over budget, time and what could be included. He made ambitious use of varied shooting techniques rather than settling with giving *Jam* a conventional sketch-show identity: cameras swept in from the side and then stood up in one scene, and in the next the cast might be made to look small and isolated through long tracking shots, static cameras mounted as if recording CCTV footage, reversed negatives and silhouettes. That marked the show out as different from other comedies to start with, but the true character of *Jam*, like that of the radio version, was established only in post-production.

Adrian Sutton came in about two-thirds of the way through the schedule for the soundtrack: 'I wasn't entirely convinced at the start of it that *Jam* would work,' he says, 'specifically because the reason that *Blue Jam* works so well is that there aren't any pictures.' Like everyone else, he had to wait for the show to come out of the digital post-production environment, where scenes were fractured, rendered in night vision, distorted, jerkily animated, saturated with colour and actors given ghostly trails as they moved, pulling the hallucinatory vision of the show out of Morris's head. 'It's designed to be hypnotic, so that it weaves itself in, and compelling, so that you stay with it,' explained Morris. 'And quite often the jokes are going off under ground – normally you're given a cue to laugh at things and here there aren't any cues.'[10]

Cramming visual detail into each scene remained important, even though much of it would eventually be obscured by the digital processing. A prop buyer panicked over Morris's request for a shark destined for an introductory sequence in which a musician in a band of grotesques in a barn was to mime playing it with a small reed. Unable to find anything suitable in London, the buyer was about to get a 200-pound specimen from a fisherman they had tracked down in Cornwall, before another member of the production crew pointed out that in the desperation to get the right species they'd missed the impracticality of the size. The actor ended up with a skinned rabbit stitched into an oboe, which worked fine – you wouldn't really have been able to tell the species in the final broadcast, what with the low lighting, the scene playing back at a varying speed and David Cann kneeling distractingly in the foreground, virtually naked, dripping with protoplasm and screaming in terror. But it was a mark of how diligent the crew were in trying to achieve Morris's effects in full.

Even though the greater part of their efforts was glimpsed only fleetingly, the fetid atmosphere of *Jam* lingered in the mind longer than individual scenes or jokes. They had to construct a world that was only heard in *Blue Jam*. On occasion, even some of the crew were unconvinced about the viability of creating certain images. Spurting penises were one memorable example. They were to be fitted to actors playing unfortunate porn stars with a fatal disorder called the 'gush' that doomed them to ejaculate until all the protein drained from their bodies. Art director Dick Lunn, the son of children's TV legend Wilf Lunn of *Vision On* – who as an inventor working with Tony Hart surely had to deal with far fewer requests to make actors look as if they were orgasming to death – pointed out the restrictions on broadcasting erections. Morris's immediate response, that the rule shouldn't apply to fakes, was an example of what Charlie Brooker describes as a standard Chris Morris technique for overcoming doubts and technical challenges.

He just ignored them: 'And then somehow reality seems to shift around to reflect what he wants to achieve,' says Brooker. 'One thing I've learned from him is that if someone's telling you you can't do something and it's not for a creative reason, just ignore them as much as you can and keep driving forward. Chris always wants to find a way of doing things. That's probably why if most TV is quite bland there is a lot of flavour in his stuff. It's alive and vibrant in a way that most shows haven't been for a very long time.'

For the gush, casts were taken from a jumbo-sized dildo for the prosthetic penis, the actors' pubic hair was shaved and their genuine genitals were stowed in the hollow of the model scrotum. Synthetic semen was supplied via a pipe taped to the actor's leg and, after tests in the Talkback basement, the power of the pump at the other end of the pipe had to be lowered when it delivered a jet strong enough to take someone's eye out. The actors playing the agonized stars were attended to by real porn actresses, and yet, in the end, the careful penis construction was shown only in the briefest of cutaways. Morris contributed his scenes after a long and fraught day on set, but immediately settled into a relaxed Euro-porn-star accent. 'It took him three days to die,' he says of an afflicted star. 'All the while he was firing the fuck juice. And when they weighed his body he was maybe twenty kilos, which is no more than two or three squirrels.'

The disconcerting atmosphere of *Jam* also partly came through its locations, such as the eerie surroundings of former asylum Horton Hospital near Epsom. One-time patients occasionally wandered into the grounds, feeling compelled, the crew learned, to return to a place where they'd spent so much of their lives. The 'Welcome in *Jam*' of the first episode, where Morris is 'freezer-drawered' in and out of a cadaver storage unit, was filmed in the asylum's old morgue. Along with discarded medical equipment lay a crumpled book containing details of deceased patients. One of the old wards had walls that were padded, but only to the height of four feet – it had been the children's ward. Later, a young actor heard about this and said they weren't surprised as they'd heard their screams. Nobody else had.

Jam went out between the end of March and April 2000 without an advert break or credits to interrupt the mood and the mad jumble of visuals and jokes. It didn't go out quite as late as the Radio 1 version, though it similarly escaped the attentions of those who had criticized *Brass Eye*, despite playing with notions far more horrifying than even those that would be explored in the *Special*. But the languid pace and the stylized look of the programme provided an effective cover for the humour as art, so that the subject matter went unremarked. And the lack of celebrity-baiting made it even less of a candidate for the headlines. All of which seemed only to contribute to the sense of unreality in watching the shows, as if what you were witnessing sliding out dream-like on a major broadcaster somehow couldn't really be happening.

Not all of the sketches transferred convincingly from the radio. The one in which a dead baby is 'fixed' by a plumber had long shadows in the child's bedroom and an ominous tangle of steaming pipes in the cot. But nothing could look as horrific as the vision you would have yourself to accompany the noises of a decaying baby plumbed into the central heating so he's 'nice and warm', with a tap in his head which can be turned to make him give a watery gurgle. Rather than compare the two versions, though, it was better to come to the TV series fresh and absorb the reused sketches as part of the overall and distinct mood of *Jam*, where even the ones that worked better on the radio were carried by the performances of the cast. They were understated throughout and never mugged for easy laughs. David Cann as a doctor had

NOW, WHAT SEEMS TO BE THE PROBLEM?

an ability to visibly radiate sincere concern which added another dimension to the sketches.

If the visual version of *Blue Jam* was a success, Chris Morris had less luck creating a remix album. The idea was that musicians signed to his friends at Warp were to be supplied with his original sketches which they would then work into their own pieces of music. But despite the intriguing reports of Chris Morris in discussion with Aphex Twin and his long-time video collaborator Chris Cunningham, two artists whose output was as hallucinogenic as anything from *Blue Jam*, the project foundered. Only two tracks were completed and released, Matt Elliott's 'Push off My Wire' and Amon Tobin's 'Bad Sex', featuring the 'Cackle my Gladys'ing of the *Blue Jam* lovers. In the end, Morris settled for releasing a straight collection of the broadcast sketches through Warp towards the end of 2000. As a small company, they fitted in with the way he did things, resulting in a minimal look for the CD cover, in the face of requests from retailers who wanted the title and his name prominently displayed. Even with relatively little promotion *Blue Jam* still went on to sell more than 25,000 copies.

Warp hosted the BBC-banned Archbishop speech cut-up on their website to coincide with the launch of the CD, and President Bush was later given an Archbishop-onceover with a take on his war on terror called 'Bushwhacked'. It was released as a 12-inch single to a certain amount of unease in the company. Greg Eden says, 'There was definitely a feeling that it might result in either MI5 or Al-Qaeda crashing through the Warp office doors, but of course these things go completely unnoticed unless somebody in the media picks up on it.'

Morris made a brief guest return to Radio 1 the month after the release of the *Blue Jam* CD to DJ on Mary Anne Hobbs's *Breezeblock* show. The selection over two sets ranged from underground club tracks to ambient music closer in spirit to *Blue Jam*, interspersed with electronic squalls and samples and a couple of celebrity hits. It was the last time he appeared on radio. But even having thoroughly deconstructed the medium he loved with *Blue Jam*, he told friends from the show that he retains a great affection for it. He has, he said to them, never ruled out making a return.

12

IF THE PRINTED WORD HAS ANY MEANING, THEN IT MUST COME FROM THE VERY EDGE OF FUCKY BUM BOO BOO

IN APRIL 1999 A NEW COLUMNIST STARTED AT THE *OBSERVER*. His byline picture showed Richard Geefe to be dark and good-looking, and his writing revealed a cruel streak, all new laddish adventures flavoured with literary pretension. But as casually misogynistic as he was in his description of seducing women in his various cars and his modish if bland loft apartment, there was also a world-weariness alongside his emotional disconnection. His work first appeared just under two months after the final series of *Blue Jam* concluded, though there was nothing in his writing that hinted at a connection to the show, much less to the dark bruises of its mono-logues. There was little to connect him to anything at all, which seemed rather odd to his fellow writers on the paper. Nobody had read anything he had written prior to his Second Class Male column. Nobody knew him personally. He'd only ever been properly introduced to one person on the staff and that was the man who commissioned him, editor Roger Alton – though it was rumoured that Geefe had once delivered his copy to the offices while drunk.

Most of his adventures seemed to take place while under the influence, and for such a reclusive hack he did seem remarkably unreserved about relating his unstable lurches from one pointless liaison to the next. Titillating the liberal *Observer* readership with his determinedly non-PC attitudes, he explains that he's given up homeless women, 'though I still like to clock them alfresco for fantasy reference when I'm with someone dull but clean'. He follows sad-looking foreign women on the Tube. 'I don't bother them, you understand. I just stay on the train for as long as they do so I can bathe in the exquisite tragedy of their remote erotolachrymalia.'

Geefe claimed that he was compelled to tell the truth, which seemed to manifest itself as an unbearably bleak view of life. But if the truth brings death, he says, it is 'better than the living death of lies. Sod it if I lose my friends, if they can't take the truth they're not worth half an air kiss.' Consumed by increasing self-loathing, he lashes out at those around him, impersonating his female best friend's date on the phone to convince her of a non-existent romantic interest. His hoax pushes the friend to the point where she turns up at his flat in the middle of the night having taken an overdose. 'I had the sangfroid to heave her on to a couch, sit down and write this,' Geefe reports, 'clocking casually that I still had another hour to empty her stomach (if she had told me correctly what time she filled it).'

And then Geefe disappeared. Only six columns had been published. In the last he'd written about how difficult he was finding it to get out of bed in the mornings and that when he did eventually manage to leave his flat he lost track of what happened to him for the rest of the morning. When he returned to the paper after a week, it was explained that his absence was due to a suicide attempt. Geefe himself revealed he was still planning to kill himself, but had agreed with the editor to wait for six months 'on the spurious grounds that some fucker (probably him) may benefit from my burbling'.

Richard Geefe had come from nowhere to being the world's first commissioned suicide in a remarkably short period. And little more than another week elapsed before the *Independent* denounced him as a fake. Of the true identity of Geefe, the paper said only that it was a 'much-respected' writer. But they did report that behind the scenes at the *Observer* a 'delegation' of journalists had been complaining that Geefe's creation 'violated the trust between the paper and its readers'. Roger Alton says now there were far fewer staff complaints than reported, although he does admit that some came to see him about the column. 'And why not?' he says. 'There was a bit of argy-bargy, but you would expect it. Some were baffled, some were annoyed, some amused. But that's what happens. People disagree and that's fine.'

So the columns continued. And on 20 June Geefe referenced the criticism when he reported that when he had second thoughts his editor responded, 'The *Observer* has a bond of trust with its readers, who are now relying on me to commit suicide and would rightly be appalled if I said I was going to live after all. And I began to see that morally, and in every other conceivable way, the editor was actually right.'

A furious article soon followed in London's *Evening Standard*, condemning the columns for dishonesty, but saving most of its criticism for Roger Alton and the damage it suggested he had done to the *Observer*'s reputation. It accused him of being a news snob who wanted to belittle confessional writers and pointed at Chris Morris as the real author of the columns almost as an afterthought.

But the true history of Richard Geefe was rather more involved. He had another parent, in Morris's monologue-writing partner Robert Katz, and his story had been the subject of greater planning than his critics suggested. Richard Geefe had been conceived more than a year before he appeared in the *Observer* and made his debut in a *Blue Jam* monologue of April 1998. The narrator character is invited to join the journalist at a dinner party given in honour of his brave suicide column. It's a gathering that is Hogarthian in its pungent depiction of gluttonous self-celebration. As the braying guests greedily consume twitching oysters, the journalist's nihilism and contempt for his audience seem only to increase their unquestioning adoration as, 'sousing his oysters in vodka and setting them alight before hurling them down his throat, [he] now added a cigarette to the turmoil and belched the word "Bollocks"'. Morris's narrator, ever anxious and confused, is himself only a missed prescription away from disaster, but it is the star guest who finally does what he has written in his columns he will do, with the assistance of the narrator – 'about an hour later I revealed that [the journalist] hadn't just gone for a walk, he'd gone to divorce his head'.

The suicide journalist's transition to a real newspaper came out of occasional informal meetings between Morris and Roger Alton. Their wide-ranging discussions sometimes included various ideas for articles: 'He's the only person around I can think of who makes us look at the way we live and the society we live in in a completely new way,' says Alton. 'He is a revolutionary and a visionary.'

Richard Geefe gradually moved from taking a supporting role in *Blue Jam* to centre stage, with the *Observer*'s staff kept in the dark all the while by Morris's insistence on complete secrecy, 'much to their annoyance,' says Alton. That only the editor and one senior colleague knew the true identity of the (not very) mild-mannered Geefe did little to improve the opinion of him later expressed in print.

The criticism was that Geefe parodied journalists who wrote about personal suffering. The *Evening Standard* article had been written by India Knight, whose friend Ruth Picardie had reported for the *Observer* on life with terminal cancer, bringing her experiences into her weekly articles and dealing with the miserable daily realities of pain, suffering and humiliation with the self-deprecating wit of the confessional journalist. But though Richard Geefe was usually unsympathetic as a character, he never seemed to be more than a rather helpless spectator of his own life. The real monster was the editor – he had, after all, commissioned a writer to kill himself. He is a Mephistophelian character haranguing from the sidelines, phoning Geefe to remind him of the importance of keeping to his decision to wait for a few months before killing himself and warning of the possible legal consequences of not doing so. He even provides a housemate to keep Geefe company – and ensure he doesn't make another attempt at going before the columns have been completed. Sometimes he appears in his own right in the columns, in introductory paragraphs justifying his decision to keep the story going as Geefe's mental state deteriorates. Each point on the journey had been mapped by Morris to mock the way in which Geefe's sadness and darkness were ruthlessly exploited. The emotional disintegration was sensitively realized – it was the absurdly morbid commission which was the target, highlighting the uneasy relationship between the plight of the writer and his worth to the paper.

'A very flattering picture of myself . . .' says Alton. 'No, it's a joke. He is making a serious point about the media being a voracious and often manipulative thing. Of course it applies to me. I'm always saying to people in extremis, "Oh, you must write about that." I don't know any journalist who doesn't.' It was, as one colleague of Morris imaginatively puts it, 'cool' of Alton to 'willingly lube up'. And perhaps it was altruistic or maybe even some form of masochism – though in interview Alton betrays a more straightforward reason for taking on Morris. As the talk turns to the best lines from a classic *On the Hour* newspaper hoax, his composed front of journalistic neutrality melts into hoots of compulsive, wheezing laughter and he has to take his glasses off to wipe away the helpless tears before he can continue. Alton was just delighted to have one of Morris's creations in the paper and left Morris and Robert Katz alone for what he describes as the 'delicate process' of crafting Geefe.

The journalist's byline picture came from Barnaby's Picture Library – taken as inspiration for the archive in Stephen Poliakoff's *Shooting the Past* – near Talkback. Katz found an Austrian ski instructor who looked as if he would be suitably anonymous to British readers – though it was later used as evidence against Geefe when a sharp member of the *Observer*'s picture staff questioned its provenance. It was also Katz who delivered the copy to the offices, but even after it had been filed Morris would continue refining.

Morris set up a fake book deal with Fourth Estate, a publisher of *Guardian* and *Observer* books. Morris already knew editorial director Clive Priddle, who liked the character and the idea, although he had to be reassured by Morris that he wouldn't find himself forced to honour his bid on the proposed collection of columns. Morris phoned the book trade journal *Publishing News* pretending to be a 'media insider' outraged at the news that an unknown journalist such as Geefe should be given a book deal with Fourth Estate on the strength of just a few columns in the *Observer*. Clive Priddle obligingly provided a quote to back up the story, and to his intense relief it prompted another publisher to top his offer.

'It was a classic pop culture bid for the memoir of this tortured soul,' says Priddle now, less surprised at the interest of the book trade in a non-existent author than he was at the reaction of some of his freelance copy editors when the truth was revealed. A number wrote to say they were long-time *Observer* readers and thought it was cruel. For Priddle it was 'slightly sobering' to see the joke cause such offence. He'd seen the point of the deal to be the relationship between publisher and market. When Ruth Picardie and fellow columnist John Diamond were approached in 1997 about collecting their writings on their illness, one publisher explained, 'Cancer is hot.'

But any reader of Richard Geefe might well have felt that they had been deliberately taken in in a way that was different from anything Morris had done before. This time his target unambiguously included its audience. With *Brass Eye* the viewer was always in on the joke, even if the celebrities never guessed. Geefe was different. It hit both sides – those in the newspaper office and the Sunday-morning readers. It was the hoax in which Morris was at his most solitary, only the tightest circle around him aware of what was really going on. More people might have seen his television shows, but proportionally Richard Geefe was the character who caught out the most, as if Morris were determined to eliminate the last suggestion that his comedy was on anybody's side. You could only be on Morris's team if you were sharp enough to spot the clues. But he himself would claim there were as many for Geefe's readers as there had been for *Brass Eye* interviewees.

'How could anyone have seriously thought that the editor of a national newspaper would hire someone to commit suicide?' he said to the *Sunday Times*. 'What I found disturbing was the number of people who said they felt betrayed when they realised it wasn't true. What are they saying – that they wanted him to die?'[1] It was a somewhat disingenuous response. Readers invested considerably in the words of their favourite columnists. Writers such as Ruth Picardie articulated what readers felt, and you didn't have to wish someone dead or approve of the paper's editorial policy to connect with the way they articulated their situation. It was this that gave a greater meaning to what were often called 'ego columns', as *Guardian* media journalist Roy Greenslade had observed of Picardie's work some two years earlier. Though even there, as he describes praise for her column, there is something ambiguous about the relationship between reader and journalist, an undercurrent of sympathy becoming sensation: 'One woman told me that reading Ruth was both unbearable and compulsive,' he wrote in August 1997. 'Every week, she tells herself not to look and, having done so, tells herself again not to go on.'[2] Morris felt uneasy about something so personal being consumed by complete strangers: 'I could understand somebody who's close to someone who is dying of a terminal disease being emotionally racked by it,' he said, 'but I don't understand how a reader can feel they can connect with a thousand perfectly polished words under a picture. That's putting a dramatizing gloss on a real situation. People reading someone's grief story demand that their relationship with that column is treated with the same respect as someone whose best friend is dying.'[3]

Roger Alton saw Geefe being what he describes as 'people's response to the media and their response to that – that quite complicated thing'. He recalls relatively few reader complaints about the columns and says that once all was eventually revealed the reaction was very favourable. By comparison, there would later be far more complaints arising from the one-off special Morris wrote with Armando Iannucci in 2002 following the 11 September attacks.

The difference between the reader response to Richard Geefe and the later piece – 'Six Months that Changed a Year', 'An absolute atrocity special' – was that there was by then a much larger internet readership. American readers were far louder in expressing their anger at the pull-out section. In addition, much less time was taken over the piece, written by the pair with contributions from Arthur Mathews, and it showed. It was conceived over four days and the scope was ambitious. Iannucci was particularly interested in the belief that the attacks had somehow changed everything, Blair's obsession with America and the concept of a war on terror which turns into a standard bombing mission. But they were allocated what turned out to be an inadequate number of in-house design staff. 'We probably didn't execute that as well as Chris would have liked,' admits one of his friends at the *Observer*. 'I think he found it a tiny bit frustrating.'

The same accusation could not be made of Richard Geefe, where far more care was taken to render his decline into a crushing depressive episode. He describes the days of 'smothering dread' leading up to his first suicide attempt, painting his trendy loft black, helplessly watching the mail pile up and refusing to talk to his friends on the phone. He seizes on any shreds of hope with a touching vulnerability: '. . . anything that feels like a reason to live at the moment,' he says, 'it glimmers for an instant – easy to see because it is alone – and then vanishes like a mirage . . .'

In his later columns Geefe records being filmed by a BBC crew, his documentary to be called *Time to Go: A Chronicle of Courage*. The crew capture his increasingly demented attempts to finish his book to coincide publication with his death – 'committing myself to what I'll be doing, how I will feel about it and my exact method of blapping my lulu. It's driving me nuts.' In one of his occasional asides, the editor admits that he has a 50 per cent interest in the book deal.

The last full column followed the *Evening Standard* naming of Morris. On 4 July the *Observer* reprinted the collected works with a final short piece from the editor explaining that Geefe had killed himself before the agreed date. There were tributes from friends who were with him on his final night at a dinner party, leaving readers in what had also been the setting for the original *Blue Jam* monologue. Both versions of the character had been halfway through the commissioned run of their column, giving them a final, bitter triumph over the editor who had thought their life was just another regular feature under his control.

Geefe's life might have been truncated, but the weekly columns had turned into Morris's first extended narrative. It was an indication of his growing interest in developing complete stories, as well as being yet another outlet for ideas from *Blue Jam*. In opening up the recesses of the mind late at night, it had found all the things which are usually hidden at more respectable hours – self-loathing, the horror of being alive – and used them as inspiration for a comedy that never diminished them as subjects. When the columns concluded, *Blue Jam*'s transfer to television was still six months away. But if *Jam*'s visual derangements weren't to attract controversy, the following year everything changed. Chris Morris revived *Brass Eye*.

13

17.8 PER CENT SAFER

BRASS EYE RETURNED FOR A ONE-OFF SPECIAL IN JULY 2001 with the same powerful blend of rapid-fire gags, documentary parody and celebrity deception. Chris Morris was taking a risk in returning to a format which had, after all, been successful partly through its originality and unexpectedness and which could have come back seeming admired but maybe little more than worthy. Even four years on the series remained a landmark achievement, and its extravagantly mangled news-speak was, like *The Day Today* before it, still much quoted. Its transition from audacity to adoration had been instantaneous. Morris's presenter character might have become a familiar sort of anti-hero, which could fatally detract from his impact. Everything rested on why the show had been brought back, and it was the choice of subject which made the show compelling all over again.

In using *Brass Eye* to look at the way in which paedophilia had become such a predominant issue, Morris placed himself at the centre of the unsayable. *Brass Eye* came only a year after a tabloid-led campaign of anti-paedophile marches and violence, when any dissenting voices were denounced at best as liberal apologists and at worst as defenders of abusers. Morris's was virtually the only voice of sustained response, and *Brass Eye* was attacked with unparalleled ferocity. It became the headline story of the summer. The programme even divided Morris's own long-time contributors. He hadn't pressurized anyone to take part and approached cast and crew with the expectation that some wouldn't want to be involved. Everyone knew that they were taking a stand simply by having a credit in the show; making an act of calculated defiance against the popular press which was unlikely to go unpunished. Graham Linehan asked for his name to be taken off on viewing the completed *Brass Eye*: 'I felt you didn't have to press the accelerator quite so hard to the floor with a subject like paedophilia to have it work,' he says. 'There was a lot of stuff that was quite harsh and unpleasant. I thought it was like throwing a live grenade. I chickened out a little bit . . . Maybe it's something that couldn't have been helped. As an experiment, it was brave and worthwhile but you could say that it didn't quite come off. The subject matter in the end took over.' Having being born in Ireland and lived for much of his early life in Dublin, Linehan didn't feel he would have the instinct to judge the nuances of English life well enough to predict the reaction to the show – although you could have spent your whole life in the country and still not quite have believed the scenes of mobs going on nightly paedophile hunts in late 2000. What if *Brass Eye* stirred all that up again? 'I didn't know what the results would be. I didn't know if I'd get attacked in the street,' Linehan says. 'The level of stupidity was so high around all that.'

David Quantick's thoughts about the show ran along the same lines, and he even uses the same explosive metaphor as Linehan, but the conclusions he reached were very different. 'I think some of the jokes in it are completely out of order, but they're hilarious,' he says, citing the opening with real-life paedophile Sidney Cooke reported as being blasted into space in a rocket which inadvertently also holds a small child. NASA comments, 'This is the one thing we didn't want to happen.'

'Absolutely unjustifiable, but I think it's really funny,' says Quantick. 'Unjustifiable, because what that is basically saying is, "Isn't it funny that this real man has raped children?" So, morally, appalling, but worth it because it's a very good gag. You could say it's satirizing something but it's not, but that's fine. It's a perfectly valid show because it satirized media attitudes to paedophilia and the hypocrisy and the way they are making money out of children's pain. Some of the jokes are dodgy, but I don't care . . . Anything can be a subject for humour. It's like letting off a grenade. You then go in and see who's dead and what it's achieved. Has it knocked down any useful walls or has it just created a load of mess?'

Jane Bussmann agrees: 'It was making fun of the media's reaction to paedophilia. If you give in to boundaries, you are letting them win. If you really care about an issue, if you think it's bad, the best way to reduce its badness is to mock it. It's as old as history itself. If you think a person is evil, laugh at them and then see how much they like it. Being caught by the cops is a random fate for a paedophile, but being mocked in a comedy is a certainty that you can create and execute.'

Runner James Serafinowicz early on asked that his name be changed to James Sezchuan, as his grandfather had only a couple of years earlier been the subject of worldwide coverage of charges accusing him of being a war criminal. Though the charges against him were dropped after it was ruled he was unfit to stand trial,[1] such was the apprehension about the show's reception that James imagined 'Nazi grandson in paedophile outrage' headlines if he kept his distinct surname (and the story was indeed revived when his brother's *Peter Serafinowicz Show* aired in 2007).

It was in recognition of how much was invested in supporting what Morris was doing that even though Quantick and Bussmann didn't get any material in the final show he gave them a credit: 'It could have backfired quite badly,' reflects Quantick now, 'if we'd been assassinated by loonies.' But though the sense of violence in the air was very real, it hadn't solely been that which provided the inspiration for the show. Morris had been thinking about doing something on attitudes to children with *Brass Eye* even before 2000.

New contributing writer Charlie Brooker was transfixed by the way the show coalesced over the months: 'It seemed to be happening by osmosis,' he says, 'in that I don't think there was a definite point I could say where he told me specifically what he was doing and asked for ideas. The show drifted in a bit like a cloud and you think, Surely that's not going to happen . . . Jesus Christ! And then it *is* happening . . .'

The roots of *Brass Eye* lay in the country's general uneasy sense of its relationship with children, who were more often viewed as empty vessels to be filled with good or evil than as individuals. It was an instinctive reaction which held them to be either innocents to be kept away from a brutal world or monsters like the 10-year-old killers of toddler James Bulger in 1993. Five years after his murder, the age of criminal responsibility in England and Wales was lowered from fourteen to ten. But as soon as young people approached an age of official maturity they could be leered at, as the *Star* would do in the wake of the *Special*, publishing a picture of 15-year-old singer Charlotte Church and her cleavage, showing 'how quickly she's grown up'. (The facing page attacked *Brass Eye*'s 'perv spoof'.)

The darkest fears for the well-being of the young were confirmed by a series of scandals in state care in the late 1980s and 1990s. London boroughs came in for particular criticism – seventeen years elapsed before reports on one particularly sadistic head of a home in Islington were followed up. Investigations showed how systems of child protection had been lax; the abused were often not believed, incompetence was covered up. Just as damaging were the allegations that became mired in uncertainty and often bitter controversy, such as the diagnosis of abuse in the late 1980s in Cleveland. Truth was hard to find, and in that vacuum unease flourished.

There was a growing sense that not enough was being done about predatory paedophiles. And when they were caught and convicted, there was further concern about whether they would be released and go on to reoffend. Of all the fears and threats that faced children, it was the image of that most dangerous paedophile which was most terrifying.

The most direct influences on the format of the *Special* were emotive documentaries which used such predatory paedophiles as source material. They were often powerful programmes, but it wasn't so much how far they succeeded on their own terms which concerned *Brass Eye* as the inevitably manipulative techniques they used to get there. Specific programmes were given to Morris's writers to watch, among them a Channel 4 *Dispatches* of October 1998 which featured paedophile Sidney Cooke with what Morris later described as 'camp relish'.[2] *Dispatches* editor Dorothy Byrne had commissioned the programme as Cooke's release date approached amid public debate about where he should be housed. Her starting point was to question whether he should be released at all. It had been alleged that he had committed other offences for which he hadn't yet been charged, so she conceived the programme as a counterpoint to investigations into miscarriages of justice which resulted in the conviction of innocent people. This would be *Crimewatch* in reverse – *Dispatches* knew its criminal and appealed, successfully, for information relating to his activities. 'The popular genre in TV was getting people out of prison,' explained Byrne. 'So it was actually a very daring programme because it resulted in a dreadful paedophile *going* to prison.'[3]

Even unadorned, Sidney Cooke's story of squalid perversion and murder provided a narrative as compulsive as it was horrifying. Yet *Dispatches* had horror-movie touches that Cooke hardly required – portentous music, dramatic pauses, gravelly voiceovers and eerie shots of menacing housing estates in reconstructions of his hide-outs. Even some of what seemed to be *Brass Eye*'s wilder flights of invention proved to be little more than direct transplants. A real-life victim of Cooke is described as so traumatized that he will only speak off camera and then only while holding a small toy animal in front of his face – as presenter David Jessel solemnly relates this prurient detail, he holds his hands up protectively by way of demonstration. In *Brass Eye*, an interviewee talks to Morris only via her sister disguised as a blue toy troll.

Both programmes were presented as live from an office dominated by a blow-up photograph of their featured paedophile leering down in black and white. The real Sidney Cooke was a fairground worker who spent years in parks and amusement arcades ('Places where *your* children may have been') and the *Special* captured *Dispatches*' sensationalism in hinting darkly at details of the story which would be simply too vile for the audience to bear in full, the sort of programme that never reassured where it could play up threats, throwing a spotlight on to monsters and making the victims look freakish in their shadows. It all served to reinforce the idea that the official system of child protection was inadequate and required the media to do its job. The volatility of public fury in the face of this became clear almost two years later, on 1 July 2000, when 8-year-old Sarah Payne was abducted in Sussex and murdered, and the *News of the World* took up its anti-paedophile campaign.

The aim was to get a version of the US law which allowed communities to be told when a paedophile moved into the area. Between July and September, the paper printed endless stories about the most abusive UK paedophiles, promising to name all 110,000 on the sex offenders' register – 'virtually one for every square mile of the country'.[4] Ignoring those who said that attacks by strangers were far outnumbered by abuse within the home, every week they published photos of fugitive paedophiles, despite being refused permission to do so by the police. The paper was filled with headlines such as 'What to do if there is a pervert on your doorstep' and 'Ten facts to shock every parent'.[5]

Though the paper denied it was encouraging vigilantism, within a day of the first report, mobs hunted the 'named and shamed' paedophiles, and many offenders fled their homes in panic. Celebrities such as Esther Rantzen and GMTV's Eamonn Holmes backed the campaign: 'If you had a person living next door who had a contagious disease, you'd be told,' Holmes said. 'Why should this be different?'[6] In Manchester an offender killed himself when his home was surrounded. Another had his flat attacked in Portsmouth on the Paulsgrove estate, which had the most energetic rabble and a long, if largely speculative, list of paedophiles. Cars were torched, innocent families were targeted. 'They should be burned alive,' offered one Paulsgrove woman as she protested about a local man, while nearby a young girl chanted, 'Burn him, stab him, kill him.'[7]

A march held in gentrified Balham in London near where Chris Morris lived was inevitably called 'posh Paulsgrove' in the press, but the unmediated emotion on display was pretty much the same. Morris had gone along to find out what protesters really thought of paedophilia beyond the headlines and was told by one parent that they would rather their child were murdered. It was a comment that played a decisive part in convincing him that there was something worth looking into, along with the personal contact he'd had himself with officers investigating child abuse allegations at his old school, Stonyhurst. He'd felt that the investigation – which resulted in no convictions – was also driven by panic. Morris returned to Balham in filming the *Special*, dressed in a top hat and riding gear and inhaling helium gas, obtained for the production at great trouble at the last moment. He went door to door in a sequence that didn't make the final programme, warning people of a paedophile moving in nearby who wore strange clothes and spoke in a squeaky voice.

Morris later said: 'The very specific nature of *Brass Eye* is in identifying a thoughtless, knee-jerk reaction to an issue. If you tackle drugs or paedophilia, then you're dealing with something where people's brains are nowhere near the point of debate.'[8] Debate was actively discouraged during the *News of the World* campaign, when those judges, MPs and newspapers who suggested that perhaps there might not be a paedophile under every cot in the country were named in the paper and ridiculed by its editor Rebekah Wade as 'feeble men'.[9] It seemed as if just the act of walking past children's playgrounds might result in being the subject of a hunt by a baying crowd of demented parents. A paediatrician had to leave her town after vigilantes got confused about her job title and scrawled 'paedo' over her front door.

The *News of the World* never formally agreed to drop its campaign, despite protests from groups representing both offenders and children. In practice, as the lynch mobs spread, the naming and shaming aspect was quietly dropped – at least until the following year, when it would be revived specially for the cast and crew of the *Special* – and the headlines died out, leaving a sense that the traditional image of the English as a reserved people was not necessarily to be relied on.

By the beginning of the following year, pre-production had begun on the *Special*, known within Talkback and Channel 4 only as *Trombone*. The reputation of the original series guaranteed goodwill, but also brought its own risks. Chris Morris had become a legendary figure in the industry, and there was a generation who had grown up. with his shows and would have wanted to work with him whatever he was doing. Ali MacPhail joked that he was surrounded by fans rather than colleagues. He thought she had a point. 'Mm. Maybe you're right,' he told her. 'I can walk to the water cooler and people fall about laughing these days.' To ensure that the show wasn't thrown together on autopilot, Morris canvassed impartial advice from friends such as Armando Iannucci, who introduced his long-time producer and friend Sarah Smith. Experienced and with a cool head, she could be relied on to point out the gratuitous. She became the *Special*'s script consultant. 'He wanted to make the right points and only the right points,' she says, 'and he wanted to be careful about why he was doing it, and I think he just wanted to be challenged along the way whether or not the stuff was in there because it appeals to someone's evil comic instinct as opposed to guessing at something specific. It was really important in that show that it did have a fundamental satirical intent.' And quite apart from anything else, it was enjoyable for her to engage in Morris's extended debates about comedy without the stressful responsibility of having to run the show herself. 'I just went in and sat with him every now and then and argued.'

It was an enviable freedom from the point of view of those who were returning to full-time front-line duties: 'By the end of *Jam* I was absolutely exhausted,' says line producer Philippa Catt, 'and I'd lost loads of weight. Going back to *Brass Eye*, I was quite excited at the prospect of working with Chris again, but the whole politics of all the money shit and having to fight about [it] all the time – everything is so intense.' Faced with the prospect of having to mediate between Morris and Peter Fincham at Talkback for months, she decided to walk away and had almost made it to liberty before Chris and Sally Debonnaire convinced her over the course of a weekend to return.

Many other familiar faces returned to the show, including Jump Design, whose minimalist opening sequence reflected a more self-conscious mode of current affairs presentation. They were partnered once again on the musical side by Jonathan Whitehead.

Among the new contributors was Charlie Brooker, who was probably the most notable addition to Morris's circle, despite not getting a particularly large amount of material in the *Special* itself. But his involvement marked the start of a productive new writing partnership which would culminate in 2005's *Nathan Barley*. Like Morris, Brooker was wildly creative and a naturally comic writer. Production crew who have worked with both men say that Brooker demonstrates the same inspiring leadership quality, and he would get his own TV team behind him for his later *Screenwipe* show, pulling together to create last-minute bits of extra invention. His early career was also spent in the media rather than in performing comedy. As a teenager, Brooker had contributed cartoons to *Viz*-alike comic *Oink!* He later worked as a games journalist for *PC Zone* magazine, where he was given a regular slot for his artwork which prompted the entire publication to be withdrawn the month he created a fake advert for a zoo that encouraged animal abuse. He had doctored Argos catalogue images of kids with animal toys to look like the results of the wanton slaughter players could inflict on wildlife as Lara Croft in *Tomb Raider*. 'There wasn't any satirical point to be made there,' he says. 'I just liked the idea that it was wilfully unpleasant. That becomes amusing in itself, when it's that unnecessary.' He also investigated the comic potential of prank calls, a series of which he made as irritating customers calling computer helplines which were featured on a *PC Zone* cover disk. Off the back of that he was asked to co-present a technology show on TV.

But it was his spoof TV listings webpage that gave him cult status and brought him to Morris's attention. *TV Go Home*'s layout imitated the reassuring look of the *Radio Times*, but read as if years of churning out bland, neutral programme descriptions had led the writer to be consumed by an increasingly rabid hatred of all television and of the viewing hordes.

'It was a weirdly cathartic thing to be doing,' says Brooker. 'It would be about three in the morning every other Thursday in quite a grumpy mood because I was usually knackered and I'd have to be doing something the next day. I do remember specifically there was a Valentine's edition I wrote the day after an appalling break-up, and it was so bitter that I ended up finding it amusing while I was doing it.'

He stored most of his bile for Nathan Barley, the twenty-something Trustafarian star he created for regular *TV Go Home* documentary *Cunt*: 'Wearing trousers apparently cut from charcoal-grey crêpe paper, Nathan Barley crosses a busy street clutching a mango smoothie and a punnet of takeaway sushi,' ran a typical entry, 'simultaneously listening to a speed garage compilation on his Minidisc walkman, contemplating the purchase of a Nokia WAP phone and mentally picturing himself sliding all the way up to the nutbag in a passing teenage girl in a tissue-thin summer dress.'[10] The co-host of Brooker's TV show knew Morris, showed him *TV Go Home* and introduced the two during the run-up to production of the *Brass Eye Special*.

Brooker was invited to writing meetings, and in return Morris and Peter Baynham both contributed to *TV Go Home*. Morris's pieces included a description of a Nathan Barley attempt at short film-making: '*11.39 (deckbang)*. A crack-crazed Yardie sprays an Uzi round the top deck of a number 23 bus; as the mortally-wounded passengers writhe in the blood, smoke, dribble and spilt bags, their moments of eye contact provide cues for fantasy porn vignettes in which they have sex with the person whose dying face they've just glimpsed. Music by Goldfrapp.'[11]

Nathan had been born of an undefined sense of bitterness that Brooker had felt years before towards the confident, young media types hanging out near the flat he could ill afford just off Chepstow Road in gentrified Westbourne Park. It was the kind of 'weird modern fuck who can kind of effortlessly get away with anything', says Brooker, 'and just seems to succeed and is operating behind about ten layers of irony which are constantly flipping around so you can't pin them down'. Readers would approvingly email *TV Go Home* about the sharp satire of idiotic new trends and fads which Brooker had been under the impression were entirely his own invention. The extraordinary savagery of his writing prompted further emails expressing fears for Brooker's mental well-being. 'I seem to remember Chris suggested that I should toy with the idea of making it more demented until it really looked like I was going a bit *Network*,' he says.

It was also Morris who suggested that Nathan could be developed into something more than a simple receptacle of hatred. The TV series would take five years to get to the screen, Brooker and Morris discussing how the show might work as far back as sessions for the *Brass Eye Special*, when they were joined by Peter Baynham. For a while they experimented with having a character playing the part of the rage-filled observer in *TV Go Home*, with documentary-maker Claire Ashcroft one candidate. Nathan himself was considered for the role of violent monster, but they found more humour in him being at heart a rather desperate figure. They talked about the show for so long that Brooker, unused to Morris's deep and long approaches to development, wondered at times if it would ever happen. In the meantime Brooker drew on his computer journalism experience for the *Special*, discussing such accoutrements of the modern paedophile as online games and working on rapper JLb-8, the Eminem figure who writes his tales of abuse into 'nu-ass' music and dates girls 'as young as seven'.

The cast of the *Special* included Doon Mackichan. Since the original series, she had been in Talkback's *Smack the Pony*, the show winning an international Emmy in 1999. She came to be Morris's co-host on the *Special* and, sharing with him a deep hatred of *Crimewatch*, was particularly enthused to discover they were to take off its presenting style. Her Swanchita Haze combined the disturbingly still quality of *The Day Today*'s Collaterlie Sisters with an absurdly sexualized Fiona Bruce off *Crimewatch* and dripped suggestively over every line – 'We believe his story is actually too upsetting to transmit. We only do so tonight with that proviso.'

Doon Mackichan remembers *Smack the Pony* and *Big Train* comparing notes to avoid doing the same gags, and they joined forces again as *Big Train*'s Amelia Bullmore, Julia Davis, Kevin Eldon and Mark Heap arrived on the *Special* via *Jam*. Their former co-star Simon Pegg, who had gone on to find fame with his sitcom *Spaced*, made a show-stealing appearance as Gerard Chote, studio-storming spokesman for militant paedophile organization Milit-Pede.

Pegg's scene attracted some of the greatest criticism of the show for its apparent involvement of a child playing Chris Morris's son. The boy is shown to Gerard, who denies wanting to have sex with him – but not for any moral reason. 'I just don't. I don't find him attractive,' he explains apologetically. Morris's face betrays his character's agonized confusion on hearing this news about his son – relief battling wounded pride. But the boy, like all of the young actors, was never really exposed to any adult conversations – he was filmed only in long shot and otherwise painted in during post-production. All parents were fully consulted and aware of what was happening in the show, just as had been the case in *Jam*.

In the American child beauty pageant sketch, careful precautions were taken to guard the footage of a little girl with apparent breast implants, created as special effects and then pixellated out for the broadcast – 'They jiggle,' observes father Kevin Eldon happily. The original tape was meticulously logged and then destroyed at the end of production, unlikely as it was that anyone would think of trying to obtain it. It was the adults who featured in the *Brass Eye Special* who were told less about what was going on. Some auditioned for parts without even knowing what they were going for and later turned the show down when they found out what it was. Then there were those who were invited to make a different sort of contribution as part of the traditional *Brass Eye* fake campaign – the celebrities were rounded up again.

'I thought people would be so much more alert and on their guard. And I was staggered at how gullible they were,' reported Morris. 'It's simply a case of identifying the right blind spot and exploiting it.'[12]

Gerald Howarth MP held up an advert designed to look like the prostitute cards left in telephone boxes. Next to a contact number and the slogan 'Kids! I can help you with your homework' was a picture of a man, hands on hips, wearing just pants and glasses. Runner and cameraman James Serafinowicz was quietly relieved to find his own striking resemblance to a fully clothed version of the model went unnoticed by the MP as he condemned the ad.

Morris brought back his vox popping in the form of a focus group, an appropriate update for the technique given the way the subject had itself been characterized by mass displays of public emotion. It seemed to be no more difficult for him to lead on half a dozen people at a time than it had been to do one or two. They nodded approval of the 'Singapore solution', a technological breakthrough which involved a cashew nut-sized implant in a paedophile's rectum reacting to the sound of children's voices by expanding to the size of a 42-inch colour television set.

The nightly protests of the year before were recalled in the form of reports punctuating the programme from Morris as Ted Maul outside a prison where a public riot over a paedophile prisoner named Jez North grows in ever more irrational fury, climaxing with North being grabbed by the mob from a prison van and ritually burned, *Wicker Man*-style, in a giant phallus. A sketch in counterpoint, which didn't make it to the final show, was to feature paedophile friends at home making placards for their own, small pro-child sex march while the mother of one of them prepares sandwiches and flasks of tea.

Not every target was framed so concisely. The self-confessed paedophile Morris interviewed never seemed genuine, though coaxing 'Peter' on to the show had been time-consuming and stressful for the crew, who had to appear sympathetic to hearing his views. He was accompanied to meetings by an adult friend, who remained silent until a discussion on the damage done to children. 'I've been having sex with him since I was six,' he said without prompting, 'and it's never done me any harm.' Though Peter had been a member of the Paedophile Information Exchange and had published a book justifying what he termed 'inter-generational sex', none of this came over in the programme. Rather, he seemed like an actor in the preposterously heavy disguise he had brought along for filming in the bright sunshine of a London park. He listened patiently to Morris's absurdly elongated list of names for paedophiles – 'unabummer', 'the crazy world of Arthur Brown', 'nut administrator', 'two-pin din plug', 'bush dodger', 'small-bean regarder', 'shrub racketeer' – as if the whole scenario were perfectly sensible. His comment – 'it's just another form of racism' – should have been disturbing in its self-pity but in context sounded more like a scripted punchline.

There was another moment in the show which would have gone unnoticed by the audience, and it was the one in which *Brass Eye* put itself in greatest peril, risking prosecution because members of the crew supplied their own childhood snaps for a sequence on composite images. And as Morris and Channel 4 knew, legally you couldn't give consent even as an adult for an image of yourself as a child to be used like that. Morris played a gently lisping art expert, eliciting instant decisions from the ex-head of the obscene publications branch Mike Hames on the legality of a massively enlarged child's head juxtaposed with a tiny image of a naked woman (not obscene) and a boy's head on to a dog's body with a huge penis (obscene). While the interview did expose the inevitably personal notions of taste behind apparent moral certainties, the more interesting legal paradox of the crew effectively incriminating themselves as their own abusers was lost. Hames was the best placed of anyone duped in the show to bring a prosecution. He had been a supporter of the *News of the World* campaign and written a book about paedophiles called *The Dirty Squad*.

If the programme hadn't hit all its targets in the way that the original series had, it was nevertheless packed with astonishing invention. The first cut revealed that Morris had made it almost exactly fit the required twenty-five minutes. Morris's agent Chiggy even noticed he had become more willing to compromise with how he presented material to the broadcaster. Was he finally beginning to mellow? 'He might have to at least tell them they're going to get what they think they're going to get,' she says. 'Even if they're not.'

Trombone was finally revealed as the *Brass Eye Special* on Thursday 26 July, repeated in the early hours of the following Saturday morning. Maintaining his rule of not commenting on or justifying his shows, Morris left for a holiday in the south of France immediately after the broadcast. There would still be plenty of questions for him by the time he came back.

Channel 4 presented a united front on the broadcast – there was no repeat of the internal arguments which had threatened the original series. But a furious response came from almost every other quarter, allies as well as long-time critics. It made previous criticism of Morris's work seem like polite equivocation. There was no doubt that the emotive subject matter had made it by far the harshest *Brass Eye*, and there was something for everyone to find at least awkward – the song with which the programme concludes, as a choir of children sing about not quite being 'ready yet', loses none of its power to disturb no matter how many times you witness it. And the fact that Morris had never been sentimental in the way he dealt with children on his shows over the years was never going to figure as part of the defence. There was a debate to be had, about the show as well as the issues it raised, but the media largely plugged itself straight back into the incoherent rage of the previous summer. And coverage was underscored with a curious moral fervour, as if implying that the *Special* were somehow a defence of child abuse.

For anyone who recalled the mob-rousing tabloid campaign with some horror, the fierce insight and questioning of *Brass Eye* never seemed better deployed. That some would find it unacceptable was inevitable, but those sensitivities were not alone reason enough to say that the *Special* should not have been made. What would ultimately carry it would be the approach to the subject and in that Morris's energy and the inspired seriousness he brought to the process of production were themselves a response to the critics: few, if any, other programme-makers could have made something so suspect but ultimately persuasive. If nothing else, *Brass Eye* demanded the respect of being engaged with beyond the predictable condemnation that at one point looked as if it might lead to state intervention in the programme.

Tessa Jowell, newly installed Secretary of State for Culture, Media and Sport, condemned it as 'a viewer and a parent'[13] and highlighted concerns about how such a controversial programme had been given a repeat only days after its initial showing. Home Office minister Beverley Hughes went on Radio 4's *Today* programme for an interview that, even without Morris's physical presence, seemed as if it could have been cut from *Brass Eye* itself. 'I've not seen the whole programme and to be honest I really don't want to,' said Hughes. She had read a 'detailed commentary' and 'I'm very clear that this is not the right way to deal with the subject'.

'But wait a minute, hang on, you're a minister in the government,' interrupted interviewer John Humphrys. 'You're coming on the air for not the first time in the last 24 hours to talk about this programme as a serious subject and you say you haven't seen it and you don't want to see it. Aren't people entitled to think that's an absurd statement?'

'No, I don't think so,' said Hughes, adding that there was a debate to be had on the media and paedophilia, but a comedy programme wasn't the place to start it. Fellow guest David Quantick commented that the debate she said she wanted was happening now as a result of the show. After the broadcast Morris called to say he hadn't known David would be asked to appear on the programme, but thanked him for saying the right things. Then Peter Fincham called. He had been watching days go by with no sign of the arguments diminishing. Talkback were hoping to limit the damage, Peter Fincham said, and could David please stop going on the radio to talk about the show.

The government started to show signs of anxiety about the way in which they were being portrayed as advocating censorship, and Number 10 eventually retracted much of the implied threat about regulating the broadcast of future controversial shows. Beverley Hughes's description of the show as 'unspeakably sick' was taken up as one of the *Mail*'s many headlines on the subject, and the *Sun* went on to ask if the *Special* was 'the sickest TV ever?' Co-producer Phil Clarke and production coordinator Holly Sait, alone in the office when the show went out, became the front line in heading off what turned into an endless stream of calls from journalists as a press campaign against the show got into full swing.

It soon became very personal, far more so than had been the case even in the coverage of the original series. The *Daily Mirror* claimed that some, inevitably unnamed, colleagues found Morris to be 'an arrogant, egotistical character, driven by an almost psychopathic need to shock but too cowardly to account for his actions'.[14] But if Morris was ever affected by such articles, he never showed any sign of it to friends and colleagues, and the *Mirror*'s impact was further undermined by the lack of available photographs. The paper was reduced to reprinting the image accompanying an interview Morris had done back in early 1990 with the *NME*. And as the subject of the original article concerned the dangers of back-wards messages hidden on pop records – Morris regularly spoofed that earlier example of a moral panic – the *Mirror*'s caption could accuse him of nothing more dastardly than 'proudly holding a Jason Donovan LP'.[15]

But then photographers came to doorstep him with partner Jo and their children. It was the only aspect of the media coverage which genuinely upset Morris – otherwise he might even have appreciated the irony in the press claiming to defend the children of the country while sticking long lenses into the Morris family buggy to get a story. 'Everyone felt very protective towards Chris,' says Jane Bussmann. 'Because the idea that someone as nice as Chris would be regarded as a bad person was just ludicrous. People standing outside his front door . . . the malevolence . . . it was insane.'

Co-host Doon Mackichan was also targeted. 'He was holed up in his house,' she remembers, 'and we were kind of talking each other down because our anger was so high we did just want to go and smash their cars up.' Morris sent her a case of champagne.

The women connected with the show were particularly vilified, painted by the *Mail* as somehow betrayers of their sex for not only telling vulgar jokes but controversial ones at that. Caroline Leddy, by then head of comedy at Channel 4 and responsible for commissioning the show, was according to the paper 'herself the mother of a young child', and the child actors featured alongside Doon Mackichan were 'not unlike her own'[16] – although it wasn't made clear how they might have differed.

Mackichan had already warned her mother that she would probably hear about the show and explained that she'd found it quite hard that people close to her hated it, including some *Smack the Pony* colleagues. Mackichan had been blanked in local shops and by mums in her kids' playground. Then the *Mail* tracked Doon's mother to Spain. She innocently relayed the conversation she'd had with her daughter, and the *Mail* worked it into a piece so vicious that on advice from friends Mackichan has never read it.

It wasn't until well into August that the stories eventually dried up. Ali MacPhail later received a copy of the *Brass Eye* DVD with a card from Morris: 'This is to remind you that you are as sick as I am.' But it wasn't just the usual suspects ranged against Chris Morris. The *Special* also alienated some who had been traditionally sympathetic to his work.

The *Guardian*'s Hugo Young thought, 'The satire was too deeply embedded in the shock effect to make much sense.'[17] And in the same newspaper Ros Coward addressed the subject of the show being watched by those who had been abused. 'Who on the liberal left, intent on a critique of media forms, really cares about that? They think the only problem with paedophilia in our society is that it's the subject of a moral panic, paedophiles as wildly exaggerated bogeymen.' She went on to say, 'I'm much more concerned that many people (including media liberals) still don't really believe sex abuse happens.'[18]

Channel 4's own Dorothy Byrne, later head of news and current affairs at the channel, is not so prescriptive, though she agrees wholeheartedly with Ros Coward's assertion that the content of the *Special* diminishes the threat posed by predatory paedophiles. Perhaps they might not so often affect middle-class families, she says, but she herself had become much more sensitized to the dangers during the production of the *Dispatches* on Sidney Cooke. She'd seen public spaces in less well-off areas where paedophiles would meet, and she had challenged a man who approached her own young daughter.

And yet Byrne also says that the *Special* did provoke debate. 'Comedy,' she says, 'should be about really serious things.' She is disarmingly frank in acknowledging that it accurately identified presentational tics which had her wincing as she watched. While she remains proud of the original *Dispatches*, would she make it differently today? 'Maybe we would be less dramatic now,' says Byrne after a moment's thought. 'When you saw the parody, we looked like we took ourselves too seriously. But on the other hand, you're talking about a man who abused children.' The balance – for both *Brass Eye* and the documentaries it lit with a dazzling but strangely humanizing light – was hard to calibrate.

A short series was shown in prime time on BBC2 a year later under the title *The Hunt for Britain's Paedophiles*. One man arrested during the making of the series allowed the crew accompanying the police to conduct a graphic interview with him among the pet ferrets he allowed to wander freely around his overflowing flat. Within a day of the filming he had killed himself. He left notes indicating that the interview should be used, which it duly was, the executive producer of the series telling the BBC: 'We were shocked, but that feeling subsided when one of the officers took us to one side afterwards and told us what he'd done.'[19]

The Hunt . . . was shown to far less viewer protest than *Brass Eye*, which prompted a record 2,000 complaints to Channel 4 and a further 500 to the ITC. The broadcaster had thought through its defence of every aspect of the *Special*, sketch by sketch, and at eighty pages it was longer than that submitted for the entire original series. The ITC found only that Channel 4 hadn't warned sufficiently of the contents of the programme or made it clear that child actors hadn't been harmed and the programme wasn't a documentary. The broadcaster was ordered to make an on-air apology.

Though it was nominated in the BAFTA Awards that year, *Brass Eye* continued to divide opinion, with ceremony host Chris Tarrant publicly criticizing it. When a clip was shown, it was greeted by boos from the audience. It didn't win. For Channel 4 itself, says Prash Naik, *Brass Eye* and the *Special* remain 'probably the most difficult comedy programme[s] we've ever done'. Yet even years on, he adds, '*Brass Eye* is still one of the seminal programmes that the channel quotes in terms of innovation and experimentation.' And Dorothy Byrne notes that few other broadcasters would produce such a weighty programme as *Dispatches* and then another that so comprehensively mocked it.

By 2001 Chris Morris had refined a style of news parody into something that existed on its own terms. The *Brass Eye Special* stood as much in a genre of one as it mimicked other programmes. Over the years since he'd first worked with Armando Iannucci in *On the Hour*, Morris had operated his comedy in a state of constant shift; deceiving and morphing, as much of a surprise to those who commissioned him to make it as it was to its audience. The *Special* was unmistakably the fullest exploration of that approach to humour in the way that it demanded a response even from those who said they hadn't seen it.

But while other comedy-makers have followed in the wake of *Brass Eye* to colonize the areas that he had first marked out, Morris has decisively turned away, focusing his practice on developing character through more sustained forms of comic narrative. He has become concerned with being more completely the storyteller that, from his earliest days, his material had always suggested he could be. Signposts to the direction he was later to take could be found in the artefacts of the long and terrible history of Sir Arthur Streeb-Greebling which he expertly unearthed from Peter Cook, in the succinct tales of his made-up listener letters on the Radio 1 shows and almost everywhere else you cared to look in his work, but most clearly in the monologues of his radio shows.

Morris returned to the rich source of *Blue Jam* for inspiration for his first stand-alone story and movie in 2002. The story of Rothko the dog, whose ability to talk is heard only by Morris's narrator character and gets him into considerable trouble as a result, became *My Wrongs #8245-8249 and 117*, also the inaugural release for the newly formed Warp Films. With Paddy Considine starring, *My Wrongs . . .* went on to win a BAFTA for best short. The running time might have been just fifteen minutes, but its relatively straight narrative represented a completely different mode of expression. In 1998 Morris described in characteristically stark terms the way in which he pushed himself to find new areas: 'I'll probably be staring into a void,' he told the *Guardian*. 'It's a way of finding something that you want to do, because something comes out and then you go with it. I think it's the only way to go. You can become very demoralized by confronting the void, but if you know that you're treading the same ground, you can become much worse – you walk, you talk, you go to parties or whatever, but you become dead, you become a zombie. So, you know, the life's gone.'[20]

With the success of *My Wrongs . . .*, Morris extended conventional narrative over the length of a full sitcom in the shape of *Nathan Barley*, the series he and Charlie Brooker created in 2005. And even if he had still been interested in using the sort of guerrilla techniques that had been such a part of *Brass Eye*, the practical considerations of doing a sitcom wouldn't have allowed it. There was little scope for delivering tapes on which were secreted last-minute bits of extra material, but in any case Morris showed little signs of nostalgia for the *Brass Eye* days. In 2008 came the announcement that he was to direct a full-length feature film, still in production at the time of writing. Under the title *Four Lions*, it is another co-production with Warp Films. Though the form couldn't be further away from what Morris was doing in the 1990s, *Four Lions* shares with all his work the distinctive imprint of his extensive and extended research. Preparation for the movie, said to concern UK-based Islamic fundamentalists, included lengthy discussions and correspondence with former Guantánamo Bay inmate Moazzam Begg as well as intensive study of the nuances of Islam, just as Morris and Armando Iannucci once closely observed news programmes before making *On the Hour* and *The Day Today*.

Such thoroughness underpins even Morris's earliest work with an enduring sense of solidity, but while his methods frequently seem to have more in common with those of a particularly blistering branch of investigative journalism than they do traditional comedy, his shows never came wrapped in the flag of a campaign. There is a lack of preciousness which makes them enduringly attractive; they wear the smartness of their construction lightly. They can be very much of their time, tapping into club culture as *Blue Jam* did, but they always come with their own identity rather than relying on trends for the laugh. At the heart of it all is a playful and energetic sense of the absurd that keeps the likes of *Brass Eye* fresh. It's that which remains once the shock of the unpredictable has worn off and the satirical intent understood when the headlines have faded.

Morris expanded the possibilities of what could be done with radio and television as media. More than any other single artist he utilized the full potential of the technical firepower which he had realized from his vantage point as a broadcaster and DJ. Many stylistic elements of his shows have provided inspiration for other comics, but none has managed to combine all of them to the same devastating effect.

And finally, but perhaps most startlingly, there is a profoundly emotional resonance to be found in Chris Morris's work, in the way in which he relentlessly mines his material for tangible proof that there need not be any part of human experience that is out of bounds for exploration. He charges straight through the politeness and respect habitually paid to sensitive subjects which can be enormously destructive when it means that pain and distress are allowed to fester within someone rather than being illuminated and understood. It's a tremendously optimistic achievement. Because if there really is nothing you can't talk and laugh about, then there truly is nothing to be scared of.

Mini-News

IN LEAVING *THE DAY TODAY* AFTER ONE TRIUMPHANT SERIES, the team had guaranteed that its status as a classic would never be tarnished by botched-follow-up syndrome. They had each gone on to develop their own highly successful careers in interesting and individual ways without once looking back. And yet they all retained a huge affection for the show that had made their names and jumped at the opportunity to get back together again in 2004. It was a reunion. Ten years since they'd last been together. But brief. The old firm together for one last job. Enough to cause a flutter of excitement – without putting at risk the show's immaculate reputation.

The excuse was the release of the series on DVD. And given the history of the programme's development, it was perhaps appropriate that it came about partly as a result of a BBC mistake. An Alan Partridge DVD was put out without the input of anyone connected with the series. Exasperated, Talkback insisted on handling all subsequent DVDs themselves, with *The Day Today* saved for the last and most lavishly over-the-top release.

Chris Morris was the most enthusiastic of everyone about doing extra features for the DVD, though neither he nor Armando Iannucci wanted to settle for the standard nostalgic commentary track when they could improvise new material. The challenge was to find a time to suit each member of the busy group, but they were determined to do it: 'It was more about getting everyone in the same room. That was an odd feeling, but it was nice,' says Patrick Marber.

In January 2004 they gathered in a sound studio with Iannucci's long-time producer Adam Tandy. There was some thinking the actors had to do, to get themselves back to how they did that *The Day Today* thing, but then they found the old rhythm. Riffing on suggestions from Iannucci, the new material included a live link between Morris and Marber as Peter O'Hanraha-hanrahan. Sent to cover a conference at the World Trade Center on 9/11, the reporter oversleeps and completely fails to notice the terrorist attacks. Under Morris's increasingly pointed questioning, he firmly maintains he is reporting from the Windows on the World restaurant at the very top of the North Tower, 'sipping a cappuccino'.

Peter Fincham and Sally Debonnaire arrived with a cake and photos were taken, the moody gang of the original publicity shots replaced by a bunch of mates with nothing left to prove, all thumbs aloft and big grins. Not everything had changed within the group dynamic, however: Steve Coogan and Patrick Marber were still to be found comparing notes to see which of them had done better since the series first went out.

The DVD, given a gatefold design and a paper band around the outside, was relatively expensive to produce and counted against promotion with the BBC, which had also decided that the old comedy wouldn't sell well anyway and had become resigned to not recouping the costs. Having accepted at Morris's insistence that they wouldn't have pictures of the stars on the cover, they gave the release little publicity. *The Day Today* quickly went on to sell well over 100,000 copies. It was joined four years later by a release of *On the Hour* through Warp Records, neatly packaged on CD under Morris's supervision with all material by Stewart Lee and Richard Herring fully restored. It seemed as if all the loose ends had been tied up.

Or had they? The heady emotion of the get-together had overcome some of the cast with a non-specific desire to do something together again, but it was a passing notion, swiftly tempered by a more specific feeling that the reality probably wouldn't be half as good as the idea. For Marber the sessions were 'nostalgic, fun, strange . . . sort of sweet and sad'.

And so that was it, after all. 'It seemed like a mirage,' says Adam Tandy of the recording sessions. 'They just came together for that brief moment.'

NOTES

1 No News = Good News: Balls

1 'Comic Wants a Word in Your Ear', Laurie Taylor, *The Times*, 24 December 1993.
2 Armando Iannucci in interview with Mark Lawson, 2 January 2007, BBC4.
3 'Pair of Jokers', Mark Edwards, *Sunday Times*, 6 March 1994.
4 *Independent*, 26 October 1997.
5 *New Yorker*, 5 November 2007.
6 Armando Iannucci in interview with Mark Lawson, 2 January 2007, BBC4.
7 *In Conversation With*, BBC Radio 4, March 2001.
8 *Word*, March 2005.
9 *The Times*, 24 December 1993.
10 Armando Iannucci in interview with Mark Lawson, 2 January 2007, BBC4.

2 Man Steps off Pavement

1 *Daily Mail*, 28 July 2001.
2 *The Life and Death of Rochester Sneath*, Humphry Berkeley, p. 11 (Harriman House, 1993).
3 *The Life and Death of Rochester Sneath*, Humphry Berkeley, p. 39 (Harriman House, 1993).
4 *Publish and Bedazzled*, No. 13, August 1998.
5 *On the Hour*, series one, episode one.

6   *Melody Maker*, 4 June 1994.

7   *Independent*, 28 May 1992.

8   *The Listener*, 30 April 1987.

9   *Private Eye*, #853, letters, 26 August 1994.

10 *Broadcast*, 17 July 1987.

3 NO KNOWN CURE

1   Chris Morris in conversation with Paul Lashmar, 6 March 2007, Wessex Media Group, Bournemouth University.

2   Chris Morris in conversation with Paul Lashmar, 6 March 2007, Wessex Media Group, Bournemouth University.

3   *Guardian*, 25 July 1994.

4   Chris Morris in conversation with Paul Lashmar, 6 March 2007, Wessex Media Group, Bournemouth University.

4 RAW MEAT RADIO

1   Chris Morris, GLR, 1 April 1991.

2   GLR, 24 April 1993.

3   *Independent*, 28 May 1992.

4   *The Times*, 21 August 1993.

5   *Guardian*, 11 June 1992.

6   *Time Out*, 21–28 November 1990.

7   *Time Out*, 5–12 December 1990.

8   *Guardian*, 21 August 1992.

9   *Word*, March 2005.

5 FACT X IMPORTANCE = NEWS

1   *Independent*, 19 March 1994.

2   *Melody Maker*, 4 June 1994.

3   *Time Out*, 20–26 June 2007.

4   *Independent*, 18 January 1994.

5   *The Times*, 21 August 1993.

6   *Time Out*, 12–19 January 1994.
7   *Financial Times*, 19 January 1994.
8   *Evening Standard*, 31 January 1994.
9   *Evening Standard*, 27 January 1994.
10 *Evening Standard*, 27 January 1994.
11 *Guardian*, 25 August 2007.
12 *Guardian*, 10 January 1994.
13 *Guardian*, 21 February 2003.

6 PUTTING A SPINE IN A BAP

1   *The Times*, 20 January 1994.
2   *Independent*, 6 February 1995.
3   *Independent*, 18 April 1998.
4   Armando Iannucci in interview with Mark Lawson, 2 January 2007, BBC4.
5   *Sunday Times*, 6 March 1994.
6   *The Times*, 24 December 1993.
7   *New Musical Express*, 15 June 1996.
8   *Daily Mirror*, 5 July 1996.
9   *Daily Mirror*, 5 July 1996.
10 *The New Yorker*, 5 November 2007.
11 *Sunshine on Putty*, Ben Thompson, p. 50 (Harper Perennial, 2004).
12 *Independent*, 6 February 1995.
13 *Observer*, 31 December 1995.

7 WHY BOTHER?

1   *Publish and Bedazzled*, No. 13, August 1998.
2   *Guardian*, 25 July 1994.
3   *Independent*, 18 January 2004.
4   *Peter Cook: A Biography*, Harry Thompson, p. 457 (Hodder & Stoughton, 1997).
5   *Publish and Bedazzled*, No 13, August 1998.
6   *How Very Interesting*, ed. Paul Hamilton, Peter Gordon and Dan Kieran, p. 428 (Snowbooks, 2006).
7   *Guardian*, 17 January 1994.

8 *Independent,* 18 January 1994.
9 *Evening Standard,* 27 April 2000.
10 *Publish and Bedazzled,* No. 13, August 1998.
11 *Guardian,* 25 July 1994.
12 *Time Out,* 1–8 June 1994.
13 *Guardian,* 8 July 1994.
14 *Guardian,* 25 July 1994.
15 *Guardian,* 25 July 1994.
16 *Guardian,* 8 July 1994.
17 *Guardian,* 25 July 1994.

8 BLATANTLY HIDING THE GROUND

1 *Guardian,* 25 July 1994.
2 *Guardian,* 25 July 1994, John Dugdale 'Taped Up for Auntie'
3 *Macmillan,* Alistair Horne, vol. ii, p. 371 (Macmillan, 1989).

9 NOT SO MUCH THE NEINTIES AS THE JA DANKETIES

1 Chris Morris in conversation with Paul Lashmar, 6 March 2007, Wessex Media Group, Bournemouth University.
2 *Word,* March 2005.
3 Chris Morris in conversation with Paul Lashmar, 6 March 2007, Wessex Media Group, Bournemouth University.
4 Will Self, *Observer,* 9 March 1997.
5 *Guardian,* 27 April 1998.
6 *Hansard,* (House of Commons) written answers part 10, column 169 (23 July 1996).
7 Issued by the Independent Television Commission.

10 BRASS EYE

1 *Time Out,* 20–27 November 1996.
2 *Guardian,* 27 April 1998.
3 *Storm over Four,* Channel 4, 1 January 1998.

4   *It Seemed Like a Good Idea at the Time*, Michael Grade, pp. 258–9 (Macmillan, 1999).

5   *Guardian*, 25 November 1996.

6   *Guardian*, 25 November 1996.

7   *NME*, 30 November 1996, p.9.

8   *Melody Maker*, 29 November 1997.

9   *Sunday Times*, 23 February 1997.

10 *The Times*, 14 February 1997.

11 Chris Morris in conversation with Paul Lashmar, 6 March 2007, Wessex Media Group, Bournemouth University.

12 *Channel 4 at Twenty-five*, More4, 30 September 2007.

13 *It Seemed Like a Good Idea at the Time*, Michael Grade, pp. 258–9 (Macmillan, 1999).

14 *Independent*, 15 March 1997.

15 Peter Fincham at Rose d'Or Festival, 2004.

16 *Observer*, 9 March 1997.

17 *ITC Programme Code 2.8* (1998 edition). The '*Brass Eye* clause': 'A different kind of set-up situation is one where the subject consents to being recorded for a different purpose from that covertly intended by the programme-makers.

    'The use of such material without the subject's permission can only be justified if it is necessary in order to make an important point of public interest. Consent to proceed should, where practicable, be given before recording by the licensee's most senior programme executive or the designated alternative. Such consent is required again before transmission.'

18 *Melody Maker*, 29 November 1997.

19 *Independent*, 20 April 2000.

20 *Guardian*, 27 April 1998.

21 *Guardian*, 27 April 1998.

11 Now, What Seems to Be the Problem?

1   *Guardian*, 27 April 1998.

2   Chris Morris in conversation with Paul Lashmar, 6 March 2007, Wessex Media Group, Bournemouth University.

3   *Guardian*, 27 April 1998.

4   *Guardian*, 27 April 1998.

5   *Melody Maker*, 29 November 1997.

6 *Independent*, 20 April 2000.
7 *Guardian*, 27 April 1998.
8 *Mail on Sunday*, 21 December 1997.
9 *Radio Times*, 21 March 1998.
10 *Independent*, 20 April 2000.

12 IF THE PRINTED WORD HAS ANY MEANING, THEN IT MUST COME FROM THE VERY EDGE OF FUCKY BUM BOO BOO

1 *Sunday Times*, 27 June 1999.
2 *Guardian*, 10 August 1997.
3 *Sunday Times*, 27 June 1999.

13 17.8 PER CENT SAFER

1 http://news.bbc.co.uk/1/hi/uk/309814.stm.
2 *Observer*, 5 August 2001.
3 *Channel 4 at Twenty-five*, More4, 30 September 2007.
4 *News of the World*, 23 July 2000.
5 *News of the World*, 23 July 2000.
6 *News of the World*, 23 July 2000.
7 *Independent*, 5 August 2000.
8 *Guardian* Friday Pages, p. 2, 21 February 2003.
9 *News of the World*, 13 August 2000.
10 www.tvgohome.com/1905-2000.html.
11 www.tvgohome.com, 24 September 2001.
12 *Guardian*, 21 February 2003.
13 *Guardian*, 30 July 2001.
14 *Daily Mirror*, 4 August 2001.
15 *Daily Mirror*, 31 July 2001.
16 *Daily Mail*, 5 August 2001, Nick Pryer, Gill Martin 'Why Doon, a mother of two young children, is in tears at appearing in show that shamed TV'.
17 *Guardian*, 31 July 2001.
18 *Guardian*, 31 July 2001.
19 http://news.bbc.co.uk/2/hi/uk_news/2027864.stm.
20 *Guardian*, 27 April 1998.

INDEX